Beckham's
Guide
to
Scholarships

CONTENTS

INTRODUCTION

There is plenty of money out there for you. But you must know where and how to look in order to take advantage of the many opportunities. This guide is a resource to help you match the many offerings with your own needs.

In our fifth edition, we have increased substantially the number of private sources, have eliminated those that no longer exist, and have modified entries that were incorrect. We thank all of you for writing us with updated information.

Still, the best guide in the world can be useless if you don't approach the process of funding your college education with certain attitudes and strategies. To begin, know that education in America today is still the number one priority and an absolute necessity for anyone who wants to join the tough job market. About 70 percent of all new jobs created in the United States require at least 14 years of education, according to the foundation Education is Freedom.

So you should be greatly motivated about finding help in financing your education. Here are some tips and strategies to consider.

Put some time into learning all you can about the college financial aid process. Become familiar with the system, its rules, guidelines and vocabulary. Get advice from your financial aid counselor in high school and your financial aid administrator in college. Don't be shy—ask questions!

Don't procrastinate! Apply for aid as soon as possible after January 1. The early bird always gets the worm—and sometimes the award too! For God's sake make a promise today that you will meet every deadline. Do you want to miss out on thousands of dollars because you were a week late?

Check to see if you are eligible for federal funds first, then check for private sources. Billions of federal dollars go unused each year because students think that they are ineligible, feel intimidated by the paperwork, or just don't know about the programs. Therefore, submit a FAFSA even if you think you don't qualify for aid. Being rejected for federal aid may even be a prerequisite for private awards.

Use the scholarship search engines on the Internet. They are quick and thorough—and are usually free.

Investigate innovative approaches like matching scholarships, sibling scholarships, guaranteed cost plans, installment plans, employee discounts, diversity awards, prepayment plays, special middle-income assistance programs, tuition remission for high grades, and others. Don't get bogged down with one approach.

Explore earning advanced placement credit in high school so that you don't have to pay tuition for that course.

Don't overlook awards from local organizations. They are usually announced in local newspapers. To see what aid was given recently, do a search for scholarships or financial aid at the online version of your local paper.

Try to cut your four years to three by attending summer school or by taking extra courses during the semester. On the same note, try to graduate on time rather than pay for an extra year.

Examine junior year abroad programs. Costs could be considerably less in Europe and other countries.

Consider starting at a community college, performing well, then transferring and obtaining a more prestigious diploma at half the cost. Many community colleges have direct connections and "articulation agreements" with four-year colleges.

Remember that after your first year you may be eligible for lower in- state tuition costs as a resident at a state-supported institution.

Think about cooperative education programs at 900 colleges that alternate formal on-campus study with career-related work. Earn up to $7,000 per year as you get valuable on-the-job experience.

Investigate the military offerings like reserve enlistments in the National Guard and the ROTC programs on campus.

Review programs where colleges, states, and the federal government will forgive loans for prospective teachers.

Believe in yourself and feel that you deserve every penny that you can get.

All the best,

Barry Beckham

FINANCIAL AID PROGRAMS FROM THE U.S. DEPARTMENT OF EDUCATION

WHERE TO FIND OUT ABOUT STUDENT AID

1. The financial aid administrator (FAA) at each school in which you're interested can tell you what aid programs are available there and how much the total cost of attendance will be.

2. The state higher education agency in your home state can give you information about state aid including aid from the State Student Incentive Grant (SSIG) Program, which is jointly funded by individual states and the U.S. Department of Education.

3. The agency in your state responsible for public elementary and secondary schools can give you information on the Robert C. Byrd Honors Scholarship Program (Byrd Program). To qualify for aid under the Byrd Program, you must demonstrate outstanding academic achievement and show promise of continued academic excellence.

For the address and telephone number of the appropriate state agency, contact your school's financial aid office or call 1-800-4-FED-AID (1-800-433-3243).

4. The AmeriCorps program provides full-time educational awards in return for work in community service. You can work before, during, or after your postsecondary education, and you can use the funds either to pay current educational expenses or to repay federal student loans. For more information on this program, call 1-800-942-2677 or write to:

> The Corporation for National and Community Service
> 1201 New York Avenue, NW
> Washington, DC 20525

5. Your public library is an excellent source of information on state and private sources of aid.

6. Many companies, as well as labor unions, have programs to help pay the cost of postsecondary education for employees, members, or their children.

7. Check foundations, religious organizations, fraternities or sororities, and town or city clubs. Include community organizations and civic groups such as the American Legion, YMCA, 4-H Club, Elks, Kiwanis, Jaycees, Chamber of Commerce, and the Girl or Boy Scouts.

8. Don't overlook aid from organizations connected with your field of interest (for example, the American Medical Association or the American Bar Association). These organizations are listed in the U.S. Department of Labor's

Occupational Outlook Handbook and are also listed in various directories of associations available at your public library.

9. If you (or your spouse) are a veteran or the dependent of a veteran, veterans' educational benefits may be available. Check with your local Veterans' Affairs office.

THE U.S. DEPARTMENT OF EDUCATION STUDENT FINANCIAL AID (SFA) PROGRAMS

I. Federal Pell Grants
II. Federal Stafford Loans
III. Federal PLUS Loans
IV. Federal Consolidation Loans
V. Federal Supplemental Educational Opportunity Grants
VI. Federal Work-Study
VII. Federal Perkins Loans

REMEMBER THESE KEY DEFINITIONS

Grants are financial aid you don't have to pay back.
Work-Study lets you work and earn money to help pay for school.
Loans are borrowed money that you must repay with interest.
Undergraduates may receive all three types of financial aid. Graduate students may receive loans or Federal Work-Study, but not Federal Pell Grants or FSEOG. Not all schools take part in all the programs. To find out which ones are available at a particular school, contact the financial aid office.

STUDENT ELIGIBILITY

To receive aid from the major student aid programs, you must:

1. Have financial need, except for some loan programs (see below).
2. Have a high school diploma or a General Education Development (GED) Certificate, pass a test approved by the U.S. Department of Education, or meet other standards your state establishes that are approved by the U.S. Department of Education. See your financial aid administrator for more information.
3. Be enrolled or accepted for enrollment as a regular student working toward a degree or certificate in an eligible program. (You may not receive aid for correspondence or telecommunications courses unless they are part of an associate, bachelor's, or graduate degree program.)
4. Be a U.S. citizen or eligible non-citizen.

5. Have a valid Social Security number.

6. Make satisfactory academic progress.

7. Sign a statement of educational purpose and a certification statement on overpayment and default (both found on the Free Application for Federal Student Aid [FAFSA]).

8. Register with the Selective Service, if required.

FINANCIAL NEED

Aid from most of the major government programs is awarded on the basis of financial need (except for subsidized Stafford, all PLUS and Consolidation loans).

When you apply for federal student aid, the information you report is used in a formula, established by the U.S. Congress, that calculates your Expected Family Contribution (EFC), an amount you and your family are expected to contribute toward your education. If your EFC is below a certain amount, you'll be eligible for a Federal Pell Grant, assuming you meet all other eligibility requirements.

There isn't a maximum EFC that defines eligibility for the other financial aid programs. Instead, your EFC is used in an equation to determine your financial need:

Cost of attendance
– Expected Financial Contribution (EFC)
= Financial need

Your financial aid administrator (FAA) calculates your cost of attendance (COA) and subtracts the amount you and your family are expected to contribute toward that cost. If there's anything left over, you're considered to have financial need. In determining your need for aid from the SFA programs, your FAA must first consider other aid you're expected to receive.

Your FAA can adjust the EFC formula's data elements or adjust your COA if he or she believes your family's financial circumstances warrant it based on the documentation you provide. However, the FAA does not have to make such an adjustment. See Special Circumstances for more information.

You can get a booklet called the "Expected Family Contribution (EFC) Formulas," which describes how the EFC formulas are calculated, by writing to:

Federal Student Aid Information Center
P.O. Box 84
Washington, DC 20044

I. FEDERAL PELL GRANTS

What Is a Federal Pell Grant?

A Federal Pell Grant, unlike a loan, does not have to be repaid. Pell Grants are awarded only to undergraduate students who have not earned a bachelor's or professional degree. (A professional degree would be a degree in a field such as pharmacy or dentistry.) For many students, Pell Grants provide a foundation of financial aid to which other aid may be added.

How Do I Qualify?

To determine if you're eligible financially, the U.S. Department of Education uses a standard formula, established by Congress, to evaluate the information you report when you apply. The formula produces an Expected Family Contribution (EFC) number. Your Student Aid Report (SAR) contains this number and will tell you if you're eligible.

How Much Money Can I Get?

Awards for the 2004-2005 award year (July 1, 2004, to June 30, 2005) will have a maximum amount of $4,050. You can receive only one Pell Grant in an award year. How much you get will depend not only on your EFC but also on your cost of attendance, whether you're a full-time or part-time student, and whether you attend school for a full academic year or less. You may not receive Pell Grant funds from more than one school at a time.

II. FEDERAL STAFFORD LOANS

Stafford Loans are either subsidized or unsubsidized. A subsidized loan is awarded on the basis of financial need. The federal government pays interest on the loan ("subsidizes" the loan) until you begin repayment and during authorized periods of deferment.

An unsubsidized loan is not awarded on the basis of need. You'll be charged interest from the time the loan is disbursed until it is paid in full. If you allow the interest to accumulate, it will be capitalized—that is, the interest will be added to the principal amount of your loan and will increase the amount you have to repay. If you choose to pay the interest as it accumulates, you'll repay less in the long run.

You can receive a subsidized Stafford Loan and an unsubsidized Stafford Loan for the same enrollment period.

Who Can Get a Stafford Loan?

If you're a regular student enrolled in an eligible program of study at least half-time, you may receive a Stafford Loan. You must also meet other general eligibility requirements.

How Much Can I Borrow?

If you're a dependent undergraduate student, you can borrow up to these amounts:

—$2,625 if you're a first-year student enrolled in a program of study that is at least a full academic year;
—$3,500 if you've completed your first year of study, and the remainder of your program is at least a full academic year; or
—$5,500 a year if you've completed two years of study, and the remainder of your program is at least a full academic year.

If you're an independent undergraduate student or a dependent student whose parents are unable to get a PLUS Loan, you can borrow up to these amounts:

—$6,625 if you're a first-year student enrolled in a program of study that is at least a full academic year (at least $4,000 of this amount must be in unsubsidized loans);
—$7,500 if you've completed your first year of study, and the remainder of your program is at least a full academic year (at least $4,000 of this amount must be in unsubsidized loans); or
—$10,500 a year if you've completed two years of study, and the remainder of your program is at least a full academic year (at least $5,500 of this amount must be in unsubsidized loans).

If you're a graduate student, you can borrow up to $18,500 each academic year (at least $10,000 of this amount must be in unsubsidized Stafford Loans).
The total debt you can have outstanding from all Stafford Loans combined is:

—$23,000 as a dependent undergraduate student;
—$46,000 as an independent undergraduate student (no more than $23,000 of this amount may be in subsidized loans); or
—$138,500 as a graduate or professional student (no more than $65,000 of this amount may be in subsidized loans). The graduate debt limit includes any Stafford Loans for undergraduate study.

What's the Interest Rate Charged on These Loans?

If you have a Stafford Loan that was first disbursed on or after July 1, 1994, the interest rate could change each year of repayment, but it will never exceeded 8.25 percent. The interest rate is adjusted each year on July 1. You'll be notified of interest rate changes throughout the life of your loan.

Direct Stafford Loans

How Do I Apply for a Direct Stafford Loan?

First, complete the 2004-2005 Free Application for Federal Student Aid (FAFSA) or Renewal FAFSA. After your FAFSA is processed, your school will review the results and will inform you of your loan eligibility.

Second, complete the promissory note provided by your school or the Direct Loan Servicing Center. Remember, the promissory note is a legal document requiring you to repay the loan. Read it carefully before you sign.

Loan payments are made to the U.S. Department of Education. For more information on repayment options, write for a copy of the Direct Loans Repayment Book at the following address:

Federal Student Aid Information Center
P.O. Box 84
Washington, DC 20044

FFEL Stafford Loans

How Do I Apply for a FFEL Stafford Loan?

First, complete the 2004-2005 Free Application for Federal Student Aid (FAFSA) or Renewal FAFSA. After your FAFSA is processed, your school will review the results and will inform you of your loan eligibility.

Second, complete the Federal Stafford Loan Application and promissory note available from your school, a lender, or your state guaranty agency. Remember, the promissory note is a legal document requiring you to repay the loan. Read it carefully before you sign.

Third, take your completed Federal Stafford Loan Application and Promissory Note to the school you plan to attend. After the school completes its portion of the application, you (or the school on your behalf) must send the application to a lender for evaluation.

How Can I Find a Lender?

Contact the guaranty agency that serves your state. For your agency's address and telephone number, and for more information about borrowing, call the Federal Student Aid Information Center's toll-free number: 1-800-4-FED-AID (1-800-433-3243).

Other Sources:

AMS Education Loan Trust: 1-800-637-3060

Bank of America Loan Center: 1-800-344-8382

Bank One, Indiana, N.A.: 1-800-288-6144

National College Funding Services, Inc., has developed an innovative college assistance program that includes a savings plan. Unlike many banks and groups that earn huge profits on loan interest and collection fees, NCFS sells its loans immediately to Sallie Mae. Contact Ivor Holmquist, NCFS, 7534 Ritchie Highway, Suite 5, Glen Burnie, MD 21061 or telephone (410) 321-1864 or (410) 761-0790.

University Support Services, Inc., offers a PLATO student loan program with $25,000 yearly maximums and a consolidation program lowering monthly loan payments up to 35 percent using a 20-year repayment period: 1-800-230-4080 or E-mail: ussinfo@aol.com.

USA Group issues, guarantees, and services educational loans: 1-800-LOAN-USA or E-mail: loanapps@usagroup.com.

III. FEDERAL PLUS LOANS (LOANS FOR PARENTS)

Federal PLUS Loans (PLUS Loans) enable parents with good credit histories to borrow to pay the educational expenses of each child who is a dependent undergraduate student enrolled at least half-time. PLUS Loans are available through both the Direct Loan and FFEL programs. Most of the benefits to parent borrowers are identical in the two programs.

Are There Any Borrowing Requirements My Parents Have to Meet?

Yes. To be eligible to receive a PLUS Loan, your parents generally will be required to pass a credit check. If they don't pass the credit check, they might still be able to receive a loan if someone, such as a relative or friend who is able to pass the credit check, agrees to endorse the loan, promising to repay it if your parents should fail to do so. Your parents might also qualify for a loan even if they don't pass the credit check if they can demonstrate that extenuating circumstances exist. You must meet the general eligibility requirements for federal student financial aid. Your parents must also meet some of these general requirements. For example, your parents must meet citizenship requirements and may not be in default or owe a refund to any SFA programs.

How Much Can My Parents Borrow?

The yearly limit on either type of PLUS Loan is equal to your cost of attendance minus any other financial aid you receive. For example, if your cost of attendance is $6,000 and your receive $4,000 in other financial aid, your parents could borrow up to—but no more than—$2,000.

What's the Interest Rate on PLUS Loans?

The interest rate is variable, but it will never exceed 9 percent. The interest rate is adjusted each year on July 1. Your parents will be notified of interest rate changes throughout the life of their loan(s). Interest is charged on the loan from the date the first disbursement is made until the loan is paid in full.

Do My Parents Need to Find a Lender?

No. Under the Direct Loan Program, their lender will be the U.S. Department of Education. Your school assists the federal government in administering the Direct Loan Program by distributing the loan application, processing the loan, and delivering the loan funds.

FFEL PLUS LOANS

How Do My Parents Apply for an FFEL PLUS Loan?

Your parents must submit a completed PLUS Loan Application (available from your school, a lender, or your state guaranty agency) to your school. After the school completes its portion of the application, it must be sent to a lender for evaluation. Because your financial need does not have to be evaluated, you do not need to file a FAFSA, unless your school requires it.

How Can My Parents Find a Lender?

Your parents should contact the guaranty agency that serves your state. For your agency's address and telephone number, and for more information about borrowing, call the Federal Student Aid Information Center's toll-free number: 1-800-4-FED-AID (1-800-433-3243).

IV. CONSOLIDATION LOANS

Consolidation Loans allow a borrower to combine different types of federal student loans to simplify repayment. (A borrower with just one loan can also choose to consolidate it.) Both the Direct Loan Program and the FFEL Program offer consolidation loans. However, Direct Consolidation Loans and FFEL Consolidation Loans are very different and are discussed separately here.

Direct Consolidation Loans

A Direct Consolidation Loan is designed to help student and parent borrowers simplify loan repayment. Even though you might have several different federal student loans, you'll make only one payment a month for all the loans you consolidate. You can even consolidate just one loan into a Direct Consolidation Loan to get benefits such as flexible repayment options.

What Kinds of Loans Can Be Consolidated Under a Direct Consolidation Loan?

Most federal student loans and PLUS Loans (including FFEL program loans) can be consolidated. All the federal loans discussed are eligible for consolidation. The Direct Loan Servicing Center can give you a complete listing of eligible loans. The toll-free telephone number of the Servicing Center's Consolidation Department is 1-800-848-0982.

FFEL Consolidation Loans

An FFEL Consolidation Loan is designed to help student and parent borrowers consolidate several types of federal student loans with various repayment schedules into one loan. With an FFEL Consolidation Loan, you'll make only one payment a month. FFEL Consolidation Loans are available from participating lenders, such as banks, credit unions, and savings and loan associations.

CAMPUS-BASED PROGRAMS

The three programs discussed in this section are called campus-based programs because they're administered directly by the financial aid office at each participating school. Not all schools participate in all three programs. The Federal Supplemental Educational Opportunity Grant (FSEOG) Program awards grants, the Federal Work-Study (FWS) Program offers jobs, and the Federal Perkins Loan Program offers loans. Even though each program is different, they have these characteristics in common:

1. How much aid you receive depends on your financial need, on the amount of other aid you'll receive, and the availability of funds at your school. Unlike the Federal Pell Grant Program, which provides funds to every eligible student, each school participating in any of the campus-based programs receives a certain amount of funds for each campus-based program each year. When that money is gone, no more awards can be made from that program for that year.

2. Each school sets its own deadlines for students to apply for campus-based funds. The deadlines will usually be earlier than the U.S. Department of Education's deadline for filing a federal student financial aid application. Ask your FAA about the school's deadlines. You may miss out on aid from these programs if you don't apply early!

V. FEDERAL SUPPLEMENTAL EDUCATIONAL OPPORTUNITY GRANTS (FSEOG)

What Is a Federal Supplemental Educational Opportunity Grant?

A Federal Supplemental Educational Opportunity Grant (FSEOG) is for undergraduates with exceptional financial need—that is, students with the lowest Expected Family Contributions (EFCs)—and it gives priority to students who receive Federal Pell Grants. An FSEOG doesn't have to be paid back.

How Much Can I Get?

You can get between $100 and $4,000 a year, depending on when you apply, your level of need, and the funding level of the school you're attending.

VI. FEDERAL WORK-STUDY

What Is Federal Work-Study?

The Federal Work-Study (FWS) Program provides jobs for undergraduate and graduate students with financial need, allowing them to earn money to help pay education expenses. The program encourages community service work and work related to your course of study.

How Much Can I Make?

Your FWS salary will be at least the current federal minimum wage, but it may be higher, depending on the type of work you do and the skills required. Your total FWS award depends on when you apply, your level of need, and the funding level of your school.

VII. FEDERAL PERKINS LOANS

What Is a Federal Perkins Loan?

A Federal Perkins Loan is a low-interest (5 percent) loan for both undergraduate and graduate students with exceptional financial need. Your school is your lender, and the loan is made with government funds. You must repay this loan to your school.

How Much Can I Borrow?

Depending on when you apply, your level of need, and the funding level of your school, you can borrow up to:

—$4,000 for each year of undergraduate study. The total amount you can borrow as an undergraduate is $20,000.
—$6,000 for each year of graduate or professional study. The total amount you can borrow as a graduate/professional student is $40,000. (This includes any Federal Perkins Loans you borrowed as an undergraduate.)

QUESTIONS YOU SHOULD NOT BE AFRAID TO ASK— YOU HAVE THE RIGHT TO RECEIVE THE FOLLOWING INFORMATION FROM THE SCHOOL:

—The financial assistance that is available, including information on all federal, state, local, private, and institutional financial aid programs.
—The procedures and deadlines for submitting applications for each available financial aid program.
—How a school selects financial aid recipients.
—How the school determines your financial need.
—How the school determines each type and amount of assistance in your financial aid package.

—How and when you'll receive your aid.

—How the school determines whether you're making satisfactory academic progress, and what happens if you're not.

—If you're offered a Federal Work-Study job, what the job is, what hours you must work, what your duties will be, what the rate of pay will be, and how and when you'll be paid.

—The location, hours, and counseling procedures of the school's financial aid office.

A QUICK OVERVIEW OF YOUR FEDERAL AID OPTIONS

Federal Student Aid Program	Type of Aid	Program Details	Annual Award Amounts
Federal Pell Grant	Grant: does not have to be repaid	Available almost exclusively to undergraduates; all eligible students will receive the Federal Pell Grant amounts for which they qualify.	$400 to $4,050 for 2004-05; 2005-06 amount will depend on program funding.
Federal Supplemental Educational Opportunity Grant (FSEOG)	Grant: does not have to be repaid	For undergraduates with exceptional financial need; priority is given to Federal Pell Grant recipients; funds depend on availability at school.	$100 to $4,000
Federal Work-Study	Money is earned while attending school; does not have to be repaid	For undergraduate and graduate students; program encourages community service work and work related to course work. Jobs can be on campus or off campus; students are paid at least minimum wage.	No annual minimum or maximum award amount
Federal Perkins Loan	Loan: must be repaid	Loans at 5% interest for both undergraduates and graduate students; payment is owed to the school that made the loan.	$4,000 maximum for undergraduate students; $6000 maximum for graduate students; no minimum award amount
Subsidized FFEL or Direct Stafford Loan	Loan: must be repaid; must be at least a half-time student	Subsidized: U.S. Department of Education pays interest while borrower is in school and during grace deferment periods; must demonstrate financial need.	$2,625 to $8,5000, depending on grade level
Unsubsidized FFEL or Direct Stafford Loan	Loan: must be repaid; must be at least a half-time student	Unsubsidized: Borrower is responsible for interest during life of the loan; financial need not a requirement.	$2,625 to $18,500, depending on grade level (includes any subsidized amounts received for the same period)
FFEL or Direct PLUS Loan	Loan: must be repaid	Available to parents of dependent undergraduate students enrolled at least half time.	Maximum amount is cost of attendance minus any other financial aid the student receives; no minimum award amount.

GLOSSARY OF TERMS

IMPORTANT TERMS USED BY
THE U.S. DEPARTMENT OF EDUCATION

Academic Year: The time period schools use to measure a quantity of study. For example, a school's academic year may consist of a fall and spring semester, during which a student must complete 24 semester hours. Or it could consist of four quarters of six semester hours. Academic years vary from school to school, and even from educational program to educational program at the same school.

Citizenship: You must be one of the following to receive federal aid:
U.S. citizen
U.S. national (includes natives of American Samoa or Swain's Island)
U.S. permanent resident who has an I-151, I-551, or I-551C (Alien Registration Receipt Card)
If you're not in one of these categories, you must have an Arrival-Departure Record (I-94) from the U.S. Immigration and Naturalization Service (INS) showing one of the following designations in order to be eligible:
"Refugee"
"Asylum Granted"
"Indefinite Parole" and/or "Humanitarian Parole"
"Cuban/Haitian Entrant, Status Pending"
"Conditional Entrant" (valid only if issued before April 1, 1980)
Other eligible non-citizen with a Temporary Resident Card (I-688)
Or you can be eligible based on the Family Unity Status category with an approved I-797 (Voluntary Departure and Immigrant Petition).
If you have only a Notice of Approval to Apply for Permanent Residence (I-171 or I-464), you aren't eligible for federal student aid.
If you're in the U.S. on a F1 or F2 student visa only, or on a J1 or J2 exchange visitor visa only, you can't get federal student aid. Also, persons with G series visas (pertaining to international organizations) are not eligible for federal student aid.
Citizens and eligible non-citizens may also receive loans from the FFEL and Direct Loan Programs at participating foreign schools.
Citizens of the Federated States of Micronesia, the Republic of the Marshall Islands, and Palau are eligible only for Federal Pell Grants, Federal Supplemental Educational Opportunity Grants (FSEOG), or Federal Work-Study (FWS). These applicants should check with their financial aid administrators for more information.

Cost of Attendance (COA): The total amount it will cost a student to go to school—usually expressed as a yearly figure. It is determined using rules established by the U.S. Congress. The COA includes tuition and fees; on-campus room and board (or a housing and food allowance for off-campus students); and allowances for books, supplies, transportation, loan fees (if applicable), dependent care, costs related to disability, and miscellaneous expenses. Also included are reasonable costs for eligible study abroad programs. An allowance (determined by the school) is included for reasonable costs connected with a student's employment as part of a cooperative education program. For students attending less than half-time, the COA includes only tuition and fees and an allowance for books, supplies, transportation, and dependent-care expenses. Talk to the FAA at the school you're planning to attended if you have any unusual expenses that might affect your cost of attendance.

Default: Failure to repay a loan according to the terms agreed to when you signed a promissory note. Default also may result from failure to submit requests for deferment or cancellation on time. If you default, your school, the lender or agency that holds your loan, the state, and the federal government can take action to recover the money, including notifying national credit bureaus of your default. This notice may affect your credit rating for a long time, and you may find it very difficult to borrow from a bank to buy a car or a house. Furthermore, the lender or agency holding your loan may ask your employer to deduct payments from your paycheck. Also, you may be liable for expenses incurred in collecting the loan. If you decide to return to school, you're not entitled to receive any more federal student aid or any deferments. The U.S. Department of Education may ask the U.S. Internal Revenue Service to withhold your income tax refund, and the amount of your refund will be applied to what you owe.

Eligible Program: A course of study that leads to a degree or certificate and meets the U.S. Department of Education's requirements for an eligible program. To get federal financial aid, you must be enrolled in an eligible program, with two exceptions:

1. If a school has told you that you must take certain coursework to qualify for admission into one of its eligible programs, you can get a Direct Loan or an FFEL Loan (or your parents can get a PLUS Loan) for up to 12 consecutive months while you're completing that coursework. You must be enrolled at least half-time, and you must meet the usual student aid eligibility requirements.

2. If you're enrolled at least half-time in a program to obtain a professional credential or certification required by a state for employment as an elementary or secondary school teacher, you can get a Federal Perkins Loan, Federal Work-Study, an FFEL Stafford Loan, a Direct Loan (or your parents can get a PLUS Loan) while you're enrolled in that program.

Financial Aid Package: The total amount of financial aid (federal and nonfederal) a student receives.

General Education Development (GED) Certificate: A certificate students receive if they've passed a specific, approved high school equivalency test. Students who don't have a high school diploma but who have a GED may still qualify for federal student aid. A school that admits students without a high school diploma must make a GED program in the vicinity of the school available to these students and must inform them about the program.

Guaranty Agency: The organization that administers the FFEL Program for your state. The federal government sets loan limits and interest rates, but each state is free to set its own additional limitations, within federal guidelines. This agency is the best source of information on FFEL Program Loans in your state. To find out the name, address, and telephone number of the agency serving your state, as well as information about borrowing, call the Federal Student Aid Information Center at 1-800-4-FED-AID (1-800-433-3243).

Half-Time: At schools measuring progress by credit hours and semesters, trimesters, or quarters, half-time enrollment is at least six semester hours or quarter hours per term. At schools measuring progress by credit hours but not using semesters, trimesters, or quarters, half-time enrollment is at least 12 semester hours or 18 quarter hours per year. At schools measuring progress by clock hours, half-time enrollment is at least 12 hours per week. Note that schools may choose to set higher minimums than these.
You must be attending school at least half-time to be eligible to receive Direct or FFEL Program Loans. Half-time enrollment is not a requirement to receive aid from the Federal Pell Grant, Federal Supplemental Educational Opportunity Grant (FSEOG), Federal Work-Study (FWS), and Federal Perkins Loan programs.

Promissory Note: The binding legal document you sign when you get a student loan. It lists the conditions under which you're borrowing and the terms under which you agree to pay back the loan. It will include information about your interest rate and about deferment and cancellation provisions. It's very important to read and save this document because you'll need to refer to it later when you begin repaying your loan.

Regular Student: One who is enrolled in an institution to obtain a degree or certificate. Generally, to receive aid from the programs discussed in this book, you must be a regular student. (For some programs, there are exceptions to this requirement. See the definition of eligible program.)

Satisfactory Academic Progress: To be eligible to receive federal student aid, you must maintain satisfactory academic progress toward a degree or certificate. You must meet your school's written standard of satisfactory progress. Check with your school to find out its standard.

If you received federal student aid for the first time on or after July 1, 1987, and you're enrolled in a program that's longer than two years, the following definition of satisfactory progress also applies to you: You must have a C average by the end of your second academic year of study or have an academic standing consistent with your institution's graduation requirements. You must continue to maintain satisfactory academic progress for the rest of your course of study.

Selective Service Registration: If required by law, you must register, or arrange to register, with the Selective Service to receive federal student aid. The requirement to register applies to males who were born on or after January 1, 1960, are at least 18 years old, are citizens or eligible non-citizens, and are not currently on active duty in the armed forces. (Citizens of the Federated States of Micronesia, the Marshall Islands, or Palau are exempt from registering.)

HELPFUL HINTS FROM THE U.S. DEPARTMENT OF EDUCATION

MYTHS ABOUT APPLYING FOR FINANCIAL AID FROM THE GOVERNMENT.

Read these before you say, "I'm not going to bother filling out the *Free Application for Federal Student Aid* because..."

"...my parents make too much money, so I won't qualify for aid."

Reality: There is no income cut-off to qualify for federal student aid. Many factors besides income—from the size of your family to the age of your older parent—are taken into account. Your eligibility is determined by a complicated mathematical formula, not by your parents' income alone. And remember: when you fill out the *Free Application for Federal Student Aid* (FAFSA), you're also automatically applying for funds from your state, and possibly from your school as well. Don't make assumptions about what you'll get— fill out the application and find out.

"...only students with good grades get financial aid."

Reality: While a high grade point average will help a student get into a good school and may help with academic scholarships, most of the federal student aid programs do not take a student's grades into consideration. Provided a student maintains satisfactory academic progress in his or her program of study, federal student aid will help a student with an average academic record complete his or her education.

"...you have to be a minority to get financial aid."

Reality: Funds from federal student aid programs are awarded on the basis of financial need, **not** on the basis of race. The FAFSA doesn't even collect this kind of information about an applicant.

"...the form is too hard to fill out."

Reality: The FAFSA is easier than ever, especially if you fill it out online at **www.fafsa.ed.gov**. There are detailed instructions for every question, and the form walks you through step by step, asking only the questions that apply to you. If you need help, you can access real-time, private online chat with a customer service representative. If you're filling out the paper FAFSA, you can get help from a high school counselor, from the financial aid office at the school you plan to attend, or from our toll-free number: 1-800-4-FED-AID. And remember, the FAFSA and all these sources of advice are FREE.

AVOIDING IDENTITY THEFT

How does identity theft happen? Criminals use their access to personal data such as names, telephone numbers, Social Security Numbers, and bank and credit card information. Using the stolen data, the criminal can fraudulently obtain credit cards, buy items over the Internet, and even establish cellular phone accounts. Complaints to the Federal Trade Commission about identity theft have doubled each year since the Commission began compiling its complaint database.

Reduce Your Risk

—Apply for federal student aid by filling out the *Free Application for Federal Student Aid* (FAFSA) at http://www.fafsa.ed.gov.
—After completing the FAFSA electronically, remember to exit the application and close the browser.

—Keep your U.S. Department of Education (ED) PIN in a secure place. (Get your PIN at http://www.pin.ed.gov.)
—Don't reveal your PIN to anyone, even if that person is helping you fill out the FAFSA. The only time you should be using your PIN is when you are on ED Web sites, which are secure.
—Review your financial aid award documents and keep track of the amount of aid applied for and awarded.
—Shred receipts and copies of documents with personal information if they are no longer needed.
—Immediately report all lost or stolen identification (credit card, driver's license, etc.) to the issuer.

Report Identity Theft

If you become a victim of identity theft or suspect that your student information has been stolen, contact:

U.S. Department of Education
Office of Inspector General Hotline
1-800-MIS-USED (1-800-647-8733)
complain online: http://www.ed.gov/misused

Federal Trade Commission
1-877-IDTHEFT (1-877-438-4338)
complain online: http://www.consumer.gov/idtheft

Social Security Administration
1-800-269-0271
http://www.ssa.gov/pubs/idtheft.htm

Equifax Credit Bureau
1-800-525-6285
http://www.equifax.com

Experian Information Solutions (Formerly TRW)
1-888-397-3742
http://www.experian.com

TransUnion Credit Bureau
1-800-680-7289
http://www.transunion.com

Visit www.fsa.gov for these and other helpful hints regarding federal aid.

USEFUL SOURCES OF INFORMATION

INTERNET SITES

fastWeb offers a free searchable database of more than 180,000 private aid sources.

http://www.fastweb.com/

Go College offers free searches of their scholarship database of more than 7,000 sources. For searches of their complete database, the fee is $9.

http://www.gocollege.com/

Sallie Mae gives students exclusive Internet access to CASHE (College Aid Sources for Higher Education), one of the most respected and comprehensive sources of financial aid resources.

http://scholarships.salliemae.com/

The Financial Aid Information Page, by Mark Kantrowitz, co-author of *The Prentice Hall Guide to Scholarships and Fellowships for Math and Science Students,* provides a free, comprehensive guide to student financial aid.

http://www.finaid.com/

The *Free Scholarship Search Service* offers a wealth of information and a searchable database.

http://www.freschinfo.com/

The Mining Company Guide to College Admissions directed by Suzanne Newmann (collegeapps.guide@miningco.com) includes valuable essays and links.

http://collegeapps.miningco.com/

BOOKS

The Scholarship Scouting Report: An Insider's Guide to America's Best Scholarships
by Ben Kaplan
HarperResource; 1st edition (February 1, 2003)
$21.95

Money-Winning Scholarship Essays and Interviews: Insider Strategies from Judges and Winners
> by Gen S. Tanabe, Kelly Y. Tanabe
> SuperCollege (April 1, 2002)
> $27.17

Paying for College Without Going Broke, 2005 Edition (Princeton Review Series)
> by Kalman A. Chany, Geoff Martz
> Princeton Review (October 12, 2004)
> $43.95

Scholarships 2002 (Scholarships (Kaplan))
> by Gail Schlachter, R. David Weber, Douglas Bucher (Introduction)
> Kaplan (September 1, 2001)
> $29.95

College Cost & Financial Aid Handbook 2005 : All-New 25th Edition (College Costs and Financial Aid Handbook)
> by College Board
> College Board; 25th Rev edition (August 16, 2004)
> $23.95

Free $ for College for Dummies
> by David Rosen, Caryn Mladen
> For Dummies; 1st edition (June 1, 2003)
> $19.99

How to Go to College Almost for Free
> by Ben Kaplan
> HarperResource; 2nd edition (September 1, 2001)
> $22.00

Scholarships, Grants & Prizes 2005 (Peterson's Scholarships, Grants & Prizes)
> by Joe Krasowski (Editor), Craig Heinz (Editor), Jill C. Schwartz (Editor)
> Peterson's Guides; 9th edition (June 1, 2004)
> $29.95

The Scholarship Book: The Complete Guide to Private-Sector Scholarships, Fellowships, Grants, and Loans for Undergraduates (Scholarship Book)
   by Ellen Schneid (Contributor), Daniel J. Cassidy (Editor)
   Prentice Hall Press; (July 1, 2004)
   $30.00

STATE AGENCIES

Alabama Commission on Higher Education
100 North Union Street
P.O. Box 302000
http://www.ache.state.al.us/

Montgomery, AL 36130-2000
334.242.1998
Fax 334.242.1998

Alaska Commission on Postsecondary Education
3030 Vintage Blvd.
Juneau, Alaska 99801-7100
800.441.2962
Fax 907.465.5316
http://alaskaadvantage.state.ak.us/

Arizona Commission for Postsecondary Education
2020 North Central Avenue, Suite 550
Phoenix, AZ 85004
602.258.2435
Fax 602.258.2483
http://www.arkansashighered.com/

Arkansas Deparment of Higher Education
114 East Capitol Avenue
Little Rock, AR 72201
501.371.2000
http://www.arkansashighered.com/

California Student Aid Commission
P.O. Box 419026
Rancho Cordova, CA 95741-9026
888.294.0153
Fax 916.526.8002
http://www.csac.ca.gov/

Colorado Commission on Higher Education
1380 Lawrence Street, Suite 1200
Denver, Colorado 80204
303.866.2723
http://www.state.co.us/cche_dir/hecche.html

Connecticut Department of Higher Education
61 Woodland Street
Hartford, CT 06105-2326
860.947.1855
Fax 860.947.1311
http://www.ctdhe.org/

Delaware Higher Education Commission
Carvel State Office Building
820 N. French Street
Wilmington, DE 19801
800.292.7935
Fax 302.577.6765
http://www.doe.state.de.us/high-ed/about.htm

Florida Department of Education Office of Student Financial Assistance
1940 North Monroe Street, Suite 70
Tallahassee, FL 32303-4759
800.366.3475
Local: 850.410.5200
http://
www.floridastudentfinancialaid.org/
osfahomepg.htm

Georgia Student Finance Commission
2082 East Exchange Place
Tucker, Georgia 30084
770.724.9000 or 800.505.GSFC
Fax 770.724.9089
http://www.gsfc.org/Main/
dsp_main.cfm

Hawaii Postsecondary Education Commission
University of Hawaii at Manoa
Bachman Hall
2444 Dole Street
Honolulu, HI 96822
808.956.6625

Idaho State Board of Education
P.O. Box 83720
Boise, ID 83720-0037
208.334.2270
Fax 208.334.2632
http://www.idahoboardofed.org/
scholarships.asp

Illinois Student Assistance Commission
1755 Lake Cook Road
Deerfield, IL 60015-5209
800.899.ISAC
http://www.collegezone.com/

Indiana State Student Assistance Commission
150 West Market Street, Suite 500
Indianapolis, IN 46204
317.232.2350
Outside 317 area code:
888.528.4719
Fax 317.232.3260
http://www.in.gov/ssaci/

Iowa College Student Aid Commission
200 - 10th Street, 4th Floor
Des Moines, IA 50309-2036
800.383.4222
Fax 515.242.3388
http://www.iowacollegeaid.org/

Kansas Board of Regents
1000 SW Jackson St., Suite 520
Topeka, KS 66612-1368
785.296.3421
http://www.kansasregents.org/
financial_aid/index.html

Kentucky Higher Education Assistance Authority
P.O. Box 798
Frankfort, KY 40602-0798
800.928.8926
http://www.kheaa.com/

Louisiana Student Financial Assistance
P.O. Box 91202
Baton Rouge, LA 70821-9202
800.259.LOAN(5626)
Fax 225.922.0790
http://www.osfa.state.la.us/

Maine Finance Authority
5 Community Drive
P.O. Box 949
Augusta, ME 04332-0949
207.623.3263 or 800.228.3734
Fax 207.62395
http://www.famemaine.com/html/
education/index.html

Maryland Higher Education Commission
Office of Student Financial
Assistance
839 Bestgate Road, Suite 400
Annapolis, Maryland 21401
410.260.4565 or 800.974.1024
Fax 410.260.3200
http://www.mhec.state.md.us/
financialAid/index.asp

Massachusetts Board of Higher Education
Office of Student Financial
Assistance
454 Broadway, Suite 200
Revere, MA 02151-3034
617.727.9420
Fax 617.727.0667
http://www.mass.edu/a_f/home.asp

Michigan Higher Education Assistance Authority
Bureau of Student Financial Aid
Office of Information and Resources
P.O. Box 30466
Lansing, MI 48909-7966
877.323.2287
http://www.michigan.gov/
mistudentaid

Minnesota Higher Education Services Office
1450 Energy Park Drive, Suite 350
Saint Paul, MN 55108-5227
651.642.0567
http://www.mheso.state.mn.us/
main.cfm?pageID=891

Mississippi Office of Student Financial Aid
3825 Ridgewood Road
Jackson, MS 39211-6453
601.432.6997
Toll free in Mississippi:
800.327.2980
http://www.ihl.state.ms.us/
financialaid/default.asp

Missouri Department of Higher Education
Missouri Student Assistance
Resource Services
3515 Amazonas Dr.
Jefferson City, MO 65109-5717
800.473.6757
Fax 573.751.6635
http://www.dhe.mo.gov/

Montana Higher Education Student Assistance Foundation
2500 Broadway
Helena, MT 59620-3104
800.852.2761 ext. 6657
Fax 406.444.0684
http://www.mhesac.org/MHESAC/

**Nebraska Coordinating
Commission for Postsecondary
Education**
P.O. Box 95005
Lincoln, Nebraska 68509-5005
402.471.2847
Fax 402.471.2886
http://www.ccpe.state.ne.us/
PublicDoc/CCPE/Default.asp

**Nevada State Treasurer College
Programs**
Sawyer Office Building
555 E. Washington Ave., Suite 4600
Las Vegas, NV 89101
888.477.2667
Las Vegas: 702.486.2025
Fax 702.486.3246
http://nevadatreasurer.gov/college/
programinfo.asp

**New Hampshire Higher Education
Assistance Foundation**
4 Barrell Court
P.O. Box 877
Concord, NH 03302-0877
603.225.6612 or 800.525.2577
Fax 603.224.2581
http://www.nhheaf.org/

**New Jersey Commission on Higher
Education**
P.O. Box 542
Trenton, NJ 08625-0542
609.292.4310
Fax 609.292.7225 or 609.633.8420
http://www.state.nj.us/
highereducation/

**New Mexico Educational
Assistance Foundation**
3900 Osuna Road NE
Albuquerque, NM 87109
800.279.5063 or 505.345.3371
http://www.nmeaf.org/

**New York Higher Education
Services Corporation**
99 Washington Ave.
Albany, NY 12255
888.NYS.HESC (888.697.4372) or
518.473.1574
http://www.hesc.com/bulletin.nsf/

**North Carolina State Education
Assistance Authority**
P.O. Box 14103
Research Triangle Park, NC 27709
919.549.8614
Fax 919.549.8481
http://www.ncseaa.edu/

North Dakota University System
10th Floor, State Capitol
600 East Boulevard Ave., Dept. 215
Bismarck, ND 58505-0230
701.328.2960
Fax 701.328.2961
http://www.ndus.nodak.edu/
default.asp

Ohio Board of Regents
State Grants and Scholarships
Department
P.O. Box 182452
Columbus, OH 43218-2452
888.833.1133
Local: 614.466.7420
Fax 614.752.5903
http://www.regents.state.oh.us/sgs/

Oklahoma State Regents for Higher Education
655 Research Parkway, Suite 200
Oklahoma City, OK 73104
800.858.1840
Oklahoma City: 225.9131
http://www.gsfc.org/Main/
dsp_main.cfm

Oregon Student Assistance Commission
1500 Valley River Drive, Suite 100
Eugene, OR 87401
541.687.7395
800.452.8807
http://www.ossc.state.or.us/

Pennsylvania Higher Education Assistance Authority
American Education Services
Education Services Group
1200 N 7th St.
Harrisburg, PA 17102-1444
Toll free U.S. & Canada:
800.699.2908
International: 717.720.3600
http://www.pheaa.org/index.html

Rhode Island Higher Education Assistance Authority
560 Jefferson Blvd.
Warwick, RI 02886
800.922.9855
401.736.1100
Fax 401.732.3541
http://www.riheaa.org/

South Carolina Higher Education Tuition Grants Commission
101 Business Park Boulevard
Suite 2100
Columbia, SC 29203-9498
803.896.1120
Fax 803.896.1126
http://www.sctuitiongrants.com/

South Dakota Board of Regents
306 East Capitol Ave., Suite 200
Pierre, SD 57501-2545
605.773.3455
http://www.sdbor.edu/

Tennessee Student Assistance Corporation
404 James Robertson Parkway
Suite 1950, Parkway Towers
Nashville, TN 37243-0820
Local: 615.741.1346
In state for grant information:
800.342.1663
In state for loan information:
800.447.1523
Out of state for loan information:
800.257.6526
Fax 615.741.6101
http://www.state.tn.us/tsac/

Texas Higher Education Coordinating Board
P.O. Box 12788
Austin, TX 78711
512.427.6101
Fax 512.427.6127
http://www.thecb.state.tx.us/

Utah System of Higher Education
60 South 400 West
Salt Lake City, UT 84101-1284
801.321.7101
http://www.utahsbr.edu/

**Vermont Student Assistance
Corporation**
P.O. Box 2000
Champlain Mill
Winooski, VT 05404
800.642.3177
Local: 802.655.9602
Fax 802.654.3765
http://services.vsac.org/ilwwcm/
connect/VSAC

**State Council of Higher Education
for Virginia**
101 N. 14TH St.,
James Monroe Bldg.
Richmond, VA 23219
804.225.2600
Fax 804.225.2604
http://www.schev.edu/

**Washington State Higher
Education Coordinating Board**
Student Financial Aid Division
P.O. Box 43430
Olympia, WA 98504-3430
888.535.0747
http://www.hecb.wa.gov/

**West Virginia Higher Education
Policy Commission**
1018 Kanawha Boulevard East,
Suite 700
Charleston, West Virginia 25301
304.558.2101
Fax 304.558.5719
http://www.hepc.wvnet.edu/

**Wisconsin Higher Educational
Aids Board**
P.O. Box 7885
Madison, WI 53707-7885
608.267.2206
Fax 608.267.2808
http://heab.state.wi.us/

GUIDE TO SCHOLARSHIPS

001

ADHA INSTITUTE

Who Can Apply: The minority scholarship is available to students enrolled in certificate/associate or bachelor's degree dental hygiene programs. Must have a 3.0 GPA and show financial need. Deadline May 1.
How Much Money Can I Get: $1,500
Whom Do I Contact: ADHA Institute for Oral Health, 444 N. Michigan Avenue, Suite 3400, Chicago, IL 60611, (312) 440-8900.

002

AFRICAN METHODIST EPISCOPAL CHURCH

Who Can Apply: Scholarships are available through local congregations. The AME church has over 8,000 congregations worldwide.
How Much Money Can I Get: Varies
Whom Do I Contact: African Methodist Episcopal Church, 2311 N Street, NW, Washington, DC 20037, (202) 337-3930.

003

AFRICAN METHODIST EPISCOPAL ZION CHURCH

Who Can Apply: This organization's 1.5 million members, encompassing 2,500 churches, provide scholarships for its college-bound members.
How Much Money Can I Get: Varies
Whom Do I Contact: African Methodist Episcopal Zion Church, 1200 Windermere Drive, Pittsburgh, PA 15218, (412) 242-5842.

004

UNIVERSITY OF AKRON

The Janet B. Purnell and W. Howard Fort Scholarship
Who Can Apply: Entering black students with a 3.0 GPA.
How Much Money Can I Get: $1,500
Whom Do I Contact: Director of Minority Affairs, Office of Minority Affairs, University of Akron, 302 E. Buchtel Avenue, Akron, OH 44325, (216) 375-7658.

005

ALABAMA A&M UNIVERSITY

Abigail K. Hobson Memorial Scholarship Award
Who Can Apply: Student majoring in Family and Consumer Sciences who demonstrates a need for financial aid, has an above average scholastic

record, and has desirable personal qualities.
How Much Money Can I Get: $500
Whom Do I Contact: Alabama A&M University, Alabama A&M University, Attn.: Financial Aid Office, P.O. Box 907, Normal, AL 35762, (256) 372-5400.

006

ALABAMA A&M UNIVERSITY
Academic Scholarship
Who Can Apply: Awards are based on SAT or ACT scores and a minimum high school 3.0 GPA.
How Much Money Can I Get: $3,160 to full tuition, fees, room, and board
Whom Do I Contact: Alabama A&M University, Attn.: Financial Aid Office, P.O. Box 907, Normal, AL 35762, (256) 372-5400.

007

ALABAMA A&M UNIVERSITY
Army Reserve Officers' Training Corps Scholarship (ROTC)
Who Can Apply: Students interested in learning more about military lifestyle. Awards are awarded on a competitive basis and are available for four years
How Much Money Can I Get: $100 per month for up to ten months of each academic year.
Whom Do I Contact: Alabama A&M University, Attn.: Financial Aid Office, P.O. Box 907, Normal, AL 35762, (256) 372-5400.

008

ALABAMA A&M UNIVERSITY
Athletic Scholarship
Who Can Apply: These awards are made in the sports of football, basketball, baseball, soccer, tennis, track & field, golf, softball and volleyball. The size of these awards varies.
How Much Money Can I Get: Varies
Whom Do I Contact: Alabama A&M University, Attn.: Financial Aid Office, P.O. Box 907, Normal, AL 35762, (256) 372-5400.

009

ALABAMA A&M UNIVERSITY
Department of Energy Computational Science Scholarship
Who Can Apply: Students must maintain a minimum 3.25 GPA and score a minimum 1220 SAT (27 ACT).
How Much Money Can I Get: $3,000

Whom Do I Contact: Alabama A&M University, Attn.: Financial Aid Office, P.O. Box 907, Normal, AL 35762, (256) 372-5400.

010

ALABAMA A&M UNIVERSITY
Eliza P. Patton Award
Who Can Apply: Two students majoring in Family and Consumer Sciences whose interests are Apparel, Merchandising, and Design and Nutrition and Hospitality Management where funds permit.
How Much Money Can I Get: $125
Whom Do I Contact: Alabama A&M University, Attn.: Financial Aid Office, P.O. Box 907, Normal, AL 35762, (256) 372-5400.

011

ALABAMA A&M UNIVERSITY
General Mills, Inc. -Total Quality Scholarship
Who Can Apply: Incoming freshman or existing undergraduates with a 3.0 GPA in the Food Science program.
How Much Money Can I Get: Tuition
Whom Do I Contact: Alabama A&M University, Attn.: Financial Aid Office, P.O. Box 907, Normal, AL 35762, (256) 372-5400.

012

ALABAMA A&M UNIVERSITY
L. L. Crump Scholarship
Who Can Apply: Academic merit, leadership potential, and evidence of responsible citizenship are the primary criteria for selection. Applicant must write a brief essay stating why he/she has chosen to study Planning and describe the contribution they hope to make to the profession.
How Much Money Can I Get: Varies
Whom Do I Contact: Alabama A&M University, Community Planning & Urban Studies, P.O. Box 206, Normal, Al 35762, or call (256) 858-4526.

013

ALABAMA A&M UNIVERSITY
Mathematics Scholarship
Who Can Apply: Students majoring in Mathematics can apply for this scholarship. During the summer that precedes the initial fall enrollment, scholarship recipients are required to participate in an eight-week summer program. Scholarships are renewable.
How Much Money Can I Get: $750 plus tuition, books, room and board is awarded during the summer program.

Whom Do I Contact: Alabama A&M University, Attn.: Financial Aid Office, P.O. Box 907, Normal, AL 35762, (256) 372-5400.

014

ALABAMA A&M UNIVERSITY

Mozelle Davis Award
Who Can Apply: Student with an option in Fashion Design within the Area of Apparel, Merchandising and Design.
How Much Money Can I Get: $200
Whom Do I Contact: Alabama A&M University, Attn.: Financial Aid Office, P.O. Box 907, Normal, AL 35762, (256) 372-5400.

015

ALABAMA A&M UNIVERSITY

Multicultural Scholarship
Who Can Apply: Students possessing a minimum 3.0 high school GPA and an average ACT score of 21 or higher. Candidates must submit a letter of recommendation by high school teachers and counselors and a completed Multicultural Scholars application containing an essay outlining the student's desire to major in a given food and agricultural science major and future career plans
How Much Money Can I Get: Varies
Whom Do I Contact: Alabama A&M University, Attn.: Financial Aid Office, P.O. Box 907, Normal, AL 35762. (256) 372-5400.

016

ALABAMA A&M UNIVERSITY

Performance Music Scholarship
Who Can Apply: Students who participate in choir and/or band.
How Much Money Can I Get: Varies
Whom Do I Contact: Alabama A&M University, Attn.: Financial Aid Office, P.O. Box 907, Normal, AL 35762. (256) 372-5400.

017

ALABAMA A&M UNIVERSITY

U.S. Housing and Urban Development Department Scholarship
Who Can Apply: Students demonstrating academic merit, leadership potential, and evidence of responsible citizenship.
How Much Money Can I Get: Monthly stipend of $750
Whom Do I Contact: Alabama A&M University, Attn.: Financial Aid Office, P.O. Box 907, Normal, AL 35762. (256) 372-5400. Ms. Constance Wilson at (256) 858-4992.

018
ALABAMA A&M UNIVERSITY
Wayne Hendrick Award
Who Can Apply: A student majoring in Nutrition and Hospitality Management.
How Much Money Can I Get: $1,000
Whom Do I Contact: Alabama A2&M University, Attn.: Office of Admissions, P.O. Box 908, Normal, AL 35762. (256) 372-5400.

019
ALABAMA COMMISSION ON HIGHER EDUCATION
Alabama Student Assistance Program
Who Can Apply: Undergraduate students who are Alabama residents attending eligible Alabama institutions. Nearly 80 Alabama institutions participate in the program.
How Much Money Can I Get: $300 to $2,500 per academic year
Whom Do I Contact: Alabama Commission on Higher Education, P. O. Box 302000, Montgomery, AL 36130-2000, (334) 242-1998.

020
ALABAMA DEPARTMENT OF EDUCATION
Alabama Scholarship for Dependents of Blind Parents
Who Can Apply: Students who are Alabama residents and from families in which the head of the family is blind and whose family income is insufficient to provide educational benefits for attendance at an Alabama post secondary institution
How Much Money Can I Get: Varies
Whom Do I Contact: Alabama Department of Education, Administrative and Financial Services Division, Gordon Persons Building, 50 North Ripley, Montgomery, AL 36130, (334) 242-9742.

021
ALABAMA STATE DEPARTMENT OF VETERANS AFFAIRS
Alabama GI Dependents' Educational Benefit Program
Who Can Apply: Students who are children or spouses of eligible Alabama veterans and who attend public post secondary educational institutions in Alabama. Candidates must enroll as an undergraduate student.
How Much Money Can I Get: Tuition, fees and books
Whom Do I Contact: Alabama State Department of Veterans Affairs, P.O. Box 1509, Montgomery, AL 36102-1509, (334) 242-5077.

022

ALABAMA STATE DEPARTMENT OF VETERANS AFFAIRS

Alabama National Guard Educational Assistance Program

Who Can Apply: Students who are active members in good standing with a federally recognized unit of the Alabama National Guard.

How Much Money Can I Get: $500 per term, and no more than $1,000 per year

Whom Do I Contact: Alabama State Department of Veterans Affairs, P.O. Box 1509, Montgomery, AL 36102-1509, (334) 242-5077.

023

ALABAMA STATE UNIVERSITY

Academic Scholarship

Who Can Apply: High school applicants must have a GPA of 3.51-3.75, or SAT score of 1100-1170 (24-26 ACT). Junior college transfer applicants must have a GPA of 3.51-3.75 after completion of 24 semester hours (36 quarter hours) of credit.

How Much Money Can I Get: Tuition

Whom Do I Contact: Director of Admissions, P.O. Box 271, Alabama State University, Montgomery, AL 36101.

024

ALABAMA STATE UNIVERSITY

Dean's Scholarship

Who Can Apply: High school applicants must have a GPA within the range of 3.26-3.50 or a SAT score of 990-1060 (21-23 ACT). Junior college transfer applicants must have a GPA within the range of 3.26-3.50 on a 4.0 scale after completion of 24 semester hours (36 quarter hours) of credit.

How Much Money Can I Get: Tuition

Whom Do I Contact: Director of Admissions, P.O. Box 271, Alabama State University, Montgomery, AL 36101, (334) 229-4291.

025

ALABAMA STATE UNIVERSITY

Incentive Scholarship

Who Can Apply: High school applicants must have a GPA within the range of 2.70-3.25 or a SAT score of 810-899 (17-20 ACT). Junior college transfer applicants must have a GPA within the range of 2.70-3.25, on a 4.0 scale, after completion of 24 semester hours (36 quarter hours) of credit.

How Much Money Can I Get: Tuition and books

Whom Do I Contact: Director of Admissions, P.O. Box 271, Alabama State University, Montgomery, AL 36101, (334) 229-4291.

026

ALABAMA STATE UNIVERSITY
Leadership Scholarship
Who Can Apply: High school applicants must have a GPA in the range of
2.70-2.99 or a SAT score of 770-820 (16-17 ACT). Junior college transfer
applicants must have a 2.70-2.99 GPA after completion of 24 semester hours
(36 quarter hours) of credit. Applicants must transfer from an accredited
college.
How Much Money Can I Get: $1,000
Whom Do I Contact: Director of Admissions, P.O. Box 271, Alabama State
University, Montgomery, AL 36101, (334) 229-4291.

027

ALABAMA STATE UNIVERSITY
Presidential Scholarship
Who Can Apply: High school applicants must have a minimum 3.76 GPA,
or a 1210 SAT (27 ACT). Junior college transfer applicants must possess a
minimum 3.76 GPA after completion of 24 semester hours (36 quarter hours)
of credit.
How Much Money Can I Get: $900 annually
Whom Do I Contact: Director of Admissions, P.O. Box 271, Alabama State
University, Montgomery, AL 36101, (334) 229-4291.

028

UNIVERSITY OF ALABAMA
Huntsville Scholarship
Who Can Apply: Must be a U.S. citizen, majoring in Engineering.
Renewable with a 3.0 GPA. Financial need required. Deadline December 3.
How Much Money Can I Get: $1,965
Whom Do I Contact: Admissions Office, University of Alabama, 124
University Center, Huntsville, AL 35899, (204) 894-6070.

029

UNIVERSITY OF ALABAMA
Ione Hendrick Roche Memorial Endowed Scholarship
Who Can Apply: Graduate-level and two undergraduate-level awards to
outstanding full-time female students at the University of Alabama, with
preference to minority students majoring in communications. Deadline
February 15.
How Much Money Can I Get: $1,000 renewable
Whom Do I Contact: University of Alabama, College of Communication,
P.O. Box 870172, Tuscaloosa, AL 34587-1072, (205) 348-5520.

030

UNIVERSITY OF ALABAMA

James T. and Joanne Lynagh Endowed Minority Scholarship
Who Can Apply: Outstanding full-time minority freshmen, sophomores, and juniors majoring in Communications. Deadline February 15.
How Much Money Can I Get: $1,000 renewable
Whom Do I Contact: University of Alabama, College of Communication, P.O. Box 870172, Tuscaloosa, AL 34587-1072, (205) 348-5520.

031

UNIVERSITY OF ALABAMA

New York Times **Minority Scholarship**
Who Can Apply: Freshmen must be Communication or Journalism majors. Deadline February 15.
How Much Money Can I Get: $800
Whom Do I Contact: University of Alabama, College of Communication, P.O. Box 870172, Tuscaloosa, AL 34587-1072, (205) 348-5520.

032

ALAMO COMMUNITY COLLEGE DISTRICT (ACCD)

Minority Teaching Fellowship Program
Who Can Apply: Recipients must pursue degrees on a full-time basis and not be employed. Candidates will be required to teach for at least three years in one of the district's campuses. Applicants are sought for architecture, art, business administration, chemistry, English/speech/foreign language, fine arts, government, history, math, music, natural science, political science, psychology, reading/education, social sciences, sociology, and theater/communications. Deadline April.
How Much Money Can I Get: Seven master's degree fellowships, approximately $33,000 annually
Whom Do I Contact: ACCD Minority Teaching Fellowship Program, ACCD, Human Resources, 811 W. Houston Street, San Antonio, TX 78207, (210) 220-1500.

033

ALBANY STATE COLLEGE

Alice Minor Stubbs Hawthorne Scholarship
Who Can Apply: Be enrolled in the Albany State College of Business and a major in Marketing or Management. Students must have a minimum 2.5 GPA and entering junior or senior status.
How Much Money Can I Get: Varies
Whom Do I Contact: Albany State College, Attn.: Financial Aid Department, 504 College Drive, Albany GA 31705, (229) 430-4650.

034

ALBANY STATE COLLEGE
Allied Health Sciences Scholarship
Who Can Apply: Students interested in pursuing a degree encourage in the Health Sciences Program.
How Much Money Can I Get: $1,000 yearly
Whom Do I Contact: Albany State College, Attn.: Financial Aid Department, 504 College Drive, Albany GA 31705, (229) 430-4650.

035

ALBANY STATE COLLEGE
Athletic Scholarship
Who Can Apply: Students involved in athletic sports.
How Much Money Can I Get: Varies
Whom Do I Contact: Albany State College, Attn.: Financial Aid Department, 504 College Drive, Albany GA 31705, (229) 430-4650.

036

ALBANY STATE COLLEGE
Criminal Justice Scholarship
Who Can Apply: Students majoring in Criminal Justice.
How Much Money Can I Get: $1,000 yearly
Whom Do I Contact: Albany State College, Attn.: Financial Aid Department, 504 College Drive, Albany GA 31705, (229) 430-4650.

037

ALBANY STATE COLLEGE
Georgia Public Safety Memorial Grant
Who Can Apply: Sons or daughters of any Georgia public safety officer who is killed or permanently disabled in the line of duty.
How Much Money Can I Get: Varies
Whom Do I Contact: Albany State College, Attn.: Financial Aid Department, 504 College Drive, Albany GA 31705, (229) 430-4650.

038

ALBANY STATE COLLEGE
HOPE Scholarship
Who Can Apply: Freshmen graduating from a Georgia high school with a minimum 3.0 GPA in a college preparatory curriculum.
How Much Money Can I Get: $150 per semester
Whom Do I Contact: Albany State College, Attn.: Financial Aid Department, 504 College Drive, Albany GA 31705, (229) 430-465

039

ALBANY STATE COLLEGE

HOPE Teacher Scholarship Program
Who Can Apply: Students or (teachers) who are seeking an advanced degree in a critical field of study.
How Much Money Can I Get: $10,000
Whom Do I Contact: Albany State College, Attn.: Financial Aid Department, 504 College Drive, Albany GA 31705, (229) 430-4650.

040

ALBANY STATE COLLEGE

HOPE Promise Scholarship Program
Who Can Apply: Students who commit to teach in a Georgia public school and have a cumulative 3.0 GPA or higher after the sophomore year in college.
How Much Money Can I Get: $3,000
Whom Do I Contact: Albany State College, Attn.: Financial Aid Department, 504 College Drive, Albany GA 31705, (229) 430-4650.

041

ALBANY STATE COLLEGE

HOPE Promise II Scholarship Program
Who Can Apply: Students seeking a B.A. in Education and are planning to become teachers in Georgia's public schools.
How Much Money Can I Get: $150 per semester
Whom Do I Contact: Albany State College, Attn.: Financial Aid Department, 504 College Drive, Albany GA 31705, (229) 430-4650.

042

ALBANY STATE COLLEGE

James H. Porter Academic Scholarship
Who Can Apply: Applicants must be a resident of Georgia and full-time undergraduate student with a minimum SAT score of 1100 (24 ACT) and 3.0 high school GPA of 3.0. Full-time graduate students must have a minimum undergraduate GPA of 3.5 and a minimum1110 on the GRE, 600 on the NTE or WCET of 600, or GMAT of 500. Other requirements are established by the Board of Regents.
How Much Money Can I Get: $3,000
Whom Do I Contact: Albany State College, Attn.: Financial Aid Department, 504 College Drive, Albany GA 31705, (229) 430-4650.

043

ALBANY STATE COLLEGE
Law Enforcement Personnel Dependents Grant
Who Can Apply: Eligible Georgia residents who are dependent children of Georgia law enforcement officers, prison guards, or firemen who are permanently disabled or killed in the line of duty.
How Much Money Can I Get: $2,000
Whom Do I College: Albany State College, Attn.: Financial Aid Department, 504 College Drive, Albany GA 31705, (229) 430-4650.

044

ALBANY STATE COLLEGE
Marie H. Dixon Scholarship
Who Can Apply: Applicants must possess a minimum 2.5 GPA and exhibit outstanding leadership abilities through specific activities and events. Students must also demonstrate financial need.
How Much Money Can I Get: $1,000
Whom Do I Contact: Albany State College Attn.: Office of Alumni Affairs, 504 College Drive, Albany, GA 31705, (229) 430-4658.

045

ALBANY STATE COLLEGE
Music Scholarship
Who Can Apply: Students majoring in Music.
How Much Money Can I Get: Varies
Whom Do I Contact: Albany State College, Attn.: Financial Aid Department, 504 College Drive, Albany GA 31705, (229) 430-4650.

046

ALBANY STATE COLLEGE
Presidential Scholarship
Who Can Apply: Recipients must rank in the upper five percent of their graduating high school class and must have attained a minimum SAT score of 1140 (25 ACT). A minimum 3.5 GPA is also required. Additionally, the applicant needs three letters of recommendation and a 500-word essay about the applicant's expectations of college.
How Much Money Can I Get: $5,764
Whom Do I Contact: Albany State College, Attn.: Financial Aid Department, 504 College Drive, Albany GA 31705, (229) 430-4650.

047

ALBANY STATE COLLEGE
Queen Mackey Sampson Scholarship
Who Can Apply: Students who have earned a minimum 2.5 GPA, exhibit outstanding leadership abilities through specific activities and events and demonstrates a financial need.
How Much Money Can I Get: $500
Whom Do I Contact: Albany State College, Attn.: Office of Alumni Affairs, 504 College Drive, Albany, GA 31705, (229) 430-4658.

048

ALBANY STATE COLLEGE
Regents' Opportunity Scholarship
Who Can Apply: Full-time graduate students who are residents of Georgia.
How Much Money Can I Get: Varies
Whom Do I Contact: Albany State College, Attn.: Financial Aid Department, 504 College Drive, Albany GA 31705, (229) 430-4650.

049

ALBANY STATE COLLEGE
Robert C. Byrd Scholarship Program
Who Can Apply: Students who demonstrate outstanding academic achievement.
How Much Money Can I Get: $1,500
Whom Do I Contact: Albany State College, Attn.: Financial Aid Department, 504 College Drive, Albany GA 31705, (229) 430-4650.

050

ALBANY STATE COLLEGE
Social Work Scholarship
Who Can Apply: Students interested in pursuing a degree in Social Work.
How Much Money Can I Get: $1,000
Whom Do I Contact: Albany State College, Attn.: Financial Aid Department, 504 College Drive, Albany GA 31705, (229) 430-4650.

051

ALBANY STATE COLLEGE
Transfer Scholarship
Who Can Apply: Students must be in good standing (a minimum cumulative 2.0 GPA) at the time of transfer. These scholarships are offered to students pursuing their first baccalaureate degree.
How Much Money Can I Get: $1,000

Whom Do I Contact: Albany State College, Attn.: Financial Aid Department, 504 College Drive, Albany GA 31705, (229) 430-4650.

052

ALBANY STATE COLLEGE
Ty Cobb Scholarship
Who Can Apply: Recipients must be a Georgia resident, demonstrate financial need, and possess a minimum 3.0 GPA.
How Much Money Can I Get: Tuition
Whom Do I Contact: Ty Cobb Foundation, P.O. Box 725, Forest Park, GA 30051.

053

ALBANY STATE COLLEGE
William Talley Memorial Scholarship
Who Can Apply: Black males admitted to the Teacher Education Program at Albany State College. Candidates must also have a minimum 2.5 GPA and demonstrate financial need.
How Much Money Can I Get: Varies
Whom Do I Contact: Albany State College, Attn.: Office of Alumni Affairs, 504 College Drive, Albany, GA 31705, (229) 430-4658.

054

ALFRED P. SLOAN FOUNDATION
Who Can Apply: Minority students who have completed their junior year in college and who are interested in government careers. Students must attend accredited summer institute. Deadline varies.
How Much Money Can I Get: $6,000
Whom Do I Contact: APAM Program, Alfred P. Sloan Foundation, 630 Fifth Avenue, Suite 2550, New York, NY 10111, (212) 582-0450.

055

ALPHA KAPPA ALPHA SORORITY
Who Can Apply: Qualified high school and college students. Many of the 700 local chapters offer scholarships that are almost exclusively for black women.
How Much Money Can I Get: Varies
Whom Do I Contact: Alpha Kappa Alpha Sorority, Inc., 5211 S. Greenwood Avenue, Chicago, IL 60615, (773) 684-1282.

056

ALPHA PHI ALPHA FRATERNITY
Who Can Apply: High school students involved in various educational and community projects.
How Much Money Can I Get: Varies
Whom Do I Contact: Alpha Phi Alpha Fraternity, Inc., 4432 S. Martin Luther King Drive, Chicago, IL 60653, (773) 373-1819.

057

ALPHA PHI ALPHA FRATERNITY
Who Can Apply: High school seniors of color with a B average graduating from the metro-Atlanta school system and are U.S. citizens pursuing careers in the newspaper industry and plan on attending Clark, Spelman, Morehouse, Morris Brown, Georgia State, Georgia Institute of Technology, Emory, or the University of Georgia; students intern at the *Atlanta Journal and Constitution* during summer and holiday breaks during college.
How Much Money Can I Get: Total financial support
Whom Do I Contact: Alpha Phi Alpha Fraternity, Inc., 4432 S. Martin Luther King Drive, Chicago, IL 60653, (773) 373-1819.

058

ALVERNO COLLEGE
Gardner Scholarship
Who Can Apply: Full-tuition scholarship for a Hispanic woman.
How Much Money Can I Get: Varies
Whom Do I Contact: Alverno College, Office of Student Financial Planning and Resources, 3401 S. 39 Street, Milwaukee, WI 53215, (414) 382-6000.

059

ALVERNO COLLEGE
Kraft Foundation Scholarship
Who Can Apply: Minority students who meet scholarship standards. New incoming students must participate in a scholarship opportunity day in order to be considered for scholarships.
How Much Money Can I Get: $1,800
Whom Do I Contact: Director of Financial Aid, Alverno College, Office of Financial Aid, 3401 S. 39 Street, Milwaukee, WI 53215, (414) 382-6046.

060

ALVERNO COLLEGE

Mark Scholarship
Who Can Apply: Minority students who meet Alverno's scholarship standards.
How Much Money Can I Get: Varies
WHOM DO I CONTACT: Alverno College, Office of Student Financial Planning and Resources, 3401 S. 39 Street, Milwaukee, WI 53215, (414) 382-6000.

061

ALVERNO COLLEGE

Schumann Scholarship
Who Can Apply: Minority students who meet Alverno's scholarship standards.
How Much Money Can I Get: Varies
WHOM DO I CONTACT: Alverno College, Office of Student Financial Planning and Resources, 3401 S. 39 Street, Milwaukee, WI 53215, (414) 382-6000.

062

ALVERNO COLLEGE

Wisconsin Bell Scholarship
Who Can Apply: Minority student specializing in technological areas.
How Much Money Can I Get: Varies
WHOM DO I CONTACT: Alverno College, Office of Student Financial Planning and Resources, 3401 S. 39 Street, Milwaukee, WI 53215, (414) 382-6000.

063

ALVERNO COLLEGE

Aetna Life & Casualty Foundation Scholarship Grant
Who Can Apply: Designed to help qualified minorities who, without such financial assistance, would possibly be unable to further their education.
How Much Money Can I Get: Varies
Whom Do I Contact: Alverno College, Office of Student Financial Planning and Resources, 3401 S. 39 Street, Milwaukee, WI 53215, (414) 382-6000.

064

ALVERNO COLLEGE

Brunswick Public Charitable Foundation
Who Can Apply: Scholarships for minority weekend college students.
How Much Money Can I Get: Varies
Whom Do I Contact: Alverno College, Office of Student Financial Planning and Resources, 3401 S. 39 Street, Milwaukee, WI 53215, (414) 382-6000.

065

ALVERNO COLLEGE

Cray Research Foundation
Who Can Apply: Scholarship money for minority students majoring in computer science or related disciplines.
How Much Money Can I Get: Varies
Whom Do I Contact: Alverno College, Office of Student Financial Planning and Resources, 3401 S. 39 Street, Milwaukee, WI 53215, (414) 382-6000.

066

AMERICAN ARCHITECTURAL FOUNDATION

American Architectural Foundation Minority Scholarship
Who Can Apply: Minority high school seniors entering a degree program at a school of architecture.
How Much Money Can I Get: Varies
Whom Do I Contact: Scholarship Program Director, The American Architectural Foundation, 1735 New York Avenue, NW, Washington, DC 20006.

067

AMERICAN CHEMICAL SOCIETY

Minority Scholarship
Who Can Apply: African Americans, Hispanics or Native American Indians who are college freshman, sophomores or juniors, planning to major in Chemistry, Biochemistry, or Chemical Engineering, enrolled full-time, with financial need. Deadline February.
How Much Money Can I Get: Up to $5,000 yearly, renewable
Whom Do I Contact: American Chemical Society Minority Scholars Programs, The American Chemical Society, 1155 16th Street, NW, Washington, DC 20036, (800) 227-5558.

068

AMERICAN CORRECTIONAL ASSOCIATION
The Martin Luther King Jr. Scholarship
Who Can Apply: Minority nominees enrolled in an undergraduate or graduate criminal justice program in a four-year college. Must demonstrate financial need and academic achievement.
How Much Money Can I Get: Varies
Whom Do I Contact: Martin Luther King Jr. Scholarship, American Correctional Association, 4380 Forbes Boulevard, Lanham, MD 20706-4322, (800)-222-5646.

069

AMERICAN DENTAL HYGIENISTS' ASSOCIATION
Who Can Apply: Minority students enrolled in a dental hygiene program. Applicants must have completed a minimum of one year in a dental hygiene curriculum and have a 3.0 GPA. Minimum financial need of $1,500. Deadline June 1.
How Much Money Can I Get: Varies
Whom Do I Contact: Minority Scholarships, American Dental Hygienists' Association, Institute for Oral Health, 444 N. Michigan Avenue, Suite 3400, Chicago, IL 60611, (312) 440-8900.

070

AMERICAN ECONOMIC ASSOCIATION
Federal Reserve Minority Fellowship Program
Who Can Apply: Minority Ph.D. students beginning dissertation research. Must be U.S. citizens and enrolled in an accredited economics program. Deadline March 1.
How Much Money Can I Get: $900 monthly stipend
Whom Do I Contact: The Joint Center for Political and Economic Studies, 1090 Vermont Ave., NW, Suite 1100, Washington, DC 20005, (202) 789-3500.

071

AMERICAN FOUNDATION FOR NEGRO AFFAIRS
AFNA New Access Routes to Professional Careers
Who Can Apply: Primarily for black high school students who have completed the 10th grade and who are residents of Philadelphia. Program is aimed at placing students at medical schools or laboratories to get research experience and earn money for college.
How Much Money Can I Get: Varies

Whom Do I Contact: American Foundation for Negro Affairs, 1700 Market Street, Philadelphia, PA 19103, (215) 563-1248.

072

AMERICAN FUND FOR DENTAL HEALTH
Minority Dental Student Scholarship
Who Can Apply: Minority first-year dental students attending a dental school in the U.S. accredited by the Commission on Dental Accreditation. Must demonstrate financial need, personal commitment to dentistry, school, and community services, activities, and awards. Deadline May 1.
How Much Money Can I Get: $1,000 to $2,000
Whom Do I Contact: Program Department, American Fund for Dental Health, 211 E. Chicago Avenue, Suite 820, Chicago, IL 60611, (312) 787-6270.

073

AMERICAN FUND FOR DENTAL HEALTH
Dental Scholarship for Minority Students
Who Can Apply: Applicants must have been accepted by a dental school in the U.S. accredited by the Commission on Dental Accreditation. Consideration will be given on academic performance, demonstrated financial need, personal commitment to dentistry, school and community service, activities and awards, and character references. Applications are available from the Student Affairs or Financial Aid office of the dental school to be attended. Applicants must submit the following: official application form, official transcripts of all college records, letter of acceptance from an accredited dental school, three letters of reference including one from an official of the dental school attesting to the applicant's character, personality, and academic ability, a financial needs statement, and the scores from the dental aptitude test. Deadline April 15.
How Much Money Can I Get: Varies
Whom Do I Contact: American Fund for Dental Health, 211 E. Chicago Avenue, Suite 820, Chicago, IL 60611, (312) 787-6270.

074

AMERICAN GEOLOGICAL INSTITUTE
Who Can Apply: Geoscience majors currently enrolled in accredited institutions as either undergraduate or graduate students are eligible to apply. Awards are based on academic excellence, need, and probable future success in the broad family of geoscience professions. Applicant must be a U.S. citizen.
How Much Money Can I Get: $250 to $1,500

Whom Do I Contact: University of New Orleans, Department of Geology/
Geophysiology, New Orleans, LA 70148.

075

AMERICAN GEOLOGICAL INSTITUTE, MINORITY PARTICIPATION

Who Can Apply: Applicants are judged on academic achievement, financial
need, and potential for success. Must be a U.S. citizen and majoring in one
of the following: Geology, Meteorology, Geochemistry, Planetary Geology,
Geophysics, Oceanography, Hydrology, or Earth Sciences. Deadline
February 1.
How Much Money Can I Get: Varies
Whom Do I Contact: Director of Education, American Geological Institute,
4220 King Street, Alexandria, VA 22302, (703) 379-2480.

076

AMERICAN HOME ECONOMICS ASSOCIATION FREDA DEKNIGHT FELLOWSHIP

Who Can Apply: African-American graduate students. Preference is given to
qualified applicants who plan to study in home economics communications
or work in cooperative extension. A $10 application fee must accompany
each request for fellowship materials.
How Much Money Can I Get: $1,500
Whom Do I Contact: American Home Economics Association, 2010
Massachusetts Avenue, NW, Washington, DC 20036-1028, (202) 862-8300.

077

AMERICAN HOME ECONOMICS ASSOCIATION
Flemmie P. Kittrell Fellowship
Who Can Apply: Members of minority groups in the U.S. and developing
countries pursuing graduate study. A $10 application fee must accompany
each request for fellowship materials. Must be majoring in home economics.
Deadline January 15.
How Much Money Can I Get: $3,000
Whom Do I Contact: American Home Economics Association, 2010
Massachusetts Avenue, NW, Washington, DC 20036-1028, (202) 862-8300.

078

AMERICAN INSTITUTE OF ARCHITECTS
Minority Program
Who Can Apply: Must be nominated and be a U.S. citizen. Candidates must
not have completed first year of a four-year program. Deadline January 15.

How Much Money Can I Get: Varies
Whom Do I Contact: Education Program Director, American Institute of Architects, 1735 New York Avenue, NW, Washington, DC 20006, (202) 626-7353.

079

AMERICAN INSTITUTE OF ARCHITECTS

Minority/Disadvantaged Scholarship Program
Who Can Apply: Students nominated by an architect or a counselor. Scholarships are renewable for three years.
How Much Money Can I Get: $400 to $3,000
Whom Do I Contact: Mary Felber, American Institute of Architects, 1735 New York Avenue, NW, Washington, DC 20006, (202) 626-7300.

080

AMERICAN INSTITUTE OF
CERTIFIED PUBLIC ACCOUNTANTS

Who Can Apply: Applicants must be minority students who are undergraduate accounting majors, U.S. citizens or permanent residents, and in financial need.
How Much Money Can I Get: Up to $1,500
Whom Do I Contact: Sharon Donahue, Manager, Minority Recruitment, American Institute of Certified Public Accountants, 1211 Avenue of the Americas, New York, NY 10036, (212) 575-7641.

081

AMERICAN INSTITUTE OF
CERTIFIED PUBLIC ACCOUNTANTS

Minority Doctoral Fellowship
Who Can Apply: Full-time minority students in doctoral accounting programs. Fellowships contingent upon acceptance of the candidate into a doctoral program in a recognized school of business. Must have a master's degree or completed a minimum of three years, full-time experience in accounting. Deadline April 1.
How Much Money Can I Get: $12,000 renewable
Whom Do I Contact: Minority Doctoral Fellowships, American Institute of Certified Public Accountants, 1211 Avenue of the Americas, New York, NY 10036-8775, (212) 596-6200.

082

AMERICAN INSTITUTE OF
CERTIFIED PUBLIC ACCOUNTANTS

Who Can Apply: Full-time minority students at a four-year accredited institution. Must have a minimum of 30 credit hours that include six hours in accounting with a minimum 3.0 GPA. Deadline July 1.

How Much Money Can I Get: Up to $5,000

Whom Do I Contact: Minority Doctoral Fellowships, American Institute of Certified Public Accountants, 1211 Avenue of the Americas, New York, NY 10036-8775, (212) 596-6200.

083

AMERICAN INSTITUTE OF
REAL ESTATE APPRAISERS

Appraisal Institute Education Trust Scholarship

Who Can Apply: U.S. citizens majoring (graduate or undergraduate) in Real Estate Appraisal, Land Economics, Real Estate, or allied fields. Awarded on the basis of academic merit. Deadline March 15.

How Much Money Can I Get: $3,000 for graduate level; $2,000 at the undergraduate level.

Whom Do I Contact: Appraisal Institute, 875 N. Michigan Avenue, Chicago, IL 60611-1980, (312) 335-4136.

084

AMERICAN LEGION AUXILIARY
SCHOLARSHIP PROGRAM

Who Can Apply: Students who are sons, daughters, grandsons, granddaughters of veterans of World War I, World War II, or the Korean and Vietnam Wars and who are residents of Alabama.

How Much Money Can I Get: Tuition, fees and board expenses

Whom Do I Contact: American Legion Department Headquarters, American Legion Auxiliary, 120 North Jackson Street, Montgomery, AL 36104, (334) 262-1176.

085

AMERICAN LIBRARY ASSOCIATION

LITA/OCLC Minority Scholarship in Library and Information Technology

Who Can Apply: Minorities interested in pursuing a master's degree in an ALA-accredited program.

How Much Money Can I Get: $2,500

Whom Do I Contact: American Library Association, 50 E. Huron Street, Chicago, IL 60611, (312) 944-6780.

086

AMERICAN LIBRARY ASSOCIATION

Louise Giles Minority Scholarship
Who Can Apply: Applicant must not have completed more than 12 semester hours and be enrolled in a library school offering an American Library Association accredited program. Applicants must be U.S. or Canadian citizens.
How Much Money Can I Get: $3,000
Whom Do I Contact: American Library Association, 50 E. Huron Street, Chicago, IL 60611, (312) 944-6780.

087

AMERICAN NURSES' ASSOCIATION

Clinical Fellowship Program for Ethnic/Racial Minorities
Who Can Apply: Applicants must be U.S. citizens or permanent residents. Fellowship is for doctoral study in psychiatric nursing. Deadline January 15.
How Much Money Can I Get: $7,500
Whom Do I Contact: American Nurses' Association, Ethnic/Racial Minority Fellowship Program, 2420 Pershing Road, Kansas City, MO 64108, (816) 474-5720.

088

AMERICAN NURSES ASSOCIATION

Kellogg Leadership Grant
Who Can Apply: Grant is for graduates of the minority fellowship programs seeking postdoctoral training in the form of leadership seminars and internships. Deadline January 15.
Whom Do I Contact: American Nurses Association Minority Fellowship Programs, 600 Maryland Avenue, SW, Suite 100W, Washington, DC 20024-2571, (202) 651-7246.

089

AMERICAN NURSES ASSOCIATION

Minority Fellowship Program
Who Can Apply: This program is designed for, but not limited to, minority R.N.'s interested in pursuing full-time study toward a baccalaureate degree in nursing. Recipients must be enrolled in an accredited baccalaureate nursing program. Deadline January.
How Much Money Can I Get: $2,000
Whom Do I Contact: American Nurses' Association Minority Fellowship Programs, 600 Maryland Avenue, SW, Suite 100W, Washington, DC 20024-2571, (202) 651-7246.

090

AMERICAN PHYSICAL SOCIETY

APS Minorities Scholarship Program
Who Can Apply: Minority high school seniors or college freshmen and sophomores majoring in Physics. Applicants must complete application and personal statement as well as provide references, official transcripts, and standardized test scores. Deadline February 17.
How Much Money Can I Get: $2,000 renewable
Whom Do I Contact: The American Physical Society, One Physics Ellipse, College Park, MD 20740-3844, (301) 209-3200.

091

AMERICAN PHYSICAL SOCIETY CORPORATE SPONSORED SCHOLARSHIPS FOR MINORITY UNDERGRADUATE STUDENTS IN PHYSICS

Who Can Apply: Awards sponsored by corporations and given to outstanding minority students who are majoring or plan to major in Physics.
How Much Money Can I Get: $2,000
Whom Do I Contact: The American Physical Society, One Physics Ellipse, College Park, MD 20740-3844, (301) 209-3200.

092

AMERICAN PLANNING ASSOCIATION

Planning Fellowship Program
Who Can Apply: Must be enrolled in a recognized graduate program and nominated by school. Deadline May 15.
How Much Money Can I Get: $2,000 to $5,000
Whom Do I Contact: Director of Council Programs, American Planning Association, 1776 Massachusetts Avenue, NW, Washington, DC 20036, (202) 872-0611.

093

AMERICAN POLITICAL SCIENCE ASSOCIATION

Black Graduate Fellowship Program
Who Can Apply: Applicants should be able to successfully pursue a doctoral degree in political science. Applicants with the greatest financial need will be given preference.
How Much Money Can I Get: $6,000
Whom Do I Contact: American Political Science Association, 1527 New Hampshire Avenue, NW, Washington, DC 20036, (202) 483-2512.

094

AMERICAN PSYCHOLOGICAL ASSOCIATION
APA Minority Fellowship Program in Clinical Training
Who Can Apply: Applicants must be U.S. citizens or permanent residents, enrolled full-time in an accredited doctoral program committed to a career in psychology related to ethnic minority mental health. Selection is based on clinical and/or research potential, scholarship, writing ability, ethnic minority identification, knowledge of broad issues in psychology, and professional commitment. Students of clinical and counseling psychology and students working on a master's degree only are ineligible. Recipients are obligated to provide clinical services to underserved populations within 24 months after the completion of their training and for a period equal to the length of the award. This obligation may not be fulfilled in private clinical practice. Deadline January.
How Much Money Can I Get: Varies
Whom Do I Contact: American Psychological Association, Attn.: Minority Fellowship Program, 750 First Street, NE, Washington, DC 20002-4242, (202) 336-5500.

095

AMERICAN PSYCHOLOGY ASSOCIATION
Minority Fellowship Program
Who Can Apply: Minority research-science students. Deadline January 15.
How Much Money Can I Get: Varies
Whom Do I Contact: APA Minority Fellowship Program, 1200 17th Street, NW, Washington, DC 20036, (913) 864-3881.

096

AMERICAN RESPIRATORY CARE FOUNDATION
The Jimmy Young Scholarships—Respiratory Care
Who Can Apply: Applicants must be U.S. citizens or have visas, be of a minority origin, be enrolled in an American Medical Association–approved respiratory care program, demonstrate financial need, submit at least two letters of recommendation attesting to worthiness and potential in the field (one from program director or senior faculty member, and one from medical director), and submit an original referenced paper on some facet of respiratory care.
How Much Money Can I Get: $1,000
Whom Do I Contact: American Respiratory Care Foundation, 11030 Ables Lane, Dallas, TX 75229, (214) 243-2272.

097

AMERICAN SOCIETY FOR MICROBIOLOGY

Predoctoral Minority Fellowship

Who Can Apply: U.S. citizens of color who are formally admitted as fully qualified prospective candidates for a Ph.D. degree in microbiology in an accredited institution in the United States. Financial need required. Deadline May 1.

How Much Money Can I Get: $9,250

Whom Do I Contact: Public Affairs Director, American Society for Microbiology, 1325 Massachusetts Avenue, NW, Washington, DC 20005, (202) 833-9680.

098

AMERICAN SOCIOLOGICAL ASSOCIATION

Minority Fellowship Program

Who Can Apply: U.S. citizens and permanent visa residents in a full-time sociology doctoral program. The purpose of the award is to contribute to the development of sociology by recruiting persons who will add differing orientations and creativity to the field. Deadline December 31.

How Much Money Can I Get: $10,008 plus tuition

Whom Do I Contact: Minority Fellowship Program, American Sociological Association, 1722 N Street, NW, Washington, DC 20036, (202) 833-3410, fax: (202) 785-0146.

099

AMERICAN SPEECH-LANGUAGE-HEARING FOUNDATION

Kala Singh Memorial Scholarship

Who Can Apply: Priority is given to applicants who are foreign or minority students studying communication sciences in the continental U.S. The student must be accepted for graduate study in an ASLH Educational Standards Board–accredited program, must be enrolled for full-time study, must be in need of financial aid, must be in good academic standing, must be recommended by a committee of two or more persons, and must not have received a prior scholarship from the American Speech-Language-Hearing Foundation. Deadline June 15.

How Much Money Can I Get: $2,000

Whom Do I Contact: Scholarship Committee, American Speech-Language-Hearing Foundation, 10801 Rockville Pike, Rockville, MD 20852, (301) 897-5700.

100

AMERICAN SPEECH-LANGUAGE-HEARING FOUNDATION

Young Scholars Award

Who Can Apply: College seniors who have been accepted for full-time study in a graduate program in speech-language pathology or audiology for the forthcoming academic term. Student must also be a U.S. citizen and a racial/ethnic minority and submit an original scholarly paper. Must be majoring in one of the following: speech pathology, speech/hearing, speech, or speech therapy. Deadline May 1.

How Much Money Can I Get: $2,000

Whom Do I Contact: Scholarship Committee, American Speech-Language-Hearing Foundation, 10801 Rockville Pike, Rockville, MD 20852, (301) 897-5700.

101

AMERICAN UNIVERSITY

Frederick Douglass Scholarship

Who Can Apply: Undergraduate students who have graduated from a District of Columbia high school and who demonstrate academic achievement and financial need. The scholarship ranges from partial to full tuition for recipients who are enrolled on a full-time basis. The Frederick Douglass Scholarship program is open only to applicants who are U.S. citizens and persons who hold permanent resident status. The applicant must be admissible to an undergraduate degree program at the American University and must have significant financial need. Students seeking admission should have at least a 2.5 GPA on a 4.0 scale, rank in the top half of their graduating class, and have acceptable SAT or ACT scores. Deadline February 1.

How Much Money Can I Get: Varies

Whom Do I Contact: Financial Aid Director, American University, 4400 Massachusetts Avenue, NW, Washington, DC 20016, (202) 885-6100.

102

AMERICAN UNIVERSITY

Hechinger Foundation Scholarship

Who Can Apply: Preference is given to a black undergraduate student from the District of Columbia who is majoring in business. Deadline March 1.

How Much Money Can I Get: Varies

Whom Do I Contact: American University, 4400 Massachusetts Avenue, NW, Washington, DC 20016, (202) 885-6100.

103

AMERICAN UNIVERSITY

Special Opportunity Grant

Who Can Apply: U.S.-born graduate students for up to 24 semester hours of tuition remission per year and/or a stipend for a service commitment. Deadline March 1.

How Much Money Can I Get: Varies

Whom Do I Contact: Graduate Affairs Office, American University, 4400 Massachusetts Avenue, NW, Washington, DC 20016, (202) 885-6100.

104

ANTIOCH COLLEGE

Alfred Hampton Memorial Scholarship

Who Can Apply: Minorities with strong academic records and demonstrated qualities of creativity. Must submit an essay about a challenging experience. Deadline February 1.

How Much Money Can I Get: Up to $5,000

Whom Do I Contact: Office of Admissions, Antioch College, Yellow Springs, OH 45387, (513) 757-6400.

105

ANTIOCH COLLEGE

Antioch Minority Science Scholarship

Who Can Apply: Applicants must be a Science major with a strong academic record and an interest in exploring the relationship between science and society. Deadline January 31.

How Much Money Can I Get: Full tuition

Whom Do I Contact: Office of Admissions, Antioch College, Yellow Springs, OH 45387, (800) 543-9436 outside Ohio, (513) 767-7047 call collect inside Ohio.

106

ANTIOCH COLLEGE

Atlanta Scholarship

Who Can Apply: Applicants must be an Atlanta-area resident with a strong academic record. Deadline January 31.

How Much Money Can I Get: Full tuition

Whom Do I Contact: Office of Admissions, Antioch College, Yellow Springs, OH 45387, (800) 543-9436 outside Ohio, (513) 767-7047 call collect inside Ohio.

107

ANTIOCH COLLEGE

Horace Mann Scholarship

Who Can Apply: Applicants must have a strong record as an activist on behalf of humanitarian values (e.g., peace, civil rights, environment) with a strong academic record. Deadline January 31.

How Much Money Can I Get: Full tuition

Whom Do I Contact: Office of Admissions, Antioch College, Yellow Springs, OH 45387, (800) 543-9436 outside Ohio, (513) 767-7047 call collect inside Ohio.

108

ANTIOCH COLLEGE

Upward Bound Scholarship

Who Can Apply: Applicants must have been a participant in Upward Bound or similar program and have a strong academic background. A separate admissions and scholarship application must be completed. The student must also go through a personal interview. Deadline January 15.

How Much Money Can I Get: Full tuition

Whom Do I Contact: Office of Admissions, Antioch College, Yellow Springs, OH 45387, (800) 543-9436 outside Ohio, (513) 767-7047 call collect inside Ohio.

109

APPALACHIAN STATE UNIVERSITY

Minority Presence Grant

Who Can Apply: Black North Carolina residents who enroll in a degree program on at least a half-time basis. Applicants must be entering freshman who demonstrate exceptional financial need. Students may apply by completing the university's application for student financial aid and the financial aid form. Deadline March 15.

How Much Money Can I Get: Varies

Whom Do I Contact: Financial Aid Director, Appalachian State University, Boone, NC 28608, (704) 262-2190.

110

ARISTO CLUB OF BOSTON

Competitive Scholarship

Who Can Apply: Applicants must be a black senior high school student in a Massachusetts high school who is entering a college or university in the fall and has at least a B average. The application must be in the form of a letter, signed by the applicant, and contain the following information: (1) Name,

address, and telephone number; (2) date of birth; (3) parent's names or person in loco parentis; (4) school attending and course pursuing; (5) school, church, and community activities; and (6) reasons for desiring a college education. A transcript of high school record must be filed with the application together with certified rank from the principal or headmaster. The applicant must submit at least three letters of recommendation from three reliable persons. Applicants are advised to follow through personally on these references as no application will be considered complete without them. Consideration for the award will be limited to the first 20 eligible applications received. Applicants will be notified of the time and place for an interview. Among the topics for discussion during the interview will be current events, individual background for chosen course, and personal community participation. Deadline April 20.
How Much Money Can I Get: Varies
Whom Do I Contact: Aristo Club of Boston, 193 Fayerweather Street, Cambridge, MA 02138.

111

ARIZONA MINORITY HIGH SCHOOL SCHOLARSHIPS

Who Can Apply: Arizona minority students pursuing postsecondary education.
How Much Money Can I Get: $5,500 to $6,400
Whom Do I Contact: (602) 869-8825

112

UNIVERSITY OF ARIZONA

Roy Drachman Minority Award
Who Can Apply: Students entering a journalism program. Deadline April 1.
How Much Money Can I Get: $1,000
Whom Do I Contact: University of Arizona, Department of Journalism, Tucson, AZ 85721, (602) 621-7556.

113

ARKANSAS STATE UNIVERSITY

William Randolph Hearst Minority Scholarship
Who Can Apply: Entering first-year students and beyond. Deadline April 1.
How Much Money Can I Get: $300 to $8,400 scholarship or graduate assistantship
Whom Do I Contact: Arkansas State University, College of Communications, P.O. Box 540, State University, AR 72467, (501) 972-2468.

114

UNIVERSITY OF ARKANSAS

Minority Incentive Tuition Grant
Who Can Apply: Open to black U.S. citizens. Deadline June 1.
How Much Money Can I Get: $1,000
Whom Do I Contact: Graduate School Dean, University of Arkansas, Office of Financial Aid, 2801 S. University, Little Rock, AR 72204, (501) 569-3206.

115

ARMCO MINORITIES ENGINEERING SCHOLARSHIPS

Who Can Apply: Black students who are planning to major in engineering, rank in the top third of their class, and are residents of a community where a participating Armco facility is located.
How Much Money Can I Get: $2,000
Whom Do I Contact: Armco Insurance Group, 703 Curtis Street, Middletown, OH 45043, (513) 425-5293.

116

ARMCO MINORITIES IN INSURANCE AND RISK MANAGEMENT SCHOLARSHIP

Who Can Apply: Black seniors who rank in the top half of their class and plan to major in business. Applicants must reside in a community where a participating Armco facility is located.
How Much Money Can I Get: $2,000
Whom Do I Contact: Armco Insurance Group, 703 Curtis Street, Middletown, OH 45043, (513) 425-5293.

117

ARMSTRONG WORLD INDUSTRIES

Multicultural Education Scholarship
Who Can Apply:. Minorities who are college juniors majoring in Business, Engineering, Information Systems, Chemistry, or Accounting with a cumulative 3.0 GPA and participation in school activities. Applicants must attend a college where Armstrong recruits (check school's financial aid office for more information). Deadline is the first quarter of each calendar year.
How Much Money Can I Get: Varies
Whom Do I Contact: Multicultural Education Scholarships, Armstrong World Industries, P.O. Box 3001, Lancaster, PA 17604.

118

ARMY ROTC QUALITY ENRICHMENT PROGRAM

Who Can Apply: Must be a U.S. citizen and be physically fit and have good grades. Will be commissioned as an officer after graduation. Deadline December 1.

How Much Money Can I Get: $200 a year

Whom Do I Contact: Army ROTC QEP, 11499 Chester, Suite 403, Cincinnati, OH 45246, (513) 772-6135.

119

ASBURY PARK PRESS

Minority Scholarship Program

Who Can Apply: High school seniors from Monmouth County, NJ, and from Ocean County, NJ, pursuing a communications degree. Award is renewable for up to four years.

How Much Money Can I Get: $1,500

Whom Do I Contact: Asbury Park Press, News Department, Minority Scholarship Program, 3601 Highway 66, P.O. Box 1550, Neptune, NJ 07754.

120

AT&T BELL LABORATORIES

Cooperative Research Fellowship Program

Who Can Apply: Minority graduate students who are working toward Ph.D. programs in engineering, chemistry, physics, statistics, and other areas. Deadline January 15.

How Much Money Can I Get: Full tuition, plus renewable $13,200 stipend, summer internships included

Whom Do I Contact: ESP Manager, AT&T Bell Laboratories, 600 Mountain Avenue, RM3D-303, P.O. Box 636, Murray Hill, NJ 07974-0636, (908) 582-6461.

121

AT&T BELL LABORATORIES

Engineering Scholarship

Who Can Apply: Applicants must be minority students with a 3.0 GPA majoring in Electrical or Mechanical Engineering or Computer Science. Deadline January 15.

How Much Money Can I Get: Tuition and fees

Whom Do I Contact: ESP Manager, AT&T Bell Laboratories, 600 Mountain Avenue, RM3D-303, P.O. Box 636, Murray Hill, NJ 07974-0636, (908) 582-6461.

122

AURORA UNIVERSITY
Presidential Minority Achievement Scholarship
Who Can Apply: Graduating minority high school seniors entering Aurora University as full-time students with strong SAT and ACT scores.
How Much Money Can I Get: Tuition, room and board
Whom Do I Contact: Aurora University, Attn.: Office of University Admissions, 347 S. Gladstone Avenue, Aurora, IL 60506-4892, (708) 896-1975.

123

BALL STATE UNIVERSITY
Academic Recognition Award
Who Can Apply: Awarded to out-of-state minority high school seniors who have a cumulative 3.0 GPA, rank in the top 50 percent of their class, and have taken a college preparatory curriculum.
How Much Money Can I Get: $4,380
Whom Do I Contact: Ball State University, Attn.: Office of Scholarships and Financial Aid, Lucina Hall, Room 245, Muncie, IN 47306, (317) 285-5600.

124

BALL STATE UNIVERSITY
Holmes/McFadden Memorial Award
Who Can Apply: Minority student majoring in Journalism. Deadline February 15.
How Much Money Can I Get: $1,000
Whom Do I Contact: Ball State University, Attn.: Journalism Department, 2000 University Avenue, Muncie, IN 47306, (317) 285-8200.

125

BALL STATE UNIVERSITY
Library Science Scholarship
Who Can Apply: These library training fellowship grants are provided by the U.S. Department of Education.
How Much Money Can I Get: $8,000
Whom Do I Contact: Library Science Department, Ball State University, 2000 University Avenue, Muncie, IN 47306, (317) 285-5900.

126

BALTIMORE SUN SCHOLARSHIP FOR MINORITY JOURNALISTS
Who Can Apply: Applicants must be enrolled in a four-year institution and

have a minimum 3.5 GPA. Preference given to Maryland students. Deadline December 30.

How Much Money Can I Get: $7,500

Whom Do I Contact: Human Resources Administration, *The Baltimore Sun*, 501 N. Calvert Street, P.O. Box 1377, Baltimore, MD 21278-0001, (301) 332-6268.

127

BAPTIST GENERAL CONVENTION OF TEXAS

Texas Black Baptist Scholarship Program

Who Can Apply: Applicant must be a black American, a member of a Baptist church, a graduate of a Texas school, and recommended by a pastor and teacher. In addition, the applicant must have maintained a B average in high school, given evidence of being a "genuine Christian," possess a "vital interest in the advancement of the Kingdom of God," and attend a Texas Baptist educational institution agreed upon by the scholarship committee.

How Much Money Can I Get: Up to $800

Whom Do I Contact: Baptist General Convention of Texas, 511 North Akard, Suite 1013, Dallas, TX 75201-3355, (214) 741-1991.

128

BARBER-SCOTIA COLLEGE

The United Negro College Fund Scholarship

Who Can Apply: Entering black students are eligible. Must have a strong academic background. Apply early.

How Much Money Can I Get: $100 to $2,000

Whom Do I Contact: Financial Aid Office, Barber-Scotia College, 145 Cabarrus Avenue, Concord, NC 28025, (704) 786-5171.

129

BENEDICT COLLEGE

100 Black Men of America Scholarship

Who Can Apply: Undergraduate black male at an accredited postsecondary institute or incoming Freshman black male. Recipients are required to perform 25 hours of community service prior to as well as during their applicable school year. Candidates must show leadership involvement and provide a copy of their transcript and an essay. Minimum 2.5 GPA is required. Deadline is February 28.

How Much Money Can I Get: Varies

Whom Do I Contact: Benedict College, Scholarship Office, 1600 Harden Street, Columbia, S.C. 29204, (803) 733-7431.

130

BENEDICT COLLEGE

Academic Excellence Scholarship

Who Can Apply: Students with an 800-890 SAT score (16-17 ACT) and 3.0 GPA.

How Much Money Can I Get: $2,823 annually

Whom Do I Contact: Benedict College, Scholarship Office, 1600 Harden Street, Columbia, S.C. 29204, (803)733-7431.

131

BENEDICT COLLEGE

AICPA/Accountemps Student Scholarship

Who Can Apply: Sophomore, junior, senior, or Graduate students at American Institute of Certified Public Accountants student affiliate majoring in Accounting, Finance or Information Systems possessing at least a 3.0 GPA are eligible. Each applicant must also be enrolled as a full-time undergraduate or graduate student and have completed the equivalent of at least 30 semester hours. Letters of recommendation and an essay are also required. Deadline is April 1.

How Much Money Can I Get: $2,500

Whom Do I Contact: Benedict College, Scholarship Office, 1600 Harden Street, Columbia, S.C. 29204, (803) 733-7431.

132

BENEDICT COLLEGE

Army ROTC Scholarship

Who Can Apply: Candidates must be in the upper 25% of their senior class, with a minimum 850 SAT (19 ACT) and possess leadership potential, good moral character, and be oriented toward the Army. Students must maintain a 2.5 GPA to retain full-time status. Applicants must be U.S. citizens.

How Much Money Can I Get: Full tuition and academic fees, flat rate for books and supplies, room & board, tax-exempt monthly stipend

Whom Do I Contact: Benedict College, Scholarship Office, 1600 Harden Street, Columbia, S.C. 29204, (803) 733-7431.

133

BENEDICT COLLEGE

Army ROTC Scholarship

Who Can Apply: Sophomores who have completed no more than three semesters of full-time study. Applicants must be U.S. citizens.

How Much Money Can I Get: Varies

Whom Do I Contact: Benedict College, Scholarship Office, 1600 Harden Street, Columbia, S.C. 29204, (803) 733-7431.

134

BENEDICT COLLEGE

Dean's Scholarship

Who Can Apply: Students with a 1000-1040 SAT score (20-21 ACT) and 3.0 GPA.

How Much Money Can I Get: $3,994 annually

Whom Do I Contact: Benedict College, Scholarship Office, 1600 Harden Street, Columbia, S.C. 29204, (803) 733-7431.

135

BENEDICT COLLEGE

Departmental Scholarship

Who Can Apply: Students with a 900-990 SAT score (18-19 ACT) and 3.0 GPA.

How Much Money Can I Get: $2,823 annually

Whom Do I Contact: Benedict College, Scholarship Office, 1600 Harden Street, Columbia, S.C. 29204, (803) 733-7431.

136

BENEDICT COLLEGE

Dwight David Eisenhower Transportation Fellowship

Who Can Apply: This scholarship program is sponsored by the U.S. Department of Transportation to students who have and expressed interested in the transportation industry.

How Much Can I Get: $44,000

Whom Do I Contact: Benedict College, Scholarship Office, 1600 Harden Street, Columbia, S.C. 29204, (803) 733-7431.

137

BENEDICT COLLEGE

John L. Carey Scholarship

Who Can Apply: This scholarship program provides financial assistance to liberal arts degree holders pursuing graduate studies in accounting. Scholarship is renewable for an additional year of study provided satisfactory scholastic progress is maintained. Deadline is April 1.

How Much Money Can I Get: $5,000

Whom Do I Contact: Benedict College, Scholarship Office, 1600 Harden Street, Columbia, S.C. 29204, (803) 733-7431.

138

BENEDICT COLLEGE

Medtronic Foundation Scholarship/Internship

Who Can Apply: Undergraduate sophomores or juniors with a minimum 3.3

GPA majoring in Engineering or Science. Applicants chosen will participate in a paid summer internship at Medtronic in Minnesota and upon completion, receive the scholarship. Deadline is March 15.
How Much Money Can I Get: $5,000
Whom Do I Contact: Benedict College, Scholarship Office, 1600 Harden Street, Columbia, S.C. 29204, (803) 733-7431.

139

BENEDICT COLLEGE
Mercedes-Benz USA Scholarship Program
Who Can Apply: High school seniors who have a minimum cumulative 3.0 GPA or students who will be the first generation in their families to attend college. Applicants must plan to enroll in a full-time undergraduate course at a two- or four-year university or vocational training school and be U. S. citizens.
Students must enroll no later than fall 2005.
How Much Can I Get: $2,000 non-renewable
Whom Do I Contact: Benedict College, Scholarship Office, 1600 Harden Street, Columbia, S.C. 29204, (803) 733-7431.

140

BENEDICT COLLEGE
National Security Education Program David L. Boren Scholarship
Who Can Apply: Award recipients will be selected on the basis of merit. The NSEP service requirement stipulates that an award recipient work in the Departments of Defense, Homeland Security, State, or the Intelligence Community. Academic record and potential to succeed in the proposed study abroad experience are also considered, along with commitment to international education to fulfill academic and career goals.
How Much Money Can I Get: Award amounts are based on the study abroad costs and financial aid information provided by the applicant. The maximum award is $10,000 for a semester or $20,000 for a full academic year.
Whom Do I Contact: Benedict College, Scholarship Office, 1600 Harden Street, Columbia, S.C. 29204, (803) 733-7431.

141

BENEDICT COLLEGE
Palmetto Fellows Scholarship
Who Can Apply: Sophomores and juniors with a minimum 1200 SAT score (27 ACT), 3.5 GPA and class rank in top 5%. Applicants must be S.C. residents.

How Much Money Can I Get: $6,700 annually
Whom Do I Contact: Benedict College, Scholarship Office, 1600 Harden Street, Columbia, S.C. 29204, (803) 733-7431.

142

BENEDICT COLLEGE
Patrick & Welch International Trade Scholarship
Who Can Apply: Rising junior or senior with a minimum 3.2 GPA.
Applicants must demonstrate proven interest in international trade or related area
How Much Money Can I Get: Varies
Whom Do I Contact: Benedict College, Scholarship Office, 1600 Harden Street, Columbia, S.C. 29204, (803) 733-7431.

143

BENEDICT COLLEGE
Presidential Scholarship
Who Can Apply: Students with a 1050-1090 SAT score (22-23 ACT), a 3.2 GPA and class rank in top 25% or valedictorian.
How Much Money Can I Get: $6,816 annually
Whom Do I Contact: Benedict College, Scholarship Office, 1600 Harden Street, Columbia, S.C. 29204, (803) 733-7431.

144

BENEDICT COLLEGE
S.C. Hope Scholarship
Who Can Apply: Students with a minimum 3.0 GPA. Applicants must be S.C. residents.
How Much Money Can I Get: $2,650 non-renewable
Whom Do I Contact: Benedict College, Scholarship Office, 1600 Harden Street, Columbia, S.C. 29204, (803) 733-7431.

145

BENEDICT COLLEGE
S.C. Life Scholarship
Who Can Apply: Students with two of the following: a minimum 1100 SAT score (24 ACT), 3.5 GPA and class ranking in top 30% of H.S. class.
Applicants must be S.C. residents.
How Much Money Can I Get: $5,000 annually
Whom Do I Contact: Benedict College, Scholarship Office, 1600 Harden Street, Columbia, S.C. 29204, (803) 733-7431.

146

BENEDICT COLLEGE

Sophomore Scholarship
Who Can Apply: Full-time Benedict College sophomores. Typical recipient earns a minimum 15 hours per semester and 3.6 GPA.
How Much Can I Get: $2,663
Whom Do I Contact: Benedict College, Scholarship Office, 1600 Harden Street, Columbia, S.C. 29204, (803) 733-7431.

147

BENEDICT COLLEGE

Trustee Club Scholarship
Who Can Apply: National Achievement/Merit Semifinalist with a minimum 1200 SAT score (27 ACT), a 3.5 GPA and class rank in top 10%.
How Much Money Can I Get: Tuition, most fees, textbook voucher, room & board
Whom Do I Contact: Benedict College, Scholarship Office, 1600 Harden Street, Columbia, S.C. 29204, (803) 733-7431.

148

BENEDICT COLLEGE

Trustee Scholarship
Who Can Apply: Students with 1100-1190 SAT score (24-26 ACT), a 3.25 GPA and class rank in top 25%.
How Much Money Can I Get: Tuition, textbook voucher
Whom Do I Contact: Benedict College, Scholarship Office, 1600 Harden Street, Columbia, S.C. 29204, (803) 733-7431.

149

BENEDICT COLLEGE

United Negro College Fund/CDM Scholarship
Who Can Apply: Undergraduate students majoring in Engineering who maintains a minimum 3.0 GPA.
How Much Money Can I Get: $5,000
Whom Do I Contact: Benedict College, Scholarship Office, 1600 Harden Street, Columbia, S.C. 29204, (803) 733-7431.

150

BENEDICT COLLEGE

United Negro College Fund/Citigroup Fellows Scholarship
Who Can Apply: Applicants must be second-term freshmen with a business-related major and a minimum 3.2 GPA. In addition to the scholarship,

recipients receive a Citigroup mentor and attend the annual leadership conference for fellows and mentors.

How Much Money Can I Get: $6,400

Whom Do I Contact: Benedict College, Scholarship Office, 1600 Harden Street, Columbia, S.C. 29204, (803) 733-7431.

151

BENEDICT COLLEGE

United Negro College Fund/Nestle Very Best Adopt-A-School Scholarship

Who Can Apply: This scholarship is open to all students who were in the 3rd through 6th grade during the 1998-99 school year at Nestle Adopt-A-Schools. Applicants apply during their senior year of high school. This scholarship will be renewable for up to four years if they attend school full time and maintain a minimum 2.5 GPA. Deadline is May 16.

How Much Money Can I Get: $4,000 annual scholarship if they attend a UNCF member institution. $3,000 annual scholarship if they attend any other college or university.

Whom Do I Contact: Benedict College, Scholarship Office, 1600 Harden Street, Columbia, S.C. 29204, (803) 733-7431.

152

BENEDICT COLLEGE

United Negro College Fund/UPS Corporate Scholarship

Who Can Apply: Undergraduate sophomores an juniors with a minimum 3.0 GGP majoring in Finance, Marketing, Computer Science, Human Resources, Information Technology, Industrial Engineering. Deadline is February 7. In addition to scholarship, recipients will also receive an internship at UPS corporate offices.

How Much Can I Get: At least $10,000

Whom Do I Contact: Benedict College, Scholarship Office, 1600 Harden Street, Columbia, S.C. 29204, (803) 733-7431.

153

BENNETT COLLEGE

African American Atelier/Miller Memorial Prize

Who Can Apply: The student must exhibit high academic ability and a commitment to the discipline. A minimum 3.0 GPA is required.

How Much Money Can I Get: $500

Whom Do I Contact: Bennett College, Financial Aid Office, 900 East Washington Street, Greensboro, NC 27401-3239, (800) 413-5323.

154

BENNETT COLLEGE

A.J. Fletcher Music Scholarship
Who Can Apply: Student must be Music major who exhibit outstanding talent and who achieve and maintain a minimum 3.0 GPA.
How Much Money Can I Get: Tuition
Whom Do I Contact: Bennett College, Financial Aid Office, 900 East Washington Street, Greensboro, NC 27401-3239, (800) 413-5323.

155

BENNETT COLLEGE

CRC Freshwomen Chemistry Achievement Award
Who Can Apply: Student who has attained the highest academic performance in General Chemistry: CH 101-102.
How Much Money Can I Get: $250
Whom Do I Contact: Bennett College, Financial Aid Office, 900 East Washington Street, Greensboro, NC 27401-3239, (800) 413-5323.

156

BENNETT COLLEGE

Dr. Cortis & Marie Torrance Scholarship in Home Economics
Who Can Apply: Student must be Home Economics major upon successful completion of the first semester of college study.
How Much Money Can I Get: $900
Whom Do I Contact: Bennett College, Financial Aid Office, 900 East Washington Street, Greensboro, NC 27401-3239 (800) 413-5323.

157

BENNETT COLLEGE

Gary Davis Memorial Scholarship
Who Can Apply: Student must be majoring in Mass Communications at a Historically Black College or University in the Triad. The scholarship is awarded based on academics and a written essay.
How Much Money Can I Get: Tuition
Whom Do I Contact: Bennett College, Financial Aid Office, 900 East Washington Street, Greensboro, NC 27401 (800) 413-5323.

158

BENNETT COLLEGE

Gittens/Ward Home Economics Club Scholarship
Who Can Apply:. A second semester sophomore Home Economics major who has completed not less than one semester of home economics course

work earning a minimum 3.0 GPA.
How Much Money Can I Get: $250
Whom Do I Contact: Bennett College, Financial Aid Office, 900 East Washington Street, Greensboro, NC 27401-3239, (800) 413-5323.

159

BENNETT COLLEGE
Goode Prize for Home Economics
Who Can Apply: A junior student who is considered to best exemplify the qualities and characteristics of a model home economist.
How Much Money Can I Get: $200
Whom Do I Contact: Bennett College, Financial Aid Office, 900 East Washington Street, Greensboro, NC 27401-3239, (800) 413-5323

160

BENNETT COLLEGE
G.R. Whitfield Endowed Scholarship.
Who Can Apply: High school senior with the highest GPA.
How Much Money Can I Get: $300
Whom Do I Contact: Bennett College, Financial Aid Office, 900 East Washington Street, Greensboro, NC 27401-3239, (800) 413-5323.

161

BENNETT COLLEGE
Greensboro Chapter of Links, Inc. Scholarship
Who Can Apply: A junior or senior possessing outstanding potential in the creative and performing arts. The recipient must possess documented evidence of performance ability and must have a minimum 2.5 earned cumulative GPA.
How Much Money Can I Get: $500
Whom Do I Contact: Bennett College, Financial Aid Office, 900 East Washington Street. Greensboro, NC 27401-3239, (800) 413-5323.

162

BENNETT COLLEGE
L. Guebveur-Streat Award
Who Can Apply: Student must be a sophomore or junior Home Economics major in recognition of academic and creative ability.
How Much Money Can I Get: $300
Whom Do I Contact: Bennett College, Financial Aid Office, 900 East Washington Street, Greensboro, NC 27401-3239, (800) 413-5323.

163

BENNETT COLLEGE

Lillian T. Lyons Scholarship
Who Can Apply: Student must be a Special Education major.
How Much Money Can I Get: $2,000
Whom Do I Contact: Bennett College, Financial Aid Office, 900 East Washington Street, Greensboro, NC 27401-3239, (800) 413-5323.

164

BENNETT COLLEGE

Mae Cynthia Lee and Edna J. Lee Educational Scholarship
Who Can Apply: Student must be a Teacher Education major.
How Much Money Can I Get: $2,000
Whom Do I Contact: Bennett College, Financial Aid Office, 900 East Washington Street, Greensboro, NC 27401-3239, 800-413-5323.

165

BENNETT COLLEGE

Merit Scholarship
Who Can Apply: Student must have a combination SAT score ranging from 850 to 899 or a minimum ACT score of 21. The student must have a minimum 3.0 high school GPA.
How Much Money Can I Get: $1,000 to $2,000
Whom Do I Contact: Bennett College, Financial Aid Office, 900 East Washington Street, Greensboro, NC 27401-3239, (800) 413-5323.

166

BENNETT COLLEGE

Queen Hester Bell Award
Who Can Apply: A student majoring in Secondary Teacher Education.
How Much Money Can I Get: $500
Whom Do I Contact: Bennett College, Financial Aid Office, 900 East Washington Street, Greensboro, NC 27401-3239, (800) 413-5323.

167

BENNETT COLLEGE

Presidential Scholarship
Who Can Apply: Student must have a combination SAT score of 1,000 or a minimum ACT score of 25. The student must have earned a minimum 3.5 high school GPA.
How Much Money Can I Get: Tuition
Whom Do I Contact: Bennett College, Financial Aid Office, 900 East Washington Street, Greensboro, NC 27401-3239, (800) 413-5323.

168

BENNETT COLLEGE

Tuition Scholarship
Who Can Apply: Student must have a combination SAT score ranging from 900 to 999 or an ACT score ranging from 20 to 24. The student must have earned a minimum 3.2 high school GPA.
How Much Money Can I Get: Tuition
Whom Do I Contact: Bennett College, Financial Aid Office, 900 East Washington Street, Greensboro, NC 27401-3239, (800) 413-5323.

169

BENNETT COLLEGE

WITS Award
Who Can Apply: A junior or senior English major who has a minimum 3.0 cumulative GPA, exemplifies written scholarship and support for the community.
How Much Money Can I Get: $200
Whom Do I Contact: Bennett College, Financial Aid Office, 900 East Washington Street, Greensboro, NC 27401-3239, (800) 413-5323.

170

BENTLEY COLLEGE

Freshman Minority Award
Who Can Apply: Candidates must be a U.S. citizen and show financial need. Awards are limited to eight semesters.
How Much Money Can I Get: Full tuition
Whom Do I Contact: Scholarship Coordinator, Bentley College, Admissions Office, Waltham, MA 02254, (617) 891-2244.

171

BENTLEY COLLEGE

Upperclass Minority Grant
Who Can Apply: Student must be a U.S. citizen, show need, and have family income below $30,000. Minimum GPA of 2.0 is required.
How Much Money Can I Get: Varies
Whom Do I Contact: Scholarship Coordinator, Bentley College, Financial Aid Office, Waltham, MA 02254, (617) 891-2244.

172

BETHUNE-COOKMAN COLLEGE

Air Force ROTC
Who Can Apply: Students interested in learning more about military

lifestyle. Awards are awarded on a competitive basis and are available for four years

How Much Money Can I Get: $150, tuition, books

Whom Do I Contact: Bethune-Cookman College, Attn.: Division of Social Sciences, 640 Dr. Mary McLeod Bethune Blvd., Daytona Beach, FL 32114-3099, (386) 481-2000.

173

BETHUNE-COOKMAN COLLEGE

Challenger Astronauts Memorial Award

Who Can Apply: Top-ranked high school graduates from each county.

How Much Money Can I Get: $1,500 per year

Whom Do I Contact: Office of Student Financial Assistance, Florida Department of Education, Tallahassee, FL 32399-0400.

174

BETHUNE-COOKMAN COLLEGE

Federal Direct/Stafford Subsidized Loan

Who Can Apply: Students who demonstrate financial need.

How Much Money Can I Get: Eligible freshmen may borrow up to $2,625 per year, sophomores up to $3,500; and juniors and seniors may borrow up to $5,500 per year. The maximum allowable undergraduate indebtedness over five years is $23,000.

Whom Do I Contact: Office of Student Financial Assistance, Florida Department of Education, Tallahassee, FL 32399-0400.

175

BETHUNE-COOKMAN COLLEGE

Federal Perkins Loan Program (formerly NDSL)

Who Can Apply: Undergraduate students who demonstrate financial need.

How Much Money Can I Get: Up to $6,000

Whom Do I Contact: Office of Student Financial Assistance, Florida Department of Education, Tallahassee, FL 32399-0400.

176

BETHUNE-COOKMAN COLLEGE

Federal Supplemental Educational Opportunity Grant (SEOG)

Who Can Apply: Students who demonstrate exceptional financial need and who are also Pell Grant recipients.

How Much Money Can I Get: $100 up to $1,500 per academic year.

Who Do I Contact: Office of Student Financial Assistance, Florida Department of Education, Tallahassee, FL 32399-0400.

177

BETHUNE-COOKMAN COLLEGE

Florida Mary McLeod Bethune Scholarship Fund
Who Can Apply: High school seniors with a minimum 3.0 cumulative GPA. Recipient must be a Florida resident and demonstrate financial need.
How Much Money Can I Get: $3,000 annually
Whom Do I Contact: Office of Student Financial Assistance, Florida Department of Education, Tallahassee, FL 32399-0400.

178

BETHUNE-COOKMAN COLLEGE

Florida Resident Access Grant (FRAG)
Who Can Apply: Full-time students who have been Florida residents for at least one year prior to the beginning of classes. This one-year Florida residency is also required for the parents of the dependent students. Transfer students and renewals must have a 2.0 cumulative GPA on all previous college work.
How Much Money Can I Get: Up to $1,600 per academic year
Whom Do I Contact: Office of Student Financial Assistance, Florida Department of Education, Tallahassee, FL 32399-0400.

179

BETHUNE-COOKMAN COLLEGE

Florida Student Assistance Grant Program (FSAG)
Who Can Apply: Full-time students with high financial need.
How Much Money Can I Get: $200 to $1,300 per academic year
Whom Do I Contact: Office of Student Financial Assistance, Florida Department of Education, Tallahassee, FL 32399-0400.

180

BETHUNE-COOKMAN COLLEGE

Florida Teacher Scholarship and Forgivable Loan Program
Who Can Apply: Capable and promising students and teachers to pursue careers in teaching.
How Much Money Can I Get: $1,500
Contact: Office of Student Financial Assistance, Florida Department of Education, Tallahassee, FL 32399-0400.

181

BETHUNE-COOKMAN COLLEGE

Florida Undergraduate Scholars Fund
Who Can Apply: Outstanding Florida high school graduates.

How Much Money Can I Get: $2,500 per year
Whom Do I Contact: Office of Student Financial Assistance, Florida Department of Education, Tallahassee, FL 32399-0400.

182

BETHUNE-COOKMAN COLLEGE
Lettie Pate Whitehead Foundation Scholarship
Who Can Apply: Christian females from Virginia, North Carolina, South Carolina, Tennessee, Georgia, Florida, Alabama, Mississippi, or Louisiana.
How Much Money Can I Get: Varies
Whom Do I Contact: Bethune-Cookman College, 740 Second Avenue, Daytona Beach, FL 02015, (904) 255-1401.

183

BETHUNE-COOKMAN COLLEGE
Rosewood Family Scholarship Fund
Who Can Apply: Students who demonstrate financial need.
How Much Money Can I Get: $4,000
Whom Do I Contact: Office of Student Financial Assistance, Florida Department of Education, Tallahassee, FL 32399-0400.

184

BETHUNE-COOKMAN COLLEGE
Sallie Mae Signature Loan
Who Can Apply: Students who demonstrate financial need.
How Much Money Can I Get: Tuition
Whom Do I Contact: Office of Student Financial Assistance, Florida Department of Education, Tallahassee, FL 32399-0400.

185

BETHUNE-COOKMAN COLLEGE
Vocational Gold Seal Endorsement Scholarship
Who Can Apply: Outstanding Florida public high school graduates.
Amount: $2000 per year
Contact: The Office of Student Financial Assistance, Florida Department of Education, Tallahassee, FL 32399-0400.

186

BISHOP STATE COMMUNITY COLLEGE
Academic Scholarships-Type I
Who Can Apply: High school students who have a minimum 3.3 GPA on a 4.0 scale. High school students who have GPAs between 3.0 and 3.29 and a

minimum composite 1,000 SAT score (20 ACT) also qualify for these awards.

How Much Money Can I Get: Tuition

Whom Do I Contact: Bishop State Community College, Attn.: Office of Financial Aid, Bishop State Main Campus, 351 N. Broad Street, Mobile, AL 36603-5898, (251) 690-6458.

187

BISHOP STATE COMMUNITY COLLEGE

Academic Scholarships-Type II

Who Can Apply: Students who have completed a minimum of 30 semester hours at Bishop State Community College with a minimum 3.5 GPA.

How Much Money Can I Get: Tuition

Contact: Bishop State Community College, Attn.: Office of Financial Aid, Bishop State Main Campus, 351 N. Broad Street, Mobile, AL 36603-5898, (251) 690-6458.

188

BISHOP STATE COMMUNITY COLLEGE

Alabama GI Dependents Scholarship Program

Who Can Apply: Eligible dependents (child, stepchild, spouse or un/ remarried widow/er) of disabled veterans (living or deceased) who were permanent civilian residents of Alabama prior to entry into military service. Special consideration is given to dependents of permanently and totally disabled veterans who are bona fide residents or were prior to their death. Other qualifying veterans' categories are former prisoners of war (POW), declared missing in action (MIA), and those who died in service.

How Much Money Can I Get: College fees

Whom Do I Contact: Alabama GI Dependents' Scholarship Program, P.O. Box 1509, Montgomery, AL 36102-1509, (251) 690-6458.

189

BISHOP STATE COMMUNITY COLLEGE

Athletic Scholarship

Who Can Apply: Students for active participation in baseball, cheerleading, men's basketball, softball, and women's basketball.

How Much Money Can I Get: Tuition and fees for up to 15 hours during the fall and spring semesters.

Whom Do I Contact: Bishop State Community College, Attn.: Office of Financial Aid, Bishop State Main Campus, 351 N. Broad Street, Mobile, AL 36603-5898, (251) 690-6458.

190

BISHOP STATE COMMUNITY COLLEGE
Federal Pell Grant
Who Can Apply: Undergraduate students who demonstrate financial need.
How Much Money Can I Get: Tuition
Whom Do I Contact: Bishop State Community College, Attn.: Office of Financial Aid, Bishop State Main Campus, 351 N. Broad Street, Mobile, AL 36603-5898, (251) 690-6458.

191

BISHOP STATE COMMUNITY COLLEGE
Federal Supplemental Educational Opportunity Grant
Who Can Apply: Students who demonstrate exceptional financial need.
How Much Money Can I Get: $200
Whom Do I Contact: Bishop State Community College, Attn.: Office of Financial Aid, Bishop State Main Campus, 351 N. Broad Street, Mobile, AL 36603-5898, (251) 690-6458.

192

BISHOP STATE COMMUNITY COLLEGE
Federal Work-Study Program
Who Can Apply: Students must demonstrate financial need and earn a part of their educational expenses.
How Much Money Can I Get: Tuition
Whom Do I Contact: Bishop State Community College, Attn.: Office of Financial Aid, Bishop State Main Campus, 351 N. Broad Street, Mobile, AL 36603-5898, (251) 690-6458.

193

BISHOP STATE COMMUNITY COLLEGE
Institutional Scholarship
Who Can Apply: Students in the following categories: art, band, choir, college bowl, creative writing, drama, elementary school tutoring, and leadership
How Much Money Can I Get: Tuition
Whom Do I Contact: Bishop State Community College, Attn.: Office of Financial Aid, Bishop State Main Campus, 351 N. Broad Street, Mobile, AL 36603-5898, (251) 690-6458.

194

BISHOP STATE COMMUNITY COLLEGE
Presidential Scholarship
Who Can Apply: Public high school students in Mobile and Washington

Counties. A minimum 3.5 GPA is required for the initial award.
How Much Money Can I Get: Tuition
Whom Do I Contact: Bishop State Community College, Attn.: Office of
Financial Aid, Bishop State Main Campus, 351 N. Broad Street, Mobile, AL
36603-5898, (251) 690-6458.

195
BISHOP STATE COMMUNITY COLLEGE
Technical Scholarship- Type I
Who Can Apply: High School students who will pursue a degree or
certificate in any of the Technical School division on the Carver or
Southwest Campuses. A minimum 2.5 GPA is required.
How Much Money Can I Get: Tuition
Whom Do I Contact: Bishop State Community College, Attn.: Office of
Financial Aid, Bishop State Main Campus, 351 N. Broad Street, Mobile, AL
36603-5898, (251) 690-6458.

196
BISHOP STATE COMMUNITY COLLEGE
Technical Scholarship – Type II
Who Can Apply: College students who have completed a minimum of 24
semester hours at Bishop State Community College with a minimum 3.0
GPA.
How Much Money Can I Get: Tuition
Whom Do I Contact: Bishop State Community College, Attn.: Office of
Financial Aid, Bishop State Main Campus, 351 N. Broad Street, Mobile, AL
36603-5898, (251) 690-6458.

197
THE BOSTON CHAPTER OF LINKS, INC.
Who Can Apply: Applicants must be black, show financial need, and be
from the Boston City area. Include with the application a letter of
recommendation from a dean and a completed 1040 tax form.
How Much Money Can I Get: $1,000
Whom Do I Contact: Boston Chapter of Links, Inc., 46 Brockton Street,
Mattapan, MA 02126.

198
BOSTON COLLEGE SCHOOL OF EDUCATION
Who Can Apply: Graduate school sponsors several fellowships specifically
for American minority students who have been accepted into the doctoral
programs at Boston College.

How Much Money Can I Get: Up to $11,000
Whom Do I Contact: Arline Riordan, Boston College, Chestnut Hill, MA 02167, (617) 552-4214.

199

BOSTON UNIVERSITY
WCVB-TV Boston Scholarship
Who Can Apply: Recipient must be a juniors, senior, or graduate minority student in broadcast communications who is a U.S. citizen. Recipients are selected on the basis of need and academic standing. Faculty members nominate candidates for this award during the fall semester.
How Much Money Can I Get: $2,500 and internship
Whom Do I Contact: Boston University, Office of Financial Assistance, 81 Commonwealth Avenue, Boston, MA 02115, (617) 353-3481.

200

BOSTON UNIVERSITY
RKO General Scholarship
Who Can Apply: Entering minority graduate students who are U.S. citizens. Awards are based on academic and professional promise rather than on financial need. Faculty members, counselors, and members of the communications profession nominate candidates.
How Much Money Can I Get: Full tuition
Whom Do I Contact: Boston University, Office of Financial Assistance, 81 Commonwealth Avenue, Boston, MA 02115, (617) 353-3481.

201

BOWDOIN COLLEGE
John Brown Russwurm Scholarship
Who Can Apply: All admitted black students. Award is based on academic record and recommendations.
How Much Money Can I Get: Varies
Whom Do I Contact: Office of Admissions, Bowdoin College, Brunswick, ME 04011, (207) 725-8731.

202

BOWLING GREEN STATE UNIVERSITY
Black Pioneers Scholarship
Who Can Apply: Black students who excel academically, athletically, or artistically and who demonstrate financial need. Deadline April 1.
How Much Money Can I Get: Varies
Whom Do I Contact: Bowling Green State University, Attn.: Office of

Financial Aid, 450 Student Services Building, Bowling Green, OH 43403-0145, (419) 372-2651.

203

BOWLING GREEN STATE UNIVERSITY
Diversity Achievement Award
Who Can Apply: Minority students with a minimum 3.25 GPA. Deadline April 1.
How Much Money Can I Get: $2,000
Whom Do I Contact: Bowling Green State University, Attn.: Office of Financial Aid, 450 Student Services Building, Bowling Green, OH 43403-0145, (419) 372-2651.

204

BRIAR CLIFF COLLEGE
MULTICULTURAL SCHOLARSHIPS
Who Can Apply: Awards to minority students who have demonstrated leadership. Deadline January 20.
How Much Money Can I Get: Half tuition
Whom Do I Contact: Briar Cliff College, Attn.: Director of Admissions, 3303 Rebecca Street, P.O. Box 2100, Sioux City, IA, 51104-9987, (712) 279-5427.

205

BUCKNELL UNIVERSITY
Betty Ann Quinn Fund
Who Can Apply: Any black student.
How Much Money Can I Get: $400
Whom Do I Contact: Office of Admissions, Bucknell University, Lewisburg, PA 17837, (717) 524-1101.

206

BUCKS COUNTY COMMUNITY COLLEGE
Minority Incentive Grant
Who Can Apply: Student must be a U.S. citizen carrying fewer than six credits. Subsequent MIG may be awarded for 12 credits. Must have a 2.0 GPA and financial need.
How Much Money Can I Get: Tuition and fees
Whom Do I Contact: Director of Financial Aid, Bucks County Community College, Swamp Road, Newton, PA 18940, (215) 968-8200.

207

BUSINESS AND PROFESSIONAL WOMEN'S FOUNDATION

Scholarships for Black Women Over Age 25
Who Can Apply:. Applicants must be black women who are 25 years or older and are pursuing college or other educational courses, seminars, or training opportunities that will enhance their personal or professional skills. Deadlines April and September of each year.
How Much Money Can I Get: Up to $500
Whom Do I Contact: Business and Professional Women's Foundation, 2012 Massachusetts Avenue, NW, Washington, DC 20036, (202) 293-1200.

208

CAL POLYTECH STATE UNIVERSITY

The War Veterans Scholarship
Who Can Apply: Sophomore, junior, or senior crop science, animal science, or agricultural business management students; preference to disadvantaged minority students. Student aid application for California required. Must have a 3.0 GPA. Deadline March 1.
How Much Money Can I Get: Varies
Whom Do I Contact: Financial Aid Officer, Cal Polytech State University, Financial Aid Office, San Luis Obispo, CA 93407, (805) 756-1111.

209

CALIFORNIA LIBRARY ASSOCIATION

Who Can Apply: Applicants must be pursuing a Master's of Library Science in a California library school. Financial need required. Deadline May 30.
How Much Money Can I Get: $2,000
Whom Do I Contact: California Library Association, Attn.: Scholarship Committee, 717 K Street, Suite 300, Sacramento, CA 95814-3477, (916) 447-8541.

210

CALIFORNIA SCHOOL OF PROFESSIONAL PSYCHOLOGY (CSPP)

Who Can Apply: Qualified U.S. citizens who are African American, Hispanic, American Indian, Asian American, or Pacific Islander. Awards are based on financial need and are open to students enrolled in CSPP's doctoral programs.
How Much Money Can I Get: $250 to $3,500
Whom Do I Contact: California School of Professional Psychology, Financial Aid Office, 2749 Hyde Street, San Francisco, CA 94109, (415) 346-4500.

211

CALIFORNIA STATE LIBRARY

Minority Recruitment Scholarship

Who Can Apply: Minorities in California who are interested in pursuing a Master's in Library Science degree. Deadline June 1.

How Much Money Can I Get: $1,500 to $5,000

Whom Do I Contact: California State Library, Library Development Services, 1001 6th Street, Suite 300, Sacramento, CA 95814-3324, (916) 323-4400.

212

CALIFORNIA STATE LIBRARY

Multiethnic Scholarship

Who Can Apply: Awarded to minority students of California majoring in Library Science. Deadline June 1.

How Much Money Can I Get: $1,000 to $5,000

Whom Do I Contact: California State Library, Library Development Services, Attn.: Ethnic Services Consultant, P.O. Box 942837, Sacramento, CA 94237- 0001, (916) 445-4730.

213

CALIFORNIA STATE UNIVERSITY, DOMINGUEZ HILLS

TRW Minority Scholarship

Who Can Apply: The award provides financial assistance to minority students in business administration. Student must have a minimum 2.5 GPA.

How Much Money Can I Get: Varies

Whom Do I Contact: School of Management, California State University, Dominguez Hills, 1000 E. Victoria Street, Carson, CA 90747, (213) 516-3300.

214

CALIFORNIA STATE UNIVERSITY, FULLERTON

NACME Incentive Awards

Who Can Apply: Entering freshman or transfer minorities who are U.S. citizens or permanent residents, have a 2.5 GPA, and are major in Engineering. Financial need required. Deadline August 15.

How Much Money Can I Get: $250 per year

Whom Do I Contact: California State University at Fullerton, 800 N. State College Boulevard, Fullerton, CA 92631, (714) 773-2361.

215

CALIFORNIA STATE UNIVERSITY, SACRAMENTO
Fresno Bee **Minority Journalism Scholarship**
Who Can Apply: Undergraduates and graduate students are eligible. Award is based on grades and need. Apply by February 1.
How Much Money Can I Get: $1,000
Whom Do I Contact: California State University, Department of Journalism, Sacramento, CA 98519, (916) 278-6354.

216

CALIFORNIA STATE UNIVERSITY, SACRAMENTO
KFMT-TV Scholarship
Who Can Apply: Journalism students from a minority group.
How Much Money Can I Get: $300
Whom Do I Contact: Office of Admissions, California State University, Sacramento, CA 95819, (916) 454-6723.

217

CALIFORNIA STATE UNIVERSITY, SACRAMENTO
Sigma Delta Chi Scholarship
Who Can Apply: Minority students entering the university to study journalism.
How Much Money Can I Get: $100
Whom Do I Contact: Office of Admissions, California State University, Sacramento, CA 95819, (916) 454-6723.

218

CALIFORNIA STUDENT AID COMMISSION
Cal Grant B
Who Can Apply: Full-time college students who are U.S. citizens, California residents, and in financial need.
How Much Money Can I Get: $300 to $5,250
Whom Do I Contact: California Student Aid Commission, P.O. Box 942845, Sacramento, CA 94245, (916) 322-6280.

219

CALIFORNIA TEACHERS ASSOCIATION
The Martin Luther King Jr. Scholarship
Who Can Apply: Racial/ethnic minority CTA members and their dependent children can apply. Scholarships vary each year depending on contributions and the financial need of individual applicants. Applications will be available at CTA Regional Resource Center Offices and the CTA Human

Rights Department after January 15. Must be a U.S. citizen to apply.
Deadline April 15.
How Much Money Can I Get: Varies
Whom Do I Contact: Human Rights Department, California Teachers
Association, 1705 Murchison Drive, P.O. Box 921, Burlingame, CA 94011-
0921, (415) 697-1400.

220

UNIVERSITY OF CALIFORNIA
Chancellor's Ethnic Minority Postdoctoral Fellowship
Who Can Apply: Individuals who show promise for tenure track record at
Berkeley. Deadline December 9.
How Much Money Can I Get: $31,000 to $35,000
Whom Do I Contact: Chancellor's Ethnic Minority Postdoctoral Fellowship
Program, Attn.: Office of the Chancellor, 200 California Hall, University of
California at Berkeley, Berkeley, CA 94720, (510) 642-1935.

221

UNIVERSITY OF CALIFORNIA, BERKELEY
SCHOOL OF LAW
Graduate Opportunity Program and Boalt Hall Opportunity Program
Who Can Apply: Selection is based on socioeconomic factors, family's
educational background, financial need, and academic merit.
How Much Money Can I Get: Tuition and fees and a stipend ranging from
$5,500 to $7,500 per academic year
Whom Do I Contact: University of California at Berkeley School of Law,
Boalt Hall, Berkeley, CA 94720, (415) 642-1563.

222

UNIVERSITY OF CALIFORNIA, RIVERSIDE
The Eugene Cota-Robles Award Program
Who Can Apply: The program links entering students with faculty sponsors
and provides guidance. Priority is given to outstanding doctoral program
candidates who demonstrate strong potential for university teaching and
research course work demands of first- and second-year graduate study.
How Much Money Can I Get: $12,500 stipend and payment of fees for each
of the first two years of graduate study
Whom Do I Contact: Graduate Recruitment and Outreach, Room B204
Library South, University of California, Riverside, CA 92521, (909) 787-
3680, fax: (909) 787-2238, E-mail: marie.steward@ucr.edu.

223

UNIVERSITY OF CALIFORNIA, RIVERSIDE

The Graduate Opportunity Fellowships (GOF)

Who Can Apply: Students from those groups that have been traditionally underrepresented in the university, specifically ethnic minorities and women. It is limited to students applying for a doctorate degree (or a master's degree when it is an absolute requirement for the Ph.D.), and is a multiyear award for incoming students only.

How Much Money Can I Get: This four-year award consists of a stipend of $10,000 and payment of all assessed fees for years one and four, including nonresident tuition (first year only).

Whom Do I Contact: Graduate Recruitment and Outreach, Room B204 Library South, University of California, Riverside, CA 92521, (909) 787-3680, fax: (909) 787-2238, E-mail: marie.steward@ucr.edu.

224

CALIFORNIA UNIVERSITY OF PENNSYLVANIA

The Board of Governors Minority Scholarship

Who Can Apply: Award is open to minority freshmen. It waives tuition every semester for four years. Must have a 2.5 GPA and a minimum combined SAT score of 725. Deadline April 1.

How Much Money Can I Get: Tuition

Whom Do I Contact: Admissions Office, California University of Pennsylvania, Third Street, California, PA 15419, (412) 938-4404.

225

CALVIN THEOLOGICAL SEMINARY

Barney and Martha Bruinsma Memorial Scholarship

Who Can Apply: Degree candidates who are preparing to minister primarily to their own groups are eligible. Purpose of the scholarship is to promote the ministry of the gospel through North American ethnic minority persons to their own groups. Criteria for selection includes academic ability and achievement, Christian character and commitment, potential for ministry, and financial need. Deadline March 1.

How Much Money Can I Get: $500

Whom Do I Contact: Registrar, Calvin Theological Seminary, 3233 Burton Street, SE, Grand Rapids, MI 49506, (616) 957-6036.

226

CALVIN THEOLOGICAL SEMINARY

John H. Kromming Scholarship

Who Can Apply: Minority students who reside in North America are eligible. The scholarship is applicable to a year of study in any one of the seminary's degree programs. Eligibility for the scholarship is adjusted to the need of the student and is commensurate with available funds. A recipient may apply for an additional award in a succeeding year. Selection is made on the basis of Christian character, financial need, academic ability, and potential for Christian service. Applicants must be committed to serve in ministry in the Reformed Christian Church. Deadline March 1.

How Much Money Can I Get: Varies

Whom Do I Contact: Registrar, Calvin Theological Seminary, 3233 Burton Street, SE, Grand Rapids, MI 49506, (616) 957-6036.

227

CAPITOL COLLEGE

The Carl English Scholarship

Who Can Apply: Applicants will be required to write an essay on careers in engineering technology and must be pursuing an A.A. or B.S. degree. Financial need is required. Must be black with a 2.75 GPA. Deadline April 1.

How Much Money Can I Get: $1,000 to $2,000

Whom Do I Contact: Office of Admissions, Capitol College, 11301 Springfield Road, Laurel, MD 20708, (301) 953-0060.

228

CAREER OPPORTUNITIES THROUGH EDUCATION

Equal Opportunity Publications Scholarship Program

Who Can Apply: Must be a full-time student working toward a bachelor's degree in any engineering discipline. Selection based on GPA, extracurricular activities, a personal statement, and a recommendation. Females only. Deadline February 15.

How Much Money Can I Get: $500

Whom Do I Contact: Career Opportunities Through Education, P.O. Box 2810, Cherry Hill, NJ 08034, (609) 795-9634.

229

CARLETON COLLEGE

Who Can Apply: Scholarship awards include The Fraser, The Honeywell Fund, and the *Minneapolis Star & Tribune* Fund for multicultural students entering the college.

How Much Money Can I Get: Varies

Whom Do I Contact: Carleton College, Office of Admissions, 100 South College Street, Northfield, MN 55057, (507) 663-4190.

230

CARNEGIE-MELLON UNIVERSITY

Who Can Apply: Minority students preparing for careers in insurance, specifically as actuaries.
How Much Money Can I Get: Varies
Whom Do I Contact: Office of Admissions, Carnegie-Mellon University, 5000 Forbes Avenue, Pittsburgh, PA 15213, (412) 578-2000.

231

CASE WESTERN RESERVE UNIVERSITY

Who Can Apply: Scholarship programs include the Martin Luther King, Jr., Scholarship and the Minority Engineers Industrial Opportunity program.
How Much Money Can I Get: $1,000 to $2,000
Whom Do I Contact: Office of Admissions, Case Western Reserve University, University Circle, Cleveland, OH 44106, (216) 368-2000.

232

CASE WESTERN RESERVE UNIVERSITY

Who Can Apply: Applicants must have demonstrated ability and achievement. Awarded to U.S. citizens or nationals who are American Indian, Black, Hispanic, Native Alaskan (Eskimo or Aleut), or Native Pacific Islander (Polynesian or Micronesian). A 3.0 GPA is required.
How Much Money Can I Get: $5,000
Whom Do I Contact: Case Western Reserve University, 109 Pardee Hall, Cleveland, OH 44106, (216) 368-4530.

233

CASTLETON STATE COLLEGE

Who Can Apply: Students demonstrating financial need may apply. Candidates should submit the Minority Scholarships Application and FFS/FAF to the financial aid office.
How Much Money Can I Get: $900 to $2,000
Whom Do I Contact: Financial Aid Director, Castleton State College, Castleton, VT 05735, (802) 468-5611.

234

CATHOLIC NEGRO SCHOLARSHIP FUND

Who Can Apply: This fund provides assistance to African Americans pursuing a college education. Applicants must demonstrate need.
How Much Money Can I Get: Varies
Whom Do I Contact: Catholic Negro Scholarship Fund, 73 Chestnut Street, Springfield, MA 01103.

235

CENTRAL COLLEGE

Hearst Scholarship
Who Can Apply: Applicants must rank in the top 10 percent of their class. Leadership potential and communication skills are considered. Award is renewable with 3.0 GPA. Deadline January 1.
How Much Money Can I Get: $5,500
Whom Do I Contact: Central College, Attn.: Financial Aid Director, 812 University, Pella, IA 50219, (515) 628-5268.

236

CENTRAL COLLEGE

McElroy Minority Student Scholarship
Who Can Apply: Applicant must rank in the top 10 percent of his or her class. Scholarship is awarded to a student from the KWWL television viewing area with academic promise, need, and strong moral character. Deadline January 1.
How Much Money Can I Get: $5,500
Whom Do I Contact: Central College, Attn.: Financial Aid Director, 812 University, Pella, IA 50219, (515) 628-5268.

237

CENTRAL COLLEGE

The Multicultural Achievement Scholarship
Who Can Apply: Candidates must submit three references and letter of application. An interview is also required. Award is renewable. Must be an entering minority who is in the upper three-fifths of his or her class and a U.S. citizen. Financial need required. Deadline January 1.
How Much Money Can I Get: Up to $4,000
Whom Do I Contact: Director of Admissions, Central College, 812 University Avenue, Pella, IA 50219, (515) 628-5268.

238

CENTRAL FLORIDA ASSOCIATION OF BLACKS IN CRIMINAL JUSTICE

Who Can Apply: The Association provides a scholarship to black males or females who are criminal justice or political science majors.
How Much Money Can I Get: Varies
Whom Do I Contact: Central Florida Association, P.O. Box 866, Orlando, FL 32803.

239

CENTRAL MICHIGAN UNIVERSITY
Lloyd M. Cofer Scholarship
Who Can Apply: Graduates of public schools in Detroit who show commitment to the advancement of minorities.
How Much Money Can I Get: Tuition
Whom Do I Contact: Central Michigan University, Attn.: Office of Admissions, Mt. Pleasant, MI 48859, (517) 774-3076.

240

CENTRAL MICHIGAN UNIVERSITY
Minority Advancement Scholarship
Who Can Apply: Minority students who show interest in the advancement of minorities in American society. Applicants must be full-time students.
How Much Money Can I Get: Varies
Whom Do I Contact: Central Michigan University, Attn.: Office of Admissions, Mt. Pleasant, MI 48859, (517) 774-3076.

241

CHARLES R. DREW UNIVERSITY OF MEDICINE AND SCIENCE
California Student Aid Commission (CSAC) Award
Who Can Apply: Residents of California who are U.S. citizens or eligible non-citizens. CSAC determines eligibility for grants, which are based on academic achievement and financial need.
How Much Money Can I Get: Tuition
Whom Do I Contact: Charles R. Drew University of Medicine and Science, Attn.: Financial Aid Office, 1731 East 120th Street, Los Angeles, CA 90059, (323) 563-4824.

242

CHARLES R. DREW UNIVERSITY OF MEDICINE AND SCIENCE
Chela Financial
Who Can Apply: Students will be required to submit an essay of no more than 500 words that demonstrates the student's financial need, how the student has overcome challenges in pursuing his/her educational goals, educational accomplishments, and/or demonstrated commitment and service to their campus or community.
How Much Money Can I Get: $1,000 Per Year
Whom Do I Contact: Chela Education Financing, 388 Market Street, 12th Floor, San Francisco, CA 94111, (800) 347-4352.

243

CHARLES R. DREW UNIVERSITY OF MEDICINE AND SCIENCE

Congressional Black Caucus Scholarship
Who Can Apply: High school graduates or college students.
How Much Money Can I Get: Varies
Whom Do I Contact: Office of U.S. Rep. Juanita Millender-McDonald, 970 West 190th Street, East Tower, Suite 900, Torrance, CA 90502, (310) 538-1190.

244

CHARLES R. DREW UNIVERSITY OF MEDICINE AND SCIENCE

Ebell/Flint Scholarship
Who Can Apply: Students must live and go to school in L.A County and show need of funds for attending the school choice. Candidate must be at least a sophomore and maintain a 3.25 GPA or above. He or she must carry a minimum of 12 units per term/semester.
How Much Money Can I Get: $200 for 10 months
Whom Do I Contact: The Ebell Club, 743 South Lucerne Boulevard, Los Angeles, California 90005-3707, (323) 931-1277.

245

CHARLES R. DREW UNIVERSITY OF MEDICINE AND SCIENCE

Health Professions Education Foundation Scholarship
Who Can Apply: Candidates must be a U.S. citizen or permanent resident and a California resident, be accepted to or enrolled in a certified midwifery or physician's assistant program, and be enrolled in at least 6.0 units for each semester/quarter that scholarship funds are being sought. Students must possess and maintain a minimum 2.0 GPA for each term/semester for which funds are being sought and agree to practice in a specialty for which funds have been awarded in direct patient care for at least two years in a medically undeserved area of California.
How Much Money Can I Get: $1,000 - $10,000
Whom Do I Contact: Health Professions Education Foundation, 818 K Street, Suite 210, Sacramento, CA 95814, (800) 773-1669.

246

CHARLES R. DREW UNIVERSITY OF MEDICINE AND SCIENCE

Hispanic Scholarship Fund Award
Who Can Apply: Hispanic student who is either a U.S. citizen or permanent

resident, has completed a minimum of 15 college units, and a minimum 2.7 GPA on a 4.0 scale or 3.7 on a 5.0 scale.

How Much Money Can I Get: $1,000 - $3,000 per year

Whom Do I Contact: Hispanic Scholarship Fund Headquarters, 55 Second Street, Suite 1500, San Francisco, CA 94105, (877) 473-4636.

247

CHARLES R. DREW UNIVERSITY OF MEDICINE AND SCIENCE

Scholarship Loan Fund

Who Can Apply: Must be a minority majoring in Medicine. Financial need required. Deadline May 30.

How Much Money Can I Get: $2,500

Whom Do I Contact: Charles Drew Loan Fund, Inc., P.O. Box 431427, Los Angeles, CA 90043.

248

CHARLES R. DREW UNIVERSITY OF MEDICINE AND SCIENCE

Talbots Women Scholarship

Who Can Apply: Women currently residing in the U.S. and who have earned a high school diploma or their GED at least 10 years ago (no later than September 1991). Candidates must be seeking a degree from an accredited 2- or 4-year college or university and have at least two full-time semesters remaining to complete their undergraduate degree.

How Much Money Can I Get: Five (5) $10,000 awards, Fifty (50) $1,000 awards

Contact: Talbots Women Corporate Headquarters, One Talbots Drive, Hingham, MA 02043, (781) 749-7600.

249

CHEYNEY UNIVERSITY

Board of Governors Scholarship

Who Can Apply: Non-African American students. Must have a minimum 900 SAT score and 3.0 GPA. Letter of recommendation from Cheyney University director of admissions is required.

How Much Money Can I Get: Tuition

Whom Do I Contact: Cheyney University, Attn.: Office of Financial Aid, 1837 University Circle, P.O. Box 200, Cheyney, PA 19319, (610) 399-2302.

250

CHEYNEY UNIVERSITY
Charles E. and Shirley S. Marshall Scholarship
Who Can Apply: New students with a minimum 1000 SAT score and a 3.0 GPA.
How Much Money Can I Get: $10,000 annually
Whom Do I Contact: Cheyney University, Attn.: Office of Financial Aid, 1837 University Circle, P.O. Box 200, Cheyney, PA 19319, (610) 399-2302.

251

CHEYNEY UNIVERSITY
Class of 1953 Scholarship
Who Can Apply: Students with a minimum 3.0 GPA majoring in Education.
How Much Money Can I Get: Offers two $1,000 awards per year
Whom Do I Contact: Cheyney University, Attn.: Office of Financial Aid, 1837 University Circle, P.O. Box 200, Cheyney, PA 19319, (610)-399-2302.

252

CHEYNEY UNIVERSITY
International Student Tuition Waiver
Who Can Apply: International students.
How Much Money Can I Get: Tuition
Whom Do I Contact: Cheyney University, Attn.: Office of Financial Aid, 1837 University Circle, P.O. Box 200, Cheyney, PA 19319, (610)-399-2302.

253

CHEYNEY UNIVERSITY
Investing in Pennsylvania's Future Scholarship
Who Can Apply: Low income, disadvantaged students who reside in the Pennsylvania counties of Allegheny, Armstrong, Beaver, Butler, Clarion, Clearfield, Crawford, Elk, Erie, Fayette, Greene, Jefferson, Lawrence, McKean, Mercer, Venango, Warren, Washington and Westmoreland. Renewal is automatic as long as the student maintains a minimum 2.5 GPA.
How Much Money Can I Get: $2,500
Whom Do I Contact: Cheyney University, Attn.: Office of Financial Aid, 1837 University Circle, P.O. Box 200, Cheyney, PA 19319, (610)-399-2302.

254

CHEYNEY UNIVERSITY
James Hughes Memorial Scholarship
Who Can Apply: First-year students who have graduated from the Philadelphia, PA public school system. Awards are renewable contingent

upon recipient completing an annual renewal application and funding availability.

How Much Money Can I Get: $1,500

Whom Do I Contact: Cheyney University, Attn.: Office of Financial Aid, 1837 University Circle, P.O. Box 200, Cheyney, PA 19319, (610)-399-2302.

255

CHEYNEY UNIVERSITY

Keystone Scholarship

Who Can Apply: Freshman students with a minimum 1000 SAT score and a 3.0 GPA. Students must reside in the Commonwealth of Pennsylvania. The scholarship will be renewed annually if the student maintains a 3.0 GPA or better.

How Much Money Can I Get: Up to $10,000 per year.

Whom Do I Contact: Cheyney University, Attn.: Office of Financial Aid, 1837 University Circle, P.O. Box 200, Cheyney, PA 19319, (610)-399-2302.

256

CHEYNEY UNIVERSITY

Maxine and Roland Coleman Scholarship

Who Can Apply: Students majoring in Business.

How Much Money Can I Get: $1,000 for the academic year applied equally to the fall and spring semesters.

Whom Do I Contact: Cheyney University, Attn.: Office of Financial Aid, 1837 University Circle, P.O. Box 200, Cheyney, PA 19319, (610)-399-2302.

257

CHEYNEY UNIVERSITY

Richard Humphreys Scholarship

Who Can Apply: Incoming freshman students with a minimum 900 SAT score and a 3.0 GPA.

How Much Money Can I Get: $2,000-$6,500

Whom Do I Contact: Cheyney University, Attn.: Office of Financial Aid, 1837 University Circle, P.O. Box 200, Cheyney, PA 19319, (610)-399-2302.

258

CHEYNEY UNIVERSITY

Shirley Scott Scholarship

Who Can Apply: Students majoring in Music or participating in the arts (choir, band).

How Much Money Can I Get: Varies

Whom Do I Contact: Cheyney University, Attn.: Office of Financial Aid, 1837 University Circle, P.O. Box 200, Cheyney, PA 19319, (610)-399-2302.

259
CHEYNEY UNIVERSITY
Shock Foundation Scholarship
Who Can Apply: Entering freshmen who live in the following Pennsylvania counties: Adams, Berks, Chester, Cumberland, Dauphin, Delaware, Lancaster, Lebanon, and York. The scholarship is renewable for four years.
How Much Money Can I Get: $1,000.
Whom Do I Contact: Cheyney University, Attn.: Office of Financial Aid, 1837 University Circle, P.O. Box 200, Cheyney, PA 19319, (610)-399-2302.

260
CHEYNEY UNIVERSITY
Thurgood Marshall Scholarship
Who Can Apply: Incoming freshman students with a minimum 1100 SAT (25 ACT) and 3.0 GPA.
How Much Money Can I Get: Varies
Whom Do I Contact: Cheyney University, Attn.: Office of Financial Aid, 1837 University Circle, P.O. Box 200, Cheyney, PA 19319, (610)-399-2302.

261
CHEYNEY UNIVERSITY
Verizon Scholarship
Who Can Apply: First-time students majoring in Computer Science or Technology demonstrating financial need and a minimum 900 SAT score and 3.0 GPA.
How Much Money Can I Get: Varies
Whom Do I Contact: Cheyney University, Attn.: Office of Financial Aid, 1837 University Circle, P.O. Box 200, Cheyney, PA 19319, (610)-399-2302.

262
CHEYNEY UNIVERSITY
Wallace & Earlene Arnold Scholarship
Who Can Apply: Full-time, undergraduate students who has the potential for high academic achievement during their undergraduate career. The student must also display leadership skills both on and off campus. In addition, the student must demonstrate financial need and, have a minimum 2.5 GPA and satisfactorily have completed a minimum of 30 credits at Cheyney University.

How Much Money Can I Get: $5,000.
Whom Do I Contact: Cheyney University, Attn.: Office of Financial Aid, 1837 University Circle, P.O. Box 200, Cheyney, PA 19319, (610)-399-2302.

263

CHEYNEY UNIVERSITY
W.W. Smith Charitable Trust Scholarship
Who Can Apply: Full-time undergraduate students in good academic standing and in financial need. Students must reside in the Delaware Valley. Preference for the grant will be given to previous recipients of two or more years to encourage continuity and recognition. Freshmen are required to have at a minimum 900 SAT score and a 3.0 GPA.
How Much Money Can I Get: Up to $2,500.
Whom Do I Contact: Cheyney University, Attn.: Office of Financial Aid, 1837 University Circle, P.O. Box 200, Cheyney, PA 19319, (610)-399-2302.

264

CHEYNEY UNIVERSITY
Wade Wilson Scholarship
Who Can Apply: Students participating on the athletic teams. Letter of recommendation by the team coach is required.
How Much Money Can I Get: Varies
Whom Do I Contact: Cheyney University, Attn.: Office of Financial Aid, 1837 University Circle, P.O. Box 200, Cheyney, PA 19319, (610)-399-2302.

265

CHICAGO ASSOCIATION OF BLACK JOURNALISTS SCHOLARSHIPS
Who Can Apply: Minority students interested in studying print or broadcast journalism on the undergraduate or graduate level and planning a career in journalism. They must be full-time students in an accredited college or university in the Chicago metro area. Includes northwest Indiana and southern Wisconsin.
How Much Money Can I Get: $1,000
Whom Do I Contact: Chicago Association of Black Journalists, Department of Journalism, Northern Illinois University, DeKalb, IL 60115, (815) 753-7017.

266

CHRISTIAN CHURCH (DISCIPLES OF CHRIST)
Black Scholarship Fund (Star Supporter)
Who Can Apply: African Americans interested in pursuing a career in the ministry of the Christian Church. Applicants must be members of the

Christian Church, demonstrate academic ability, have financial need, be enrolled in an accredited postsecondary institution, and submit a transcript of their academic record.

How Much Money Can I Get: Varies

Whom Do I Contact: Christian Church (Disciples of Christ), 222 S. Downey Avenue, P.O. Box 1986, Indianapolis, IN 46206.

267
CIC MINORITIES FELLOWSHIP, HUMANITIES

Who Can Apply: Each award provides full tuition for four academic years, plus an annual stipend of $8,500. Fellowship recipients must pursue programs of study leading to Ph.D. degrees and must be accepted as graduate students by at least one of the CIC Universities. Minorities who are U.S. citizens and who hold or will receive a bachelor's degree from a regionally accredited school are eligible. Students who have received a master's degree from a regionally accredited school or students currently enrolled in graduate study may apply. Currently enrolled graduate students at CIC University campuses are not eligible. Must be majoring in American studies, art history, literature, Germanic literature, linguistics, philosophy, American history, Italian studies, Spanish, romance languages, humanities, Greek/Latin, British literature, German, music theory, religion/theology, French, Portuguese, or Slavic studies/languages.

How Much Money Can I Get: $8,500 + tuition

Whom Do I Contact: Minorities Fellowship Program, Committee on Institutional Cooperation, Kirkwood Hall 114, Indiana University, Bloomington, IN 47405, (800) 457-4420.

268
CIC MINORITIES FELLOWSHIP, NATURAL SCIENCES

Who Can Apply: Each award provides full tuition for four academic years plus an annual stipend. Fellowship recipients must pursue programs of study leading to Ph.D. degrees and must be accepted as graduate students by at least one of the CIC Universities. Must be a U.S. citizen who holds or will receive a bachelor's degree from a regionally accredited school. Students who have received a master's degree from a regionally accredited school or students currently enrolled in graduate study may apply. Currently enrolled graduate students at CIC University campuses are not eligible. Must be majoring in the following: agriculture, geology, biology, mathematics, chemistry, physical science, engineering, or physics.

How Much Money Can I Get: Varies

Whom Do I Contact: Committee on Institutional Cooperation, Kirkwood Hall 114, Indiana University, Bloomington, IN 47405, (800) 457-4420.

269

CIC MINORITIES FELLOWSHIP, SOCIAL SCIENCES

Who Can Apply: Each award provides full tuition for five academic years, plus an annual stipend of $9,000. Fellowship recipients must pursue programs of study leading to Ph.D. degrees and must be accepted as graduate students by at least one of the CIC Universities. Applicants must be minority students who are U.S. citizens who hold or will receive a bachelor's degree from a regionally accredited school or must have received a master's degree from a regionally accredited school or be currently enrolled in graduate study may apply. Currently enrolled graduate students at CIC University campuses are not eligible. Must be majoring in anthropology, geography, political science, sociology, economics, history, or psychology.
How Much Money Can I Get: $9,000 + tuition
Whom Do I Contact: Minorities Fellowship Program, Committee on Institutional Cooperation, Kirkwood Hall 114, Indiana University, Bloomington, IN 47405, (800) 457-4420.

270

UNIVERSITY OF CINCINNATI

Minority Scholars Program
Who Can Apply: Selection is based on academic performance.
How Much Money Can I Get: Varies
Whom Do I Contact: Director of Corbett/Minority Scholarships, University of Cincinnati, 300 Tangeman University Center, Cincinnati, OH 45221, (513) 475-8000.

271

UNIVERSITY OF CINCINNATI

Darwin T. Turner Scholarship
Who Can Apply: Ethnic minorities. Award is based on academic performance.
How Much Money Can I Get: Ranges from $1,000 to tuition, fees, and books
Whom Do I Contact: Ethnic Programs & Services, University of Cincinnati, P.O. Box 210091, Cincinnati, OH 45221-0091, (513) 556-6008.

272

CLAFLIN UNIVERSITY

Army and Navy ROTC Organizations
Who Can Apply: Students interested in learning more about military lifestyle. Awards are awarded on a competitive basis and are available for four years.

How Much Money Can I Get: tuition, fee, books, and other. $100 per month
Whom Do I Contact: Claflin University, Office of Student Financial Aid,
400 Magnolia Street, Orangeburg, South Carolina 29115, (803) 535-5331.

273 CLAFLIN UNIVERSITY

Athletic Grant-in-Aid
Who Can Apply: Students participating in intercollegiate sports.
How Much Money Can I Get: Varies
Whom Do I Contact: Claflin University, Office of Student Financial Aid,
400 Magnolia Street, Orangeburg, South Carolina 29115, (803) 535-5331.

274 CLAFLIN UNIVERSITY

College Grant-in-Aid
Who Can Apply: Students who have scored a minimum 900 SAT score.
How Much Money Can I Get: Tuition, fees, room & board
Whom Do I Contact: Claflin University, Office of Student Financial Aid,
400 Magnolia Street, Orangeburg, South Carolina 29115, (803) 535-5331.

275 CLAFLIN UNIVERSITY

Cooperative Education Program
Who Can Apply: Qualifying students must have completed 45 credit hours
at Claflin College.
How Much Money Can I Get: Varies
Whom Do I Contact: Claflin University, Office of Student Financial Aid,
400 Magnolia Street, Orangeburg, South Carolina 29115, (803) 535-5331.

276 CLAFLIN UNIVERSITY

Evans Scholarship
Who Can Apply: These annual awards are for students who have been golf
caddies for at least 2 years at a Western Golf Association member club.
Applicants must be between their junior and senior year of high school, rank
in the top 25% of their class, have outstanding personal character (integrity
& leadership), and have financial need. In addition to application (accepted
from July 1 - Nov. 1), student must submit letters of recommendation from
the sponsoring club officials, official transcripts, parents' most recent tax
return, Financial Aid Profile, SAT and/or ACT scores. Finalists will be
interviewed. Award is renewable for up to 4 years.
How Much Money Can I Get: Tuition, room & board
Whom Do I Contact: Scholarship Coordinator, Evans Scholars Foundation,
1 Briar Road, Golf, IL 60029-0301, (312) 724-4600.

277

CLAFLIN UNIVERSITY
Performance Scholarship
Who Can Apply: Recipients must maintain a specific GPA and exemplify good moral character to retain scholarships.
How Much Money Can I Get: Varies
Whom Do I Contact: Claflin University, Office of Student Financial Aid, 400 Magnolia Street, Orangeburg, South Carolina 29115, (803) 535-5331.

278

CLAFLIN UNIVERSITY
United Negro College Fund (UNCF) Scholarship
Who Can Apply: Students who demonstrate financial need.
How Much Money Can I Get: $500 - $7500
Whom Do I Contact: Claflin University, Office of Student Financial Aid, 400 Magnolia Street, Orangeburg, South Carolina 29115, (803) 535-5331.

279

CLAFLIN UNIVERSITY
Vocational Rehabilitation Program
Who Can Apply: Students with mental and physical handicaps.
How Much Money Can I Get: Varies
Whom Do I Contact: Claflin University, Office of Student Financial Aid, 400 Magnolia Street, Orangeburg, South Carolina 29115, (803) 535-5331.

280

CLARION UNIVERSITY
The State Board of Governors Scholarship
Who Can Apply: Eligibility is based on students' need, and payment is made as a tuition credit. Must have a minimum 3.0 GPA, and other criteria include contribution to the university and participation in extracurricular activities.
How Much Money Can I Get: Varies
Whom Do I Contact: Dean of Admissions, Clarion University, Admissions Office, Clarion, PA 16214, (814) 226-2000.

281

CLARK ATLANTA UNIVERSITY
SCHOOL OF LIBRARY AND INFORMATION STUDIES
Who Can Apply: Two library training fellowship grants are provided by the U.S. Department of Education. Applicants must be black college seniors majoring in library science. Apply directly to the institution.

How Much Money Can I Get: $8,000
Whom Do I Contact: Clark Atlanta University, School of Library and Information Studies, 223 James P. Brawley Drive, Atlanta, GA 30314, (404) 653-8694.

282

CLARK COLLEGE

Scripps-Howard Scholarships in Journalism
Who Can Apply: Minority students enrolled at Clark College majoring in Journalism. Deadline March 15.
How Much Money Can I Get: $1,000
Whom Do I Contact: Clark College, Department of Communications, Atlanta, GA 30314, (404) 681-3080, ext. 238

283

CLEMSON UNIVERSITY

Amoco Foundation Scholarship
Who Can Apply: Minority or female full-time student in textiles with a 2.0 GPA. Deadline March 1.
How Much Money Can I Get: $2,000
Whom Do I Contact: Clemson University, Attn.: Financial Aid Director, G01 Sikes Hall, Clemson, SC 29634-5123, (803) 656-2280.

284

CLEMSON UNIVERSITY

Corinne Holt Sawyer Scholarship
Who Can Apply: Entering black freshman with a minimum 2.0 GPA. Deadline March 1.
How Much Money Can I Get: $1,000
Whom Do I Contact: Clemson University, Attn.: Financial Aid Director, G01 Sikes Hall, Clemson, SC 29634-5123, (803) 656-2280.

285

CLEMSON UNIVERSITY

Daniel Memorial Scholarship
Who Can Apply: Minority entering freshmen with a minimum 3.0 GPA. Deadline March 1.
How Much Money Can I Get: $1,500
Whom Do I Contact: Clemson University, Attn.: Financial Aid Director, G01 Sikes Hall, Clemson, SC 29634-5123, (803) 656-2280.

286

CLEMSON UNIVERSITY
Edward S. Moore Foundation Scholarship
Who Can Apply: Entering freshman minority students in forestry who are South Carolina residents. Applicants must have a 3.0 GPA and must be a full-time student. Deadline March 1.
How Much Money Can I Get: $2,500 renewable
Whom Do I Contact: Clemson University, Attn.: Financial Aid Director, G01 Sikes Hall, Clemson, SC 29634-5123, (803) 656-2280.

287

CLEMSON UNIVERSITY
Harvey B. Gantt Scholarship Endowment Fund
Who Can Apply:. Full-time black students with a 3.0 GPA. Preference given to South Carolina residents and entering freshmen. Deadline March 1.
How Much Money Can I Get: Varies
Whom Do I Contact: Clemson University, Attn.: Financial Aid Director, G01 Sikes Hall, Clemson, SC 29634-5123, (803) 656-2280.

288

CLEMSON UNIVERSITY
Management/Industrial Association Minority Engineering Scholarship
Who Can Apply: This award is renewable with satisfactory academic progress.
How Much Money Can I Get: $1,000
Whom Do I Contact: Financial Aid Director, Clemson University, G01 Sikes Hall, Clemson, SC 29631-4023, (803) 656-2280.

289

CLEMSON UNIVERSITY
Robert C. Edwards Scholarship
Who Can Apply: Entering freshmen with outstanding academic potential. Must have a 2.0 GPA. Award is renewable award. Deadline March 1.
How Much Money Can I Get: $3,000
Whom Do I Contact: Financial Aid Director, Clemson University, G01 Sikes Hall, Clemson, SC 29631-4023, (803) 656-2280.

290

CLEVELAND STATE UNIVERSITY
Link Program Scholarship
Who Can Apply: Incoming minority freshman student interested in the field of business, engineering, or computer and information sciences. Student

must show achievement and motivation and possess a minimum 2.5 high school GPA. Deadline April 1.
How Much Money Can I Get: $2,000
Whom Do I Contact: Career Services Cleveland State University, 2344 Euclid Avenue, Cleveland, OH 44115, (216) 687-3765, E-mail: osfa@csuohio.edu.

291
CLEVELAND STATE UNIVERSITY
National Broadcasting Corporation Fellowship in Journalism
Who Can Apply: Minority graduate student at Cleveland State or other college or university in the Greater Cleveland area. Applicant must have a GPA of 3.0 in undergraduate work. Deadline March 15.
How Much Money Can I Get: Full tuition and a monthly stipend
Whom Do I Contact: Cleveland State University, Department of Communications, Cleveland, OH 44115, (216) 687-4630.

292
CLINCH VALLEY COLLEGE
Black Virginians Scholarship
Who Can Apply: Applicants must be black students who are residents of Virginia. Selection is based on academic achievement and financial need. Freshmen and transfer students are eligible to apply. A minimum 2.0 GPA is required. Deadline May 1.
How Much Money Can I Get: Varies
Whom Do I Contact: Financial Aid Director, Clinch Valley College, P.O. Box 16, Wise, VA 24293, (703) 328-0139.

293
COALITION OF BLACK MEMBERS
OF THE AMERICAN LUTHERAN CHURCH
Who Can Apply: One of this organization's goals is to assist black students in their total education in colleges and institutions of the American Lutheran Church.
How Much Money Can I Get: Varies
Whom Do I Contact: Coalition of Black Members of the American Lutheran Church, 422 S. 5th Street, Minneapolis, MN 55415, (612) 330-3100.

294
COASTAL CAROLINA COLLEGE
Admissions Minority Scholarship
Who Can Apply: Freshman applicants must have an SAT combined score of

800 with a minimum sub score of 400 in verbal and 400 in math or a minimum ACT composite score of 18 with minimum sub scores of 18 in English and 18 in math. Applicants must have been in a college preparatory high school program and be U.S. citizens. Transfer students must have a 3.0 GPA.

How Much Money Can I Get: $100

Whom Do I Contact: Coastal Carolina College, P.O. Box 1954, Conway, SC 29526, (803) 347-3161.

295

COE COLLEGE

Who Can Apply: Awards available especially for minority students.

How Much Money Can I Get: Up to $2,600

Whom Do I Contact: Office of Admissions, Coe College, Cedar Rapids, IA 52402, (319) 399-8000.

296

COLBY COLLEGE

The Ralph J. Bunche Scholars Program

Who Can Apply: Applicants must show scholastic and leadership potential. Special grants given in addition to usual aid. Eligibility is based on need.

How Much Money Can I Get: Varies

Whom Do I Contact: Office of Admissions, Colby College, Waterville, ME 04901, (207) 873-1131.

297

COLLEGE SCHOLARSHIP SERVICE
OF THE COLLEGE BOARD

Engineering Scholarship Program for Minority Community College Graduates

Who Can Apply: Individual institutions are invited to nominate minority students for consideration. The nominee should have earned at least a 3.0 GPA, be a U.S. citizen or permanent resident, be scheduled to receive an associate degree or have completed 60 semester hours. They should also have completed calculus, one year of general physics, and one year of general chemistry. Candidates should demonstrate financial need and be planning to transfer to an accredited senior institution for full-time study in engineering science.

How Much Money Can I Get: Varies

Whom Do I Contact: College Scholarship Service of the College Board, 45 Columbus Avenue, New York, NY 10019, (212) 713-8000.

298

COLORADO COLLEGE

Who Can Apply: Award sponsored by the El Pomar Foundation assists qualified minority students with financial need.
How Much Money Can I Get: Varies
Whom Do I Contact: Office of Admissions, Colorado College, Colorado Springs, CO 80903, (303) 473-2233 or (800) 542-7214.

299

COLORADO INSTITUTE OF ART

Who Can Apply: Scholarship is open to Colorado minority students. Artwork is judged. New program offers first year tuition to winner. One scholarship will be offered each year. Interested students should contact their high school art teacher.
How Much Money Can I Get: $7,320
Whom Do I Contact: Colorado Institute of Art, Admissions Office, 200 E. Ninth Avenue, Denver, CO 80203, (303) 837-0825.

300

COLORADO SCHOOL OF MINES

Minority Engineering Scholarship
Who Can Apply: Applicants must be minorities majoring in one of the following engineering areas; chemical, metallurgy, petroleum, geological, or mechanical. Financial need required.
How Much Money Can I Get: $250 to $2,500
Whom Do I Contact: Financial Aid Director, Colorado School of Mines, Golden, CO 80401, (303) 279-0300.

301

COLORADO STATE UNIVERSITY

The Kodak Minority Academic Award
Who Can Apply: Sophomore minority engineering students with a high academic record. Must have a 3.3 GPA. The award pays 75 percent of tuition and is renewable for three years if the recipient meets the academic standards.
How Much Money Can I Get: Varies
Whom Do I Contact: Dean of Engineering, Colorado State University, Fort Collins, CO 80523, (303) 491-1101.

302

COLORADO STATE UNIVERSITY

Who Can Apply: For entering freshman minority students in the College of Agricultural Sciences with financial need, demonstrated scholarship, and

leadership. Must be a Colorado resident.
How Much Money Can I Get: Varies
Whom Do I Contact: Dean of Agricultural Sciences, Colorado State University, Fort Collins, CO 80523, (303) 491-1101.

303

COLORADO STATE UNIVERSITY

The Conoco Scholarship
Who Can Apply: Outstanding minority students majoring in Mechanical or Chemical Engineering. Must be a U.S. citizen with a 3.3 GPA. Deadline March 1.
How Much Money Can I Get: $1,000
Whom Do I Contact: Dean of Engineering, Colorado State University, Fort Collins, CO 80523, (303) 491-1101.

304

COLORADO STATE UNIVERSITY

Diversity Award
Who Can Apply: Selection is based on the degree to which a student contributes to the diversity of the environment at the university. The award is renewable if the recipient maintains a minimum 2.0 GPA and the student continues to receive diversity committee approval. Interested students should contact the office of the dean of his or her academic college or any of the six campus advocacy groups.
How Much Money Can I Get: $1,000
Whom Do I Contact: Financial Aid Director, Colorado State University, Fort Collins, CO 80523, (303) 491-1101.

305

COLORADO STATE UNIVERSITY

George and Paula Hill Book Fund
Who Can Apply: Minority students pursuing a degree in science. Selection based on financial need. Deadline April 1.
How Much Money Can I Get: $100
Whom Do I Contact: Vice President, Student Affairs, Colorado State University, Fort Collins, CO 80523, (303) 491-1101.

306

COLORADO STATE UNIVERSITY

The NACME Scholarship
Who Can Apply: Freshmen minority Engineering majors. Deadline March 1.
How Much Money Can I Get: $500

Whom Do I Contact: Dean of Engineering, Colorado State University, Fort Collins, CO 80523, (303) 491-1101.

307

UNIVERSITY OF COLORADO
The Minority Engineering Program
Who Can Apply: Undergraduate students in engineering and applied sciences.
How Much Money Can I Get: Sixty to 70 scholarships ranging from $500 to $2,000 are awarded annually.
Whom Do I Contact: University of Colorado, Minority Engineering Program, Campus Box 422, Boulder, CO 80309-0422, (800) 822-6371.

308

UNIVERSITY OF COLORADO, BOULDER
The Martin Luther King Scholarship
Who Can Apply: Consideration is automatic, and no separate application is required. Deadline March 1.
How Much Money Can I Get: Varies
Whom Do I Contact: Scholarship Coordinator, University of Colorado at Boulder, Boulder, CO 80309-0106, (303) 492-5091.

309

COLUMBIA INTERNATIONAL UNIVERSITY
Minority Grant
Who Can Apply: Award to minority full-time students. Deadline February 15.
How Much Money Can I Get: $1,200
Whom Do I Contact: Columbia International University, Attn.: Financial Aid Office, P.O. Box 3122, Columbia, SC 29230-3122, (803) 754-4100.

310

COMMUNITY FOUNDATION OF PALM BEACH/ MARTIN COUNTIES
Peck Scholarship
Who Can Apply: High achievers in French or Spanish pursuing French or Spanish as a major or minor. Applicants must be Palm Beach residents with a minimum 2.5 GPA.
How Much Money Can I Get: Varies
Whom Do I Contact: Community Foundation of Palm Beach/Martin Counties, Attn.: Program Officer, 324 Datura Street, Suite 340, West Palm Beach, FL 33401-5431, (407) 659-6800.

311

COMMUNITY FOUNDATION
OF PALM BEACH/MARTIN COUNTIES, BARNETT BANK

Who Can Apply: Awards to students in good academic standing who intend to major in business. Applicants must be Palm Beach residents with a minimum 2.5 GPA.

How Much Money Can I Get: Varies

Whom Do I Contact: Community Foundation of Palm Beach/Martin Counties, Attn.: Program Officer, 324 Datura Street, Suite 340, West Palm Beach, FL 33401-5431, (407) 659-6800.

312

CONCERNED MEDIA PROFESSIONALS, INC.

The Frank Johnson Scholarship

Who Can Apply: Minorities in Print Journalism who are juniors.

How Much Money Can I Get: $700

Whom Do I Contact: Concerned Media Professionals, Inc., P.O. Box 44034, Tucson, AZ 85733.

313

CONCERNED MEDIA PROFESSIONALS, INC.

The McDonald's Scholarship for Young Journalists

Who Can Apply: Minorities who are between 19 and 21 years old and who are majoring in Print or Broadcast Journalism at the University of Arizona.

How Much Money Can I Get: Varies

Whom Do I Contact: Concerned Media Professionals, Inc., P.O. Box 44034, Tucson, AZ 85733.

314

CONCERNED MEDIA PROFESSIONALS, INC.

Roy Drachman Scholarship

Who Can Apply: Minorities who are majoring in Print or Broadcast Journalism at the University of Arizona.

How Much Money Can I Get: $1,000

Whom Do I Contact: Concerned Media Professionals, Inc., P.O. Box 44034, Tucson, AZ 85733.

315

CONGRESSIONAL BLACK CAUCUS

Spouses Scholarship

Who Can Apply: Applicants must be residents of a congressional district represented by a member of the Congressional Black Caucus in Maryland.

Deadline March 25.
How Much Money Can I Get: Varies
Whom Do I Contact: Congressional Black Caucus Foundation, Inc., Attn.: Educational Programs Coordinator, 1004 Pennsylvania Avenue, SE, Washington, DC 20003, (202) 675-6730.

316
UNIVERSITY OF CONNECTICUT
Medical Scholarship
Who Can Apply: Minority student majoring in Medicine. Financial need required.
How Much Money Can I Get: Varies
Whom Do I Contact: Financial Aid Director, University of Connecticut, Wilbur Cross Building, Storrs, CT 06268, (203) 486-2000.

317
CONSORTIUM FOR GRADUATE STUDY IN MANAGEMENT
Who Can Apply: This award is restricted to blacks, Hispanics and Native American Indians who wish to attend Indiana University at Bloomington, University of North Carolina at Chapel Hill, University of Rochester, University of Southern California, University of Texas at Austin, Washington University at St. Louis, and the University of Wisconsin at Madison for an MBA. Applicants must be U.S. citizens. Deadline October 1 and February 1.
How Much Money Can I Get: Full tuition + expenses
Whom Do I Contact: Consortium for Graduate Study in Management, 101 N. Skinker Boulevard, P.O. Box 1132, St. Louis, MO 63130, (314) 889-6353.

318
CORGAN ASSOCIATES ARCHITECTS
African American/Hispanic Architectural Education Work/ Study Program
Who Can Apply: Applicants must be students living within the Dallas Independent School Districts.
How Much Money Can I Get: $12,000 total
Whom Do I Contact: Gary DeVries, Corgan Associates, Inc., 501 Elm Street, Dallas, TX 75202-3358, (214) 748-2000.

319

CORNELL UNIVERSITY SUMMER COLLEGE

Jerome H. Holland Scholarship
Who Can Apply: Applicants must be qualified minority high school juniors and seniors who demonstrate outstanding academic ability as well as financial need.
How Much Money Can I Get: Varies
Whom Do I Contact: Administrative Assistant, Cornell University Summer College, Box 811, B-12 Ives Hall, Cornell University, Ithaca, NY 14853, (607) 255-6203.

320

COUNCIL ON CAREER DEVELOPMENT
FOR MINORITIES

Julius A. Thomas Fellowship
Who Can Apply: Applicant must be interested in a career in the field of career counseling and placement. In addition to the $2,500 grant, a $150 allowance may be obtained for approved books and materials, and another $2,500 can be earned if the student participates in a summer internship dealing with counseling and placement. The student must attend one of the following institutions: Florida A&M University (FL), Howard University (DC), North Carolina Central University (NC), Texas Southern University (TX), Tuskegee Institute (AL), Virginia State University (Petersburg, VA), New Mexico State University (NM), California State University (Long Beach, CA), Pan American University (TX), or San Francisco State University (CA). Must be a U.S. citizen. Deadline May 1.
How Much Money Can I Get: $2,500
Whom Do I Contact: Program Manager, Council on Career Development for Minorities, 1341 W. Mockingbird Lane, Dallas, TX 75247, (214) 631-3677.

321

COUNCIL ON INTERNATIONAL
EDUCATIONAL EXCHANGE

Robert B. Bailey III Minority Student Scholarship
Who Can Apply: Applicants must demonstrate financial need and apply to a CIEE-administered study-abroad, work-abroad, or international volunteer work-camp program. Deadline varies.
How Much Money Can I Get: $500 to $1,000
Whom Do I Contact: Robert B. Bailey III Minority Student Scholarship, Council on International Educational Exchange, 205 E. 42nd Street, New York, NY 10017-5706, (212) 666-4177.

322

COUNCIL ON INTERNATIONAL EDUCATIONAL EXCHANGE

Scholarship Fund for Minority Students

Who Can Apply: This fund assists minority students who wish to participate in any CIEE educational program including study, work, voluntary service, and internship programs.

How Much Money Can I Get: Varies

Whom Do I Contact: Council on International Educational Exchange, 205 E. 42nd Street, New York, NY 10017, (212) 666-4177.

323

COURIER-JOURNAL & THE LOUISVILLE TIMES INTERNSHIP

Who Can Apply: The purpose of the minority business intern program is to expose the minority student to newspaper career opportunities. Summer interns are treated as professional staffers and are given opportunities to develop job skills and gain valuable work experience. The program is open to minority college students in their sophomore or junior years who either live or go to college in Kentucky or southern Indiana. Children of employees are eligible but receive no preferential treatment. The participating departments and number of positions vary from year to year. The internship lasts 13 weeks. Interns will work a full work-week. Days off will not necessarily be on weekends. Interns earn $200 a week. A business resume and cover letter must be submitted with the official application form. Must be majoring in photojournalism, accounting, advertising, journalism, business administration/management, or engineering. Deadline March 31.

How Much Money Can I Get: Varies

Whom Do I Contact: Human Resources Department, *The Courier-Journal* & *The Louisville Times*, 525 W. Broadway, Louisville, KY 40202, (502) 582-4803.

324

COX ENTERPRISES

Minority Journalism Scholarship

Who Can Apply: High school seniors graduating from the metro-Atlanta school system, have a B average, are U.S. citizens, plan to pursue careers in the newspaper industry, and plan to attend certain Georgia colleges are eligible to apply. Students must intern during summer and holiday breaks at selected newspaper throughout four years. See guidance counselor for current announcement.

How Much Money Can I Get: Financial support for four years

Whom Do I Contact: Scholarship Officer, Cox Enterprises, P.O. Box 4689, Atlanta, GA 30302, (404) 526-5091.

325

CREIGHTON UNIVERSITY
Black Undergraduate Scholarship
Who Can Apply: Applicants must maintain a 2.5 GPA and prove financial need.
How Much Money Can I Get: Tuition, room & board
Whom Do I Contact: Financial Aid Office, Creighton University, California at 24th Street, Omaha, NE 68178, (402) 280-2731.

326

CREIGHTON UNIVERSITY SCHOOL OF LAW
Frances M. Ryan Scholarship
Who Can Apply: Qualified minority students are eligible. Award is based on academic ability and financial need.
How Much Money Can I Get: Varies
Whom Do I Contact: Creighton University School of Law, California Street at 24th, Omaha, NE 68178, (402)280-2872.

327

CREOLE ETHNIC ASSOCIATION, INC.
Creole Scholarship Fund
Who Can Apply: Undergraduate or graduate students conducting research in the areas of genealogy, language, or Creole culture. Applicants must be U.S. citizens and are asked to fill out a genealogical chart of at least five generations. Deadline June.
How Much Money Can I Get: $1,000
Whom Do I Contact: Creole Ethnic Association, Inc., P.O. Box 2666, Church Street Station, New York, NY 10008.

328

DAILY PRESS
Scholarship for Black Journalists
Who Can Apply: Black students either interested in studying print journalism or already in print journalism. Preference is given to residents of the Virginia Peninsula.
How Much Money Can I Get: $2,500
Whom Do I Contact: Daily Press, Inc., 7505 Warwick Boulevard, P.O. Box 746, Newport News, VA 23607, (804) 244-8421.

329

DALLAS–FORT WORTH ASSOCIATION OF BLACK COMMUNICATORS

Who Can Apply: Applicants must be black entering freshmen and must reside in Dallas, Tarrant, Collin, or Denton County. Must be majoring in one of the following: Journalism, Photojournalism, Public Relations, Radio/TV Broadcasting, or Graphic Arts.
How Much Money Can I Get: $1,500
Whom Do I Contact: DFW/ABC, 400 Records Street, Belo Building, Suite 343, Dallas, TX 75265.

330

DARTMOUTH COLLEGE

Thurgood Marshall Dissertation Fellowship for African American Scholars
Who Can Apply: Applicants must have completed all other Ph.D. requirements other than the dissertation at Dartmouth College. Each fellow will be expected to complete the dissertation during the tenure of the fellowship and to participate in teaching one 10-week course during the year. Deadline March 1.
How Much Money Can I Get: $20,000+
Whom Do I Contact: Office of the Dean of the Faculty, Dartmouth College, 201 Wentworth Hall, Hanover, NH 03755, (603) 646-1110.

331

DEFIANCE COLLEGE

Who Can Apply: Awards to minority students graduating in the top 50 percent of their high school class.
How Much Money Can I Get: $1,500
Whom Do I Contact: Defiance College, Attn.: Office of Financial Aid, 701 N. Clinton Street, Defiance, OH 43512, (419) 783-2355.

332

DELAWARE VALLEY CLUB SCHOLARSHIP

Who Can Apply: A minority high school senior Delaware Valley resident who has interest in service to the community. Must have a 3.0 GPA and financial need. Deadline May 23.
How Much Money Can I Get: $750
Whom Do I Contact: Scholarship Chairperson, Delaware Valley Club, 2324 47th Street, Pennsauken, NJ 08110, (609) 662-8739.

333

DELTA SIGMA THETA, INC.

Who Can Apply: Scholarships for women from Montgomery or Prince George's County in Maryland for study at either a college or specialized vocational school.
How Much Money Can I Get: Varies
Whom Do I Contact: Delta Sigma Theta Sorority, Inc., 1707 New Hampshire Avenue, NW, Washington, DC 20009, (202) 483-5460.

334

DELTA SIGMA THETA, INC.

Myra Davis Hemmings Scholarship
Who Can Apply: Applicants must be active, dues-paying members of Delta Sigma Theta and majoring in the performing or creative arts. Applicants must submit transcripts of all college records. Deadline March.
How Much Money Can I Get: Varies
Whom Do I Contact: Delta Sigma Theta, Inc., 1707 New Hampshire Avenue, NW, Washington, DC 20009, (202) 483-5460.

335

DELTA SIGMA THETA, INC.

Potomac Valley Alumnae Chapter Scholarship
Who Can Apply: Awards are for residents of Montgomery County in Maryland who demonstrate financial need. Deadline March 31.
How Much Money Can I Get: $2,000
Whom Do I Contact: Potomac Valley Alumnae Chapter, Delta Sigma Theta Sorority, Inc., Attn.: Scholarship Committee, 9913 Sorrel Avenue, Potomac, MD 20854, (301) 299-8011.

336

DENISON UNIVERSITY

Who Can Apply: Denison University offers 41 minority student scholarships as follows: 17 Tyree Scholarships, 9 Meredity Scholarships, 12 Fisher Scholarships, and 3 Bob Good Scholarships.
How Much Money Can I Get: $1,500 to $2,500
Whom Do I Contact: Financial Aid Director, Denison University, Granville, OH 43023, (614) 587-0810.

337

DENISON UNIVERSITY

Parajon Scholarship
Who Can Apply: Awarded to Hispanic, Asian, and Native American Indian

students who show outstanding academic performance or potential.
Deadline January 1.
How Much Money Can I Get: Half tuition
Whom Do I Contact: Denison University, Attn.: Financial Aid Director,
Office of Financial Aid and Student Employment, Box H, Granville, OH
43023, (614) 587-6279.

338

DEPAUW UNIVERSITY

Who Can Apply: Applicant must be a black U.S. citizen and possess
leadership qualities. Deadline February 15.
How Much Money Can I Get: $5,000
Whom Do I Contact: DePauw University, 309 S. Locust Street,
Administration Bldg., Greencastle, IN 46135, (317) 658-4030.

339

DICKINSON SCHOOL OF LAW

Who Can Apply: The Dickinson School of Law provides two minority
scholarships for incoming students.
How Much Money Can I Get: Full-tuition. Dormitory preference and book
allowances are offered. Renewable each year.
Whom Do I Contact: Dickinson School of Law, 150 S. College Street,
Carlisle, PA 17013-2899, (717) 243-4611.

340

DIGITAL EQUIPMENT CORPORATION

Who Can Apply: Offers a minority education scholarship for students
majoring in Electrical, Mechanical, or Industrial Engineering or Computer
Science in their last two years of college.
How Much Money Can I Get: Varies
Whom Do I Contact: Digital Equipment Corporation, 2500 W. Union Hills
Drive, Phoenix, AZ 85027.

341

DIGITAL EQUIPMENT CORPORATION
MINORITIES AND WOMEN ENGINEERS

Who Can Apply: Minority and women high school juniors and seniors who
are residents of Springfield, West Springfield, Holyoke, Chicopee, Agawam,
or Westfield or are children of Digital Equipment Corporation/Springfield
employees, regardless of their place of residence, are eligible. Recipients
will be invited work at Digital/Springfield during the summer. Scholarship
support may be extended beyond freshman year if the student performs

acceptably during the summer work program and college year. Must major in Engineering. Financial need is required. Deadline February 2.
How Much Money Can I Get: Tuition + fees
Whom Do I Contact: Digital Equipment Corporation, 2500 W. Union Hills Drive, Phoenix, AZ 85027.

342

DOW JONES NEWSPAPER FUND
Minority Editing Intern Program for College Seniors
Who Can Apply: This newspaper intern program offers minority college seniors a paid summer copyediting internship on daily newspapers and a scholarship to use for graduate studies following the internship or a grant to pay outstanding school loans. Deadline November 15.
How Much Money Can I Get: Paid internship + $1,000 grant
Whom Do I Contact: Dow Jones Newspaper Fund, Inc., P.O. Box 300, Princeton, NJ 08543-0300.

343

EDUCATIONAL AND CULTURAL FUND OF THE ELECTRICAL INDUSTRY
Dr. Martin Luther King, Jr., Memorial Scholarship Award
Who Can Apply: Black high school graduates are eligible. Winners determined by SAT scores, GPA, leadership, recommendations, and personal interviews.
How Much Money Can I Get: $2,000
Whom Do I Contact: Educational and Cultural Fund of the Electrical Industry, Electric Industry Center, 158-11 Jewel Avenue, Flushing, NY 11365.

344

DRAKE UNIVERSITY
Cowles Foundation Multicultural Scholarship
Who Can Apply: Award available to minority full-time students with a minimum 3.75 GPA, combined 1210 SAT score, minimum 27 ACT score, and who are in the top fifth of their high school class. Deadline March 1.
How Much Money Can I Get: Tuition
Whom Do I Contact: Drake University, Attn.: Director of Admissions, Des Moines, IA 50311-4505, (515) 271-3181.

345

DRAKE UNIVERSITY
Des Moines Register **Minority Journalism Scholarship**
Who Can Apply: Iowa minority students.

How Much Money Can I Get: Varies
Whom Do I Contact: Drake University, School of Journalism & Mass Communications, 2507 University Avenue, Des Moines, IA 50311-9901, (515) 271-3194.

346
DRAKE UNIVERSITY LAW SCHOOL
Scholarships for Disadvantaged Students
Who Can Apply: Entering students from educationally or economically disadvantaged backgrounds who demonstrate financial need.
How Much Money Can I Get: Ten full-tuition scholarships, renewable
Whom Do I Contact: Drake University, The Law School, Cortwright Hall, Des Moines, IA 50311, (515) 271-2782.

347
DREXEL UNIVERSITY
Business Minority Award
Who Can Apply: Four-year Malcolm X Scholarship provides tuition, books, fees, and room and board.
How Much Money Can I Get: Varies
Whom Do I Contact: Office of Admissions, Drexel University, Philadelphia, PA 19104, (215) 895-2400.

348
DUKE UNIVERSITY
Who Can Apply: Award sponsored by the Gulf Oil Corporation Foundation. Scholarships are available for minority students interested in engineering and science who are in financial need.
How Much Money Can I Get: Up to $2,000
Whom Do I Contact: Office of Admissions, Duke University, Durham, NC 27708, (919) 684-3214.

349
DUKE UNIVERSITY
Reginaldo Howard Memorial Scholarship
Who Can Apply: Selection is based on academic ability and leadership skills. Awards is renewable. Applicants must be in the upper fifth of their class and have a 3.3 GPA.
How Much Money Can I Get: $6,000
Whom Do I Contact: Director of Admissions, Duke University, Durham, NC 27708, (919) 684-3214.

350

DURACELL/NATIONAL URBAN LEAGUE

Scholarship and Intern Program
Who Can Apply: Applicants must be in the upper 25 percent of their class majoring in one of the following: Marketing, Finance, Engineering, Business Administration/Management, or Sales. Deadline April 15.
How Much Money Can I Get: $10,000 and summer internships
Whom Do I Contact: The Duracell/National Urban League, 500 E. 62nd Street, New York, NY 10021-8309, (212) 310-9000.

351

DURHAM TECHNICAL INSTITUTE

Scholarship Program
Who Can Apply: In order to qualify, a student must maintain a passing grade average at or above the level for graduation. Preference will be given to those with the greatest need, minority students enrolled in college-transferable curriculum programs, displaced persons seeking new job skills, and women in nontraditional curriculum programs (in that order). Other factors to be considered will include scholastic achievement and participation in institution and community activities. Deadline varies.
How Much Money Can I Get: $400
Whom Do I Contact: Financial Aid Director, Durham Technical Institute, 1637 Lawson Street, Durham, NC 27703, (919) 596-9311.

352

EARL WARREN LEGAL TRAINING PROGRAM

Who Can Apply: Preference will be given to students enrolling in law schools in the South. Applicants must take the Law School Admissions Test. Consideration is given to applicants under 35 years of age and to those who plan to practice where there is a great need for lawyers. Must be a black U.S. citizen.
How Much Money Can I Get: $1,200
Whom Do I Contact: Earl Warren Legal Training Program, 99 Hudson Street, Suite 1600, New York, NY 10013, (212) 219-1900.

353

EARLHAM COLLEGE

The Cunningham Cultural Scholarship
Who Can Apply: Candidates must submit a recommendation from a teacher and be willing to attend April Scholar's forum. Deadline March 1.
How Much Money Can I Get: $2,500 to $4,000
Whom Do I Contact: Earlham College, Office of Admissions, Richmond, IN 47374, (317) 983-1600.

354

EARLHAM COLLEGE
Educational Enhancement Award
Who Can Apply: Indiana black and Hispanic students enrolling at Earlham. The grants are based on demonstrated financial need. Grants include a guaranteed campus job, allowing qualified students to earn a four-year Earlham degree without incurring any debt.
Whom Do I Contact: Robert L. De Veer, Dean of Admissions, Earlham College, Richmond, IN 47374, (317) 983-1600 or toll free (800) 382-6906.

355

EAST TENNESSEE STATE UNIVERSITY
Minority Scholarship
Who Can Apply: Minority students.
How Much Money Can I Get: $950
Whom Do I Contact: East Tennessee State University, Attn.: Office of Financial Aid, P.O. Box 70722, Johnson City, TN 37614-0722, (615) 929-4313.

356

EAST TEXAS STATE UNIVERSITY
The Harvey Martin Scholarship
Who Can Apply: Minority high school or college students who exhibit leadership and scholarship ability. Students must be in the upper quarter of their high school class or possess a 3.0 GPA in college work. A letter requesting consideration must be submitted to the office of special services. Deadline July 5.
How Much Money Can I Get: $200
Whom Do I Contact: Office of Special Services, East Texas State University, Commerce, TX 75428, (214) 886-5014.

357

EAST TEXAS STATE UNIVERSITY
The Placid Oil Company Scholarship
Who Can Apply: Accounting major who is a minority student (females considered minority) with a 3.0 GPA, who is active in extracurricular activities and has financial need. No application is required.
How Much Money Can I Get: $500
Whom Do I Contact: Accounting Department, East Texas State University, Commerce, TX 75428, (214) 886-5014.

358

EAST TEXAS STATE UNIVERSITY

The United Minority Student Scholarship

Who Can Apply: Entering freshmen and transfer minority students who are in the upper quarter of their high school class with a 3.25 GPA or transfer students with a 3.0 GPA on a 4.0 system. Students are sought for their leadership and scholarly abilities.

How Much Money Can I Get: $200

Whom Do I Contact: Office of Special Services, East Texas State University, Commerce, TX 75428, (214) 886-5014.

359

EASTERN COLLEGE

Who Can Apply: Scholarship applicants must be in the upper two-fifths of their class with a 2.3 GPA. Awarded on a first-come, first-served basis.

How Much Money Can I Get: $1,000 to $5,000

Whom Do I Contact: Eastern College, Minority Student Recruitment, St. David's, PA 31908, (215) 341-1376.

360

EASTERN ILLINOIS UNIVERSITY

Copley Minority Journalism Scholarship

Who Can Apply: Freshman, sophomore, and junior students are eligible. Award is based on grades and activities on student publications. Deadline March 1.

How Much Money Can I Get: $300

Whom Do I Contact: Eastern Illinois University, Journalism Department, Charleston, IL 61920, (217) 581-6003.

361

EASTERN ILLINOIS UNIVERSITY

Eric Schuster Scholarship

Who Can Apply: Award is based on financial need, new student status, intent to pursue a career in newspaper journalism, and strong academic performance. Deadline June 1.

How Much Money Can I Get: Varies

Whom Do I Contact: Eastern Illinois University, Journalism Department, Charleston, IL 61920, (217) 581-6003.

362

EASTERN ILLINOIS UNIVERSITY

James A. Saunders Minority Journalist Scholarship

Who Can Apply: All minority students. Scholarship is based on grades and

activities on student publications. Deadline March 1.
How Much Money Can I Get: $200.
Whom Do I Contact: Eastern Illinois University, Journalism Department, Charleston, IL 61920, (217) 581-6003.

363

EASTERN MENNONITE COLLEGE
American Minority Scholarship
Who Can Apply: Two scholarships are available to American minority students who have maintained a satisfactory record at Eastern Mennonite College. Applicants are required to submit a statement of service goals and demonstrate financial need. Deadline March 1.
How Much Money Can I Get: $450
Whom Do I Contact: Financial Aid Director, Eastern Mennonite College, Harrisonburg, VA 22801, (703) 433-2771.

364

EASTMAN KODAK COMPANY
Kodak Minority Academic Award
Who Can Apply: Minority freshman majoring in one of the following: Engineering, Computer Science/Data Processing, Business Administration/ Management, Chemistry or Accounting. Awards granted at 27 selected colleges.
How Much Money Can I Get: 50 percent of tuition
Whom Do I Contact: Scholarship Officer, Eastman Kodak Company, 343 State Street, Rochester, NY 14650, (716) 724-3127.

365

EASTMAN KODAK COMPANY
Kodak Scholarship and Internship Program
Who Can Apply: Available to students pursuing degrees in engineering, chemistry, polymer science, quantitative business analysis, computer science, marketing, finance, and accounting. Applicants must demonstrate academic excellence and personal leadership.
How Much Money Can I Get: Varies
Whom Do I Contact: Robert M. Belmont, Coordinator, Internship and Scholarship Program, Eastman Kodak Company, Personnel Resources, 343 State Street, Rochester, NY 14650, (716) 724-7593.

366

EDGES GROUP, INC.
Scholarship Program
Who Can Apply: This program provides assistance to black students who

are planning to major in business. Applicants who live in New York, New Jersey, or Connecticut are eligible if they meet the educational and economic criteria established by the United Negro College Fund and are interested in attending a UNCF-affiliated school.
How Much Money Can I Get: $4,000 renewable
Whom Do I Contact: EDGES Group, Inc., c/o William H. Blakely, Jr., 1221 Avenue of the Americas, New York, NY 10020, (212) 790-6058.

367

EDUCATIONAL OPPORTUNITY FUND GRANTS
Who Can Apply: Applicants must be from educationally disadvantaged backgrounds, be able to show financial need, be residents of New Jersey, and be enrolled in a New Jersey college or university.
How Much Money Can I Get: $200 to $1,200
Whom Do I Contact: New Jersey Department of Higher Education, P.O. Box 1417, Trenton, NJ 08625, (609) 292-4368.

368

ELKS NATIONAL FOUNDATION SCHOLARSHIP
Who Can Apply: High school seniors who show leadership, outstanding academic performance, and financial need. Must live within the jurisdictions of the Elks.
How Much Money Can I Get: $1,000 to $5,000
Whom Do I Contact: Improved Benevolent Protective Order of Elks of the World, P.O. Box 159, Winton, NC 29786, (919) 358-7661.

369

EMERSON COLLEGE
WCVB-TV Scholarship
Who Can Apply: Junior, senior, or graduate student in broadcast journalism who is considered disadvantaged. Preference is given to black, Spanish, Hispanic, Asian, or American Indian students. The recipient must be an American citizen or satisfactorily demonstrate that he or she plans to remain in the U.S. for his or her life work. Must have a 3.0 GPA and financial need required. Deadline April 1.
How Much Money Can I Get: $1,250
Whom Do I Contact: Financial Aid Director, Emerson College, 100 Beacon Street, Boston, MA 02116, (617) 578-8655.

370

EMORY UNIVERSITY
Martin Luther King Scholarship
Who Can Apply: The applicant must demonstrate qualities of mind and

spirit and academic and personal achievements that would honor the memory of the late civil rights leader. Must be in the upper fifth of their class and be an entering black freshman. Deadline December 1.
How Much Money Can I Get: Varies
Whom Do I Contact: Emory University, 1380 Oxford Road, NE, Atlanta, GA 30322- 1018, (404) 727-6036.

371
ENVIRONMENTAL PROTECTION AGENCY
Minority Institution Assistance Fellowship
Who Can Apply: Minority full-time undergraduates pursuing environmental careers at historically black colleges/universities. Applicants must apply two years before receiving a B.S. degree and have a cumulative 3.0 GPA.
How Much Money Can I Get: Full tuition+
Whom Do I Contact: Minority Institution Assistance Fellowships, Environmental Protection Agency, Office of Exploratory Research, Mail Stop 8703, 401 M Street, SW, Washington, DC 20460, (202) 260-5750.

372
UNIVERSITY OF EVANSVILLE
The Martin Luther King Scholarship
Who Can Apply: Minority students who show academic promise and are pursuing a professional career. Deadline March 1.
How Much Money Can I Get: Varies
Whom Do I Contact: Financial Aid Director, University of Evansville, 1800 Lincoln Avenue, Evansville, IN 47722, (812) 479-2364.

373
FAYETTEVILLE STATE UNIVERSITY
Academic Scholarship Program
Who Can Apply: Awards for all majors but especially for band, choir, art, drama, or athletics.
How Much Money Can I Get: $4,200 renewable
Whom Do I Contact: Charles Darlington, Director, Enrollment Management and Admissions, Fayetteville State University, 1200 Murchison Road, Fayetteville, NC 28301-4298, (919) 486-1371.

374
FISK UNIVERSITY
Who Can Apply: The numbers of awards vary. Must be a black college freshman. Must have a strong academic background. Apply early.
How Much Money Can I Get: $100 to $2,000

Whom Do I Contact: Fisk University, 1000 17th Avenue, North, Nashville, TN 37208-3051, (615) 329-8665.

375

FIVE COLLEGE

Fellowship Program for Minority Scholars
Who Can Apply: Minority graduate students who have completed all requirements for the Ph.D. except the dissertation. Deadline January 15.
How Much Money Can I Get: $20,000
Whom Do I Contact: Lorna M. Peterson, Five College Fellowship Program Committee, Five Colleges, Inc., P.O. Box 740, Amherst, MA 01004, (413) 256-3626.

376

FLORIDA A&M UNIVERSITY

Life Gets Better Scholarship
Who Can Apply: Students with a major in science, engineering, computer information systems, or mathematics. The program is a comprehensive recruitment program designed to identify and encourage academically talented youth to pursue their educational aspirations at Florida A&M University.
How Much Money Can I Get: Tuition, room and board and books, as well as summer internships which provide the student with unique work experience for four summer semesters at the sponsored corporation.
Whom Do I Contact: Deborah Hardy, Florida A&M University, Tallahassee, FL 32307, (904) 599-3225.

377

FLORIDA A&M UNIVERSITY

Journalism Endowment Scholarship
Who Can Apply: Students majoring in Journalism. Deadline April 15.
How Much Money Can I Get: $500 to $1,000
Whom Do I Contact: Florida A&M University, School of Journalism, Media & Graphic Arts, Tallahassee, FL 32307, (904) 599-3379.

378

FLORIDA ATLANTIC UNIVERSITY

Emily B. and Robert Murdick Scholarship
Who Can Apply: Candidates must be full-time black students with a 3.0 GPA and demonstrated financial need. Deadline July 1.
How Much Money Can I Get: $5,000
Whom Do I Contact: Florida Atlantic University, Attn.: Financial Aid Office, 500 NW 20th Street, Boca Raton, FL 33431-0991, (407) 367-3530.

379

FLORIDA ATLANTIC UNIVERSITY
Martin Luther King Scholarship
Who Can Apply: Incoming black freshmen in the upper fifth of their class.
Deadline March 1.
How Much Money Can I Get: Varies
Whom Do I Contact: Florida Atlantic University, Attn.: Office of
Admissions, 500 NW 20th Street, Boca Raton, FL 33431-0991, (407) 367-
3000.

380

FLORIDA ATLANTIC UNIVERSITY
The Minority Educational Award
Who Can Apply: Scholarships are available to encourage academic
excellence and leadership among black students who matriculate at the
university in graduate programs. Contact the dean of the college of
enrollment for additional information.
How Much Money Can I Get: Varies
Whom Do I Contact: Florida Atlantic University, Student Services
Building, Room 227, Boca Raton, FL 33431-0991, (407) 367-3000.

381

FLORIDA ATLANTIC UNIVERSITY
Minority Transfer Scholarship
Who Can Apply: Incoming black juniors who have at least a 3.0 GPA.
Deadline March 1.
How Much Money Can I Get: $775
Whom Do I Contact: Financial Aid Director, Florida Atlantic University,
Student Services Building, Room 227, Boca Raton, FL 33431-0991, (407)
367-3000.

382

FLORIDA ATLANTIC UNIVERSITY
The North Broward Hospital Scholarship
Who Can Apply: Minority or female students from Broward County
majoring in health administration. Selection is based on academic
achievement and financial need. Must have a 3.0 GPA and show financial
need. Deadline March 1.
How Much Money Can I Get: Varies
Whom Do I Contact: Health Administration Program, Florida Atlantic
University, Boca Raton, FL 33431, (407) 367-3000.

383

FLORIDA COMMUNITY COLLEGE AT JACKSONVILLE

Black Student Grant
Who Can Apply: Incoming freshmen enrolling full-time. Applicant must be a U.S. citizen. Deadline February 28.
How Much Money Can I Get: $1,150
Whom Do I Contact: Florida Community College at Jacksonville, Attn.: Scholarship Coordinator, 501 W. State Street, Jacksonville, FL 32202, (904) 632-3353.

384

FLORIDA DEPARTMENT OF EDUCATION
José Martí Scholarship Challenge Grant Fund
Who Can Apply: Awards offered to Hispanic Florida residents beginning undergraduate or graduate studies at a Florida college. Applicants must apply as a senior in high school or as a graduate student with a 3.0 GPA. Applicant must be a U.S. citizen. Deadline April 1.
How Much Money Can I Get: $2,000
Whom Do I Contact: Florida Department of Education, Assistance-State Programs, Attn.: Office of Student Financial Assistance, 1344 Florida Education Center, Tallahassee, FL 32399-0400, (904) 487-0049.

385

THE FLORIDA EDUCATION FUND
The McKnight Doctoral Fellowship Program
Who Can Apply: Fellowships are awarded in all disciplines except law, medicine, and education, with the exceptions of mathematics and science education and educational testing and measurement. Two fellowships are available in art history, art education, arts management, history, or literature to study the Barnett-Aden African American Art Collection at the Museum of African American Art in Tampa, Florida. Deadline January 15.
How Much Money Can I Get: $16,000
Whom Do I Contact: The Florida Education Fund, 201 E. Kennedy Boulevard, Suite 1525, Tampa, FL 33602, (813) 272-2772.

386

FLORIDA INSTITUTE OF TECHNOLOGY
Minority Engineering Education Effort
Who Can Apply: Applicants must be full-time students with a 2.5 GPA, majoring in engineering. Financial need required. Deadline May 1.
How Much Money Can I Get: $1,500.

Whom Do I Contact: Engineering Department, Florida Institute of Technology, Office of Financial Aid/Scholarships, 150 W. University Boulevard, Melbourne, FL 32901, (407) 768-8000.

387

FLORIDA INTERNATIONAL UNIVERSITY
Academic Opportunity Program
Who Can Apply: Incoming freshmen with a minimum GPA of 3.0, a combined SAT score of 850, and a record of school and community involvement. Deadline December 1.
How Much Money Can I Get: $1,200
Whom Do I Contact: Florida International University, Attn.: Director of Minority Student Services, University Park Campus, GC 216, Miami, FL 33199, (305) 348-2436.

388

FLORIDA INTERNATIONAL UNIVERSITY
CRC Press Scholarship
Who Can Apply: Full-time minority students with a minimum 3.0 GPA, demonstrating financial need, and majoring in English, Communications, Marketing, Sales, Retailing, or Accounting. Deadline May 1.
How Much Money Can I Get: $1,500
Whom Do I Contact: Florida International University, Attn.: Office of Financial Aid, University Park Campus, PC 125, Miami, FL 33199, (305) 348-2436.

389

FLORIDA INTERNATIONAL UNIVERSITY
The Diversity in Journalism Scholarship
Who Can Apply: Minority student from the Tampa Bay area interested in pursuing a career in journalism; presented at the Society of Professional Journalists awards banquet in September. Deadline late summer.
How Much Money Can I Get: $1,000
Whom Do I Contact: Florida International University, School of Journalism & Mass Communications, North Miami, FL 33181, (305) 940-5425.

390

FLORIDA INTERNATIONAL UNIVERSITY
Ed Bradley Scholarship
Who Can Apply: Scholarship is provided with preference to a minority undergraduate student by The Radio and Television News Directors Foundation.

How Much Money Can I Get: $5,000
Whom Do I Contact: Florida International University, School of Journalism & Mass Communications, North Miami, FL 33181, (305) 940-5425.

391

FLORIDA INTERNATIONAL UNIVERSITY
Golden Drum Scholarship
Who Can Apply: Incoming black freshmen with a minimum 3.0 GPA, a combined 900 SAT score (25 ACT), and a record of school and community involvement. Deadline December 17.
How Much Money Can I Get: $1,200
Whom Do I Contact: Florida International University, Attn.: Director of Minority Student Services, University Park Campus, GC 216, Miami, FL 33199, (305) 348-2436.

392

FLORIDA INTERNATIONAL UNIVERSITY
Greater Miami Chapter, Women in Communications, Inc. Scholarship
Who Can Apply: Female students in the School of Journalism and Mass Communications in any field of specialization. Deadline March 1.
How Much Money Can I Get: $300 and $500 per semester
Whom Do I Contact: Florida International University, School of Journalism & Mass Communications, North Miami, FL 33181, (305) 940-5425.

393

FLORIDA INTERNATIONAL UNIVERSITY
Minority Community College Transfer Scholarship (MCCTS)
Who Can Apply: Candidates must hold an AA or AS degree from an accredited Florida community college. Award is based on either financial aid or academic merit for all minorities, including women.
How Much Money Can I Get: Up to $1,600 per academic year
Whom Do I Contact: Florida International University, Equal Opportunity Program, PC 215 University Park, Miami, FL 33199, (305) 348-2785.

394

FLORIDA INTERNATIONAL UNIVERSITY
The Sarah and Solomon Rosenberg Scholarship
Who Can Apply: Black juniors or seniors who are majoring in Engineering, Computer Science, or Business. Applicants must show financial need. Deadline July 1.
How Much Money Can I Get: Varies
Whom Do I Contact: Financial Aid Director, Florida International University, Tamiami Trail, Miami, FL 33199, (305) 554-2431.

395

FLORIDA INTERNATIONAL UNIVERSITY
The Scripps-Howard Foundation Scholarship
Who Can Apply: Juniors, seniors, and graduate students majoring in Print or Broadcast Journalism. Students must send two samples of work experience in journalism, two letters of recommendation, SAT/ACT/GRE scores, and a typewritten narrative to the school.
How Much Money Can I Get: $500 to $3,000
Whom Do I Contact: Florida International University, School of Journalism & Mass Communications, North Miami, FL 33181, (305) 940-5425.

396

FLORIDA INTERNATIONAL UNIVERSITY
The South Florida Chapter of the National Academy of Television Arts and Sciences Award
Who Can Apply: Candidates must attend a college in Dade or Broward County, have a minimum 3.0 GPA and plan to concentrate in television. Deadline April.
How Much Money Can I Get: $15,000
Whom Do I Contact: Florida International University, School of Journalism & Mass Communications, North Miami, FL 33181, (305) 940-5425.

397

FLORIDA MEMORIAL COLLEGE
Who Can Apply: Applicants must be a black entering freshman with a strong academic background. Apply early.
How Much Money Can I Get: $100 to $2,000
Whom Do I Contact: Florida Memorial College, 15800 NW 42nd Street, Miami, FL 33054, (305) 625-4141.

398

FLORIDA NICARAGUAN & HAITIAN SCHOLARSHIP PROGRAM
Who Can Apply: Scholarships offered to Nicaraguan or Haitian students with a 3.0 GPA who are Florida residents and plan to attend a Florida public college. Deadline July 1.
How Much Money Can I Get: $4,000 to $5,000
Whom Do I Contact: Office of Student Financial Assistance, Florida Department of Education, 1344 Florida Education Center, Tallahassee, FL 32399-0400, (904) 487-0049.

399
FLORIDA SOCIETY OF NEWSPAPER EDITORS
Journalism Scholarship
Who Can Apply: Award is for minority senior journalism students attending a Florida college or university.
How Much Money Can I Get: $2,000
Whom Do I Contact: Managing Editor, Florida Society of Newspaper Editors, *The Tampa Tribune*, 202 Parkway Street, Tampa, FL 33606.

400
FLORIDA STATE UNIVERSITY AND THE UNIVERSITY OF FLORIDA LAW SCHOOLS
The Virgil Hawkins Fellowship
Who Can Apply: Minority students enrolled full-time at FSU and the University of Florida Law Schools. Awards are given yearly for a maximum of three years.
How Much Money Can I Get: $5,000
Whom Do I Contact: Florida State University, Attn.: Dean of Law School, 425 W. Jefferson Street, Tallahassee, FL 32306-1034, (904) 644-7338.

401
UNIVERSITY OF FLORIDA
Dow Chemical Research Scholarship
Who Can Apply: Awards are open to African Americans, Hispanic Americans, and Native American Indians who are engineering undergraduates.
How Much Money Can I Get: $1,000
Whom Do I Contact: University of Florida, Student Financial Affairs, S-103 Criser Hall, Gainesville, FL 32611.

402
UNIVERSITY OF FLORIDA
The Florida Publishing Company Minority Scholarship
Who Can Apply: Minority freshmen or sophomores from Jacksonville, North Florida, or South Georgia who are planning a career in print journalism or newspaper advertising.
How Much Money Can I Get: $3,000. Renewable if student completes paid summer internships at the Florida *Times Union.*
Whom Do I Contact: University of Florida, S-103 Criser Hall, Gainesville, FL 32611.

403

UNIVERSITY OF FLORIDA
General Electric Scholarship
Who Can Apply: Sophomore engineering students who are African American, Hispanic, or Native American Indians with leadership potential and interest in mechanical, electrical, or industrial engineering and systems or computer science. Candidate must have at least a 3.2 GPA.
How Much Money Can I Get: $5,000, renewable
Whom Do I Contact: University of Florida, Student Financial Affairs, S-103 Criser Hall, Gainesville, FL 32611.

404

UNIVERSITY OF FLORIDA
The New York Times Scholarship
Who Can Apply: Award is open to either a graduate or undergraduate student in the field of journalism. Priority is given to minority group members.
How Much Money Can I Get: $750 to $1,500
Whom Do I Contact: Office of Admissions, University of Florida, 233 Tigert Hall, Gainesville, FL 32611, (904) 392-3261.

405

UNIVERSITY OF FLORIDA
The Philip L. Graham Minority Scholarship
Who Can Apply: Minority students majoring in Telecommunications from the Jacksonville or Miami area.
How Much Money Can I Get: Four awards ranging from $1,500 to $3,000.
Whom Do I Contact: University of Florida, S-103 Criser Hall, Gainesville, FL 32611.

406

UNIVERSITY OF FLORIDA LAW SCHOOL
VIRGIL HAWKINS FELLOWSHIP
Who Can Apply: Fellowships for minority students attending University of Florida Law Schools.
How Much Money Can I Get: $5,000
Whom Do I Contact: Hawkins Fellowship Administration, Department of Education, Office of Student Financial Assistance, University of Florida, Tallahassee, FL 32399.

407

FOUNDATION OF AMERICAN COLLEGE HEALTHCARE EXECUTIVES

Ache, Albert W. Dent Scholarship

Who Can Apply: Awarded to a minority student for full-time study in a graduate program of health care management. Student must be a U.S. citizen. Deadline March 31.

How Much Money Can I Get: $3,000

Whom Do I Contact: Foundation of American College Healthcare Executives, Attn.: Albert W. Dent Scholarship, 1 N. Franklin Street, Suite 1700, Chicago, IL 60606-3461, (312) 943-0544.

408

FORD FOUNDATION POSTDOCTORAL FELLOWSHIPS FOR MINORITIES

Who Can Apply: Must be planning a career in teaching/education. Deadline January 13.

How Much Money Can I Get: Varies

Whom Do I Contact: National Research Council Office, Fellowship Office, HR 420A, 2101 Constitution Avenue, NW, Washington, DC 20418, (202) 334-2000.

409

FOUNDATION FOR EXCEPTIONAL CHILDREN SCHOLARSHIPS

Who Can Apply: For disabled, disabled minority, disabled gifted or disabled gifted minority students with financial need. Deadline February 1.

How Much Money Can I Get: Varies

Whom Do I Contact: Scholarship Committee, Foundation for Exceptional Children, 1920 Association Drive, Reston, VA 22091, (703) 620-1054.

410

FOUNDATION FOR EXCEPTIONAL CHILDREN

Stanley E. Jackson Scholarship for the Handicapped

Who Can Apply: Applicants must be handicapped and minority students who intend to enroll in full-time postsecondary education or training and are able to document financial need.

How Much Money Can I Get: $1,000

Whom Do I Contact: Foundation for Exceptional Children, 1920 Association Drive, Reston, VA 22091, (703) 630-3660.

411

FRANKLIN AND MARSHALL COLLEGE
William Gray Scholarship
Who Can Apply: Minority students are selected based on academic ability, leadership, and strong moral character.
How Much Money Can I Get: Tuition+
Whom Do I Contact: Franklin and Marshall College, Admissions Office, P.O. Box 3003, Lancaster, PA 17604-3003, (717) 291-3951.

412

THE FREEDOM FORUM
Who Can Apply: Fifty scholarships to students pursuing careers in print or broadcast journalism. Deadline January 31.
How Much Money Can I Get: $2,500 for one-year entering freshmen/ undergraduate scholarships; $4,000 for one-year graduate scholarship.
Whom Do I Contact: The Freedom Forum, Scholarship Committee, 1101 Wilson Boulevard, Arlington, VA 22209, (703) 528-0800.

413

FRIENDS UNIVERSITY
J. David Jackson Scholarship
Who Can Apply: Minority students with first preference given to Native American Indian students.
How Much Money Can I Get: Varies
Whom Do I Contact: Financial Aid Director, Friends University, 2100 University, Wichita, KS 67213, (316) 261-5887.

414

FUND FOR THEOLOGICAL EDUCATION
Who Can Apply: Candidates must be black citizens of the U.S. or Canada and official candidates for ministerial ordination within their communion. All nominees must be prepared to enroll in a master's of divinity program at a theological school that is fully accredited with the association of theological schools in the U.S. and Canada in the autumn following receipt of the award. No midyear fellowships are awarded. Stipends will vary in amount according to need. The awards are not intended to replace financial aid normally offered by institutions where the recipient is studying. Fellowships are awarded on the basis of competence and promise, not financial need. Renewals are contingent upon each fellow maintaining a high academic record as well as other evidence of promise for ministerial effectiveness. Each individual must be nominated by a minister, member of the faculty or administration, or a former fellow of programs administered by the fund. The letter of nomination

should provide the name and current address of the nominee and must be received no later than November 20 of each year.

How Much Money Can I Get: Varies

Whom Do I Contact: Fund for Theological Education, 421 Wall Street, Research Park, Princeton, NJ 08540, (609) 924-0004.

415

GARDEN CITY COMMUNITY COLLEGE

Angie Gonzáles Posey Memorial Scholarship

Who Can Apply: Candidates must be minorities with a 2.5 GPA. Nonrenewable.

How Much Money Can I Get: $200

Whom Do I Contact: Dean of Student Services, Garden City Community College, LULAC Education Center, 801 Campus Drive, Garden City, KS 67846, (316) 276-7611.

416

GE FOUNDATION

Engineering and Business Administration Scholarship Program

Who Can Apply: High achieving minority students enrolled in a transfer program at two-year colleges
with a 3.0 GPA or higher. Applicants must be nominated by college/school official and complete the
application procedures. Deadline November 15.

How Much Money Can I Get: Varies

Whom Do I Contact: Barbara Kram, Grant Program for Minority · Engineering and Business Students, The College Board, 45 Columbus Avenue, New York, NY 10023-6992, (212) 713-8000.

417

GEORGE FOX COLLEGE

Minority Award

Who Can Apply: Awarded is open to members of all minority groups.

How Much Money Can I Get: $1,000 to $2,500

Whom Do I Contact: George Fox College, Attn.: Financial Aid Office, 414 N. Meridian Street, Newberg, OR 97132-2625, (503) 538-8383.

418

GEORGE E. JOHNSON FOUNDATION
AND EDUCATIONAL FUND

Who Can Apply: Applicant must be a minority student, a citizen of the U.S., already accepted as a full-time student in an accredited four-year institution, and demonstrate financial need. Applicants must be studying business

administration, engineering, chemistry, physics, pre-dentistry, or pre-law.
How Much Money Can I Get: Varies
Whom Do I Contact: Clotte Y. Best, Assistant Administrator, Johnson
Products Co., Inc., 8522 S. Lafayette Avenue, Chicago, IL 60620-1301,
(773) 483-4100.

419

GEORGE WASHINGTON CARVER SCHOLARSHIP

Who Can Apply: Minority students graduating from select high schools in
Santa Barbara, California, with a 2.5 GPA and in financial need.
How Much Money Can I Get: Varies
Whom Do I Contact: George Washington Carver Scholarship Club, Inc., c/o
Mrs. William E. King, 626-B E. De LaGuerra, Santa Barbara, CA 93103.

420

GEORGETOWN UNIVERSITY

Law Center Minority Scholarship Fund
Who Can Apply: Minority students.
How Much Money Can I Get: Varies
Whom Do I Contact: Office of Admissions, Georgetown University, 37th &
O Streets, NW, Washington, DC 20057, (202) 625-0100.

421

GMI ENGINEERING/MANAGEMENT INSTITUTE

NACME Scholarship
Who Can Apply: Applicants must be minority U.S. citizens or permanent
residents. May be an incoming freshman or transfer student. Award is based
on need and/or merit and is renewable for up to 4 1/2 years. Financial need
required. Deadline April 15.
How Much Money Can I Get: $250 to 1,000
Whom Do I Contact: Director of Financial Aid, GMI/Engineering/
Management Institute, 1700 W. Third Avenue, Room 2-328CC, Flint, MI
48504- 4898, (800) 521-7436.

422

GOLDEN STATE MINORITY FOUNDATION
FINANCIAL AID

Who Can Apply: This scholarship is available to residents of or attending
school in Southern California. Students must be full-time and must work no
more than 25 hours per week. Must have a 3.0 GPA and major in business
administration/management. Deadline October 1 for Northern California and
March 1 for Southern California.
How Much Money Can I Get: $2,000

Whom Do I Contact: Scholarship Officer, Golden State Minority Foundation, 1999 W. Adams Boulevard, Los Angeles, CA 90018, (213) 731-7771.

423
GOLDEN STATE MINORITY SCHOLARSHIP
Who Can Apply: Qualified minority students accepted to or enrolled in a college or university in an area where the foundation conducts fundraising.
How Much Money Can I Get: Varies
Whom Do I Contact: Golden State Minority Foundation, 1999 W. Adams Boulevard, Los Angeles, CA 90018, (213) 731-7771.

424
GOLUB FOUNDATION
Tillie Golub-Schwartz Memorial Scholarship
Who Can Apply: Awarded to a full-time minority student attending a four-year school in Vermont, New York, Pennsylvania, or Massachusetts. Deadline March 15.
How Much Money Can I Get: $8,000
Whom Do I Contact: Golub Foundation, Attn.: Scholarship Committee, P.O. Box 1074, Schenectady, NY 12301, (518) 356-9375.

425
GOSHEN COLLEGE
Multicultural Leadership Scholarship
Who Can Apply: Awarded to a minority student entering college with a minimum 2.5 GPA and in the upper two-fifths of the graduating class.
How Much Money Can I Get: $1,000
Whom Do I Contact: Goshen College, Attn.: Financial Aid Director, 1700 S. Main, Goshen, IN 46526, (219) 535-7525.

426
GRACE THEOLOGICAL SEMINARY
Minority Academic Honor
Who Can Apply: Minority applicants who have achieved a 3.0 GPA or above in their baccalaureate studies and who present above-average GRE scores may qualify for a 50 percent tuition scholarship. These grants are renewable for succeeding semesters if a cumulative 3.0 GPA or above is maintained.
How Much Money Can I Get: Varies
Whom Do I Contact: Financial Aid Director, Grace Theological Seminary, 200 Seminary Drive, Winona Lake, IN 46590, (219) 267-8191.

427

HAMPSHIRE COLLEGE

Who Can Apply: This institution offers scholarships to benefit the graduates of the Springfield, Mass., public school system. Awarded to academically promising students of color who demonstrate financial need.
How Much Money Can I Get: Two awards of $3,000 to $5,000
Whom Do I Contact: Hampshire College, Attn.: Financial Aid Director, Amherst, MA 01002, (413) 582-5484.

428

HAMPSHIRE COLLEGE
Arturo Schomburg Scholarship
Who Can Apply: Awarded to students of color who show promise of strong academic performance and who exhibit potential for leadership at Hampshire College and in their own communities. Applicants must demonstrate financial need and be in upper 20 percent of class. Renewable for four years.
How Much Money Can I Get: Ten awards of $3,000 to $7,500
Whom Do I Contact: Hampshire College, Attn.: Financial Aid Director, Amherst, MA 01002, (413) 582-5484.

429

HARDIN-SIMMONS UNIVERSITY
The Texas National Baptist Scholarship Program
Who Can Apply: Candidates must be recommended by the applicant's pastor. Applicants must have graduated from a Texas high school, have a 2.0 GPA and be a black Baptist.
How Much Money Can I Get: $600
Whom Do I Contact: Financial Aid Office, Hardin-Simmons University, Drawer R/ HSU Station, Abilene, TX 79698, (915) 670-1331.

430

HAVERFORD COLLEGE
Class of 1912 Scholarship Fund
Who Can Apply: Students with financial need. When able, preference given to African or Asian students.
How Much Money Can I Get: Varies
Whom Do I Contact: Office of Admissions, Haverford College, Haverford, PA 19041-1392, (215) 896-1350.

431

HAVERFORD COLLEGE
Ira De A. Reid Scholarship
Who Can Apply: Black and Hispanic students are eligible to apply based on academic and personal promise. Dr. Reid was chairman of Haverford's sociology and anthropology department until retiring in 1966. His research centered on the conditions of blacks in the United States and in the Caribbean, and his works include *In a Minor Key* and *The Negro Immigrant*. The amount of aid depends upon financial need. All awards are in the forms of grants and do not include loans or jobs. Deadline for admission and Financial Aid Form January 31. Application fee can be waived. A campus interview is preferred.
How Much Money Can I Get: Varies
Whom Do I Contact: Director of Admissions, Haverford College, Haverford, PA 19041-1392, (215) 896-1350.

432

HAVERFORD COLLEGE
J. Henry Scattergood Scholarship Fund
Who Can Apply: Goal of scholarship is to provide financial aid and other supportive services to black students.
How Much Money Can I Get: Varies
Whom Do I Contact: Office of Admissions, Haverford College, Haverford, PA 19041-1392, (215) 896-1350.

433

HEALTH CAREERS OPPORTUNITY PROGRAM GRANTS
Who Can Apply: Assistance provided for education in health professions and students with financial need. Deadline November.
How Much Money Can I Get: Varies
Whom Do I Contact: Health Resources and Services Administration, Attn.: Bureau of Health Professions, Division of Disadvantaged Assistance, Parklawn Building, Room 8A-09, 5600 Fishers Lane, Rockville, MD 20857, (301) 443-4493, fax: (301) 443-5242.

434

HERBERT LEHMAN EDUCATION FUND
Who Can Apply: Awarded to a black senior who is planning to attend desegregated and publicly supported colleges or universities in the South, who is a U.S. citizen, and who can show financial need. Deadline April 15.
How Much Money Can I Get: $1,200

Whom Do I Contact: Herbert Lehman Education Fund, Inc., Attn.: NAACP Legal Defense, 99 Hudson Street, Suite 1600, New York, NY 10013, (212) 219-1900.

435

HOLY CROSS COLLEGE
Martin Luther King, Jr. Scholarship
Who Can Apply: Minority students are eligible to receive scholarship until through their senior year . The student has a choice of making up the difference in tuition after the scholarship is awarded with either work-study or loans.
How Much Money Can I Get: Varies
Whom Do I Contact: Holy Cross College, c/o Financial Aid Office, One College Hill, Worcester, MA 01610, (508) 793-2443.

436

UNIVERSITY OF HOUSTON
AICPA Scholarship
Who Can Apply: Full-time minority students pursuing an accounting or taxation degree. Selection based on demonstrated financial need and satisfactory academic progress. Must have a 2.0 GPA. Deadline March 1.
How Much Money Can I Get: Varies
Whom Do I Contact: College of Business Administration, University of Houston, University Park, 4800 Calhoun, 106 H, Houston, TX 77004, (713) 749-2911.

437

UNIVERSITY OF HOUSTON
The Amoco Foundation Scholarship
Who Can Apply: Full-time, first-year minority students majoring in geology or geophysics who show satisfactory academic progress. Deadline March 1.
How Much Money Can I Get: Varies
Whom Do I Contact: Geosciences Department, University of Houston, University Park, 4800 Calhoun, 214 SR Houston, TX 77004, (713) 749-3868.

438

UNIVERSITY OF HOUSTON
The Carnation Incentive Award
Who Can Apply: Full-time minority education majors on the basis of demonstrated academic progress. Must have a minimum 3.0 GPA. Deadline March 1.

How Much Money Can I Get: Varies
Whom Do I Contact: College of Education, University of Houston, University Park, 4800 Calhoun, 214 FH, Houston, TX 77004, (713) 749-7407.

439
UNIVERSITY OF HOUSTON
The Dow Chemical Company Scholarship
Who Can Apply: Full-time minority students who are majoring in chemistry. Applicants must be U.S. citizens and demonstrate satisfactory academic progress. Deadline March 1.
How Much Money Can I Get: Varies
Whom Do I Contact: Natural Science/Math Department, University of Houston, University Park, 4800 Calhoun, 214 SR, Houston, TX 77004, (713) 749-4612.

440
UNIVERSITY OF HOUSTON
Ethnic Recruitment Scholarships
Who Can Apply: Entering freshmen who are minority residents of Texas with demonstrated financial need. Applicants must have a minimum 900 combined SAT score (20 ACT). Financial need required. Deadline March 1.
Whom Do I Contact: Financial Aid Director, University of Houston, University Park, Houston, TX 77004, (713) 749-3311.

441
UNIVERSITY OF HOUSTON
The Shell Incentive Scholarship
Who Can Apply: Entering minority students on the basis of demonstrated financial need. Must be a U.S. citizen. Deadline March 1.
How Much Money Can I Get: Varies
Whom Do I Contact: Cullen College of Engineering, University of Houston, University Park, 4800 Calhoun, 202 D, Houston, TX 77004, (713) 749-2401.

442
COLLEGE OF IDAHO
Association of Affirmative Action Scholarship
Who Can Apply: Awarded annually to a minority student.
How Much Money Can I Get: $1,500
Whom Do I Contact: Financial Aid Director, The College of Idaho, 2112 Cleveland Boulevard, Caldwell, ID 83605-9990, (208) 459-5308.

443

INDIANA UNIVERSITY
Howard Jones Scholarship
Who Can Apply: Minority students in business administration or management with a minimum 3.3 GPA and financial need.
How Much Money Can I Get: $1,000
Whom Do I Contact: Indiana University, Attn.: School of Business, Business 230, Bloomington, IN 47405, (812) 855-8066.

444

INDIANA UNIVERSITY
Minority Achievers Program
Who Can Apply: Entering or transferring minority students who demonstrate superior talent and high academic potential. Deadline March 1.
How Much Money Can I Get: $2,000 to $7,000
Whom Do I Contact: Dr. Herman Hudson, MAP Scholarships, M20 Memorial Hall, Indiana University, Bloomington, IN 47405, (812) 855-7853.

445

INDIANA UNIVERSITY CENTER ON PHILANTHROPY
Doctoral Fellowships in the Study of Philanthropy
Who Can Apply: Students seeking research grants for study of Philanthropy. Deadline February 15.
How Much Money Can I Get: Varies
Whom Do I Contact: Indiana University Center on Philanthropy, Research Office, 550 W. North Street, Suite 301, Indianapolis, IN 46202-3162, (317) 274-8490.

446

INDUSTRIAL RELATIONS COUNCIL ON GOALS FELLOWSHIPS
Who Can Apply: African-American, Hispanic, or Native American Indian college seniors and U.S. citizens with undergraduate degrees in economics, psychology, sociology, or political science. Candidates must major in Industrial Relations or Human Resource Management at Cornell, Iowa, Michigan State, Ohio State, Rutgers, Illinois at Urbana, Massachusetts at Amherst, Minnesota at Twin Cities, Oregon, or South Carolina.
How Much Money Can I Get: Twenty-six awards averaging $7,800 yearly
Whom Do I Contact: Industrial Relations Council on Goals, P.O. Box 4363, East Lansing, MI 48826-4363, (800) 344-6257.

447
INROADS/NASHVILLE INC. INTERNSHIPS
Who Can Apply: Black students in their freshman or sophomore year with a 3.3 GPA and majoring in Business Administration/ Management or Engineering are eligible. The internships take place during the summer with a possibility of future full-time employment.
Whom Do I Contact: Inroads/Nashville, Inc., P.O. Box 3111, Nashville, TN 37219, (615) 255-7397.

448
INSTITUTE FOR REAL ESTATE MANAGEMENT FOUNDATION
George M. Broker Collegiate Scholarship for Minorities
Who Can Apply: Graduate and undergraduate minority students entering careers in real estate and specifically real estate management. Applicants must have declared a major in Real Estate or related field. Candidates must have completed two courses in real estate and must have at least a 3.0 GPA within major. Recommendation letters, themed essay, and official transcripts are also required. Deadline March 15.
How Much Money Can I Get: $1,000 for undergraduates, $2,500 for graduate students
Whom Do I Contact: Institute for Real Estate Management Foundation, Attn.: Foundation Coordinator, 430 N. Michigan Avenue, P.O. Box 109025, Chicago, IL 60611-4090, (312) 329-6008.

449
IOTA PHI LAMBDA BUSINESS SORORITY
Who Can Apply: Scholarships are offered to minority female undergraduates interested in business careers.
How Much Money Can I Get: Varies
Whom Do I Contact: Iota Phi Lambda Business Sorority, 811 E. 116 Street, Los Angeles, CA 90059.

450
IOTA PHI LAMBDA SCHOLARSHIP PROGRAM
Who Can Apply: Black female students interested in business.
How Much Money Can I Get: Varies
Whom Do I Contact: Iota Phi Lambda Scholarship Program, 1062 W. Pearl, Jackson, MS 39203.

451
IOTA PHI LAMBDA SCHOLARSHIP PROGRAM
Who Can Apply: Black female high school students interested in business education.
How Much Money Can I Get: Varies
Whom Do I Contact: Iota Phi Lambda Sorority, Inc., c/o Dr. Evelyn Peevy, 5313 Halter Lane, Norfolk, VA 23502.

452
IOWA STATE UNIVERSITY
Agricultural Career Awareness Scholarship
Who Can Apply: Minority student majoring in agriculture with a minimum 2.0 GPA. Deadline January 1.
How Much Money Can I Get: $1,000
Whom Do I Contact: Extension Service Agent, Iowa State University, 32 Curtiss Hall, State 4-H Office, Ames, IA 50011, (515) 294-1017.

453
IOWA STATE UNIVERSITY
Freshman Engineering Scholarship
Who Can Apply: Applicant must be a minority. Scholarship application available from student financial aid office. Deadline December 1.
How Much Money Can I Get: $500
Whom Do I Contact: Scholarship Coordinator, Iowa State University, 101 Marston Hall, College of Engineering, Ames, IA 50011, (515) 294-1019.

454
IOWA STATE UNIVERSITY
Minority Engineering Education Effort
Who Can Apply: Minority students majoring in one of the following engineering areas: chemical, electrical, mechanical, civil, or industrial. Financial need required.
How Much Money Can I Get: $250 to $2,500
Whom Do I Contact: Financial Aid Director, University of Iowa, Iowa City, IA 52242, (319) 353-2121.

455
IOWA STATE UNIVERSITY
Opportunity at Iowa Scholarship Program
Who Can Apply: Applicants must be U.S. minority students. Deadline December 8.
How Much Money Can I Get: Full tuition

Whom Do I Contact: Scholarship Chairman, University of Iowa, Office of Financial Aid, Iowa City, IA 52242, (800) 272-6412.

456

IOWA STATE UNIVERSITY
Monsanto Opportunity in Engineering Scholarship
Who Can Apply: Freshman minority students enrolled in chemical, civil, electrical, or mechanical engineering. Candidates must reside in the Midwest. Award is based on academic record and financial need. Deadline January 31.
How Much Money Can I Get: Tuition, on-campus room/board, $750 stipend for books, supplies, and fees. A co-op term with Monsanto for those who meet criteria is also available. Award is renewable for an additional three years.
Whom Do I Contact: Engineering Student Development Center, College of Engineering, 3117 Engineering Building, University of Iowa, Iowa City, IA 52242-1585, (319) 335-5763.

457

THE IVIES
Who Can Apply: The Ivies helps minority students obtain financial aid and gain admission to Ivy League universities: Dartmouth, Penn, Princeton, Cornell, Brown, Yale, Columbia, and Harvard-Radcliffe.
How Much Money Can I Get: Varies
Whom Do I Contact: The Ivies, P.O. Box 1502A, Yale Station, New Haven, CT 06502.

458

THE JACKIE ROBINSON EDUCATION AND LEADERSHIP DEVELOPMENT PROGRAM
Who Can Apply: Must show academic performance, leadership potential, financial need, and commitment to the community. Deadline April 15.
How Much Money Can I Get: Up to $20,000 for four years.
Whom Do I Contact: The Jackie Robinson Scholarship, The Jackie Robinson Foundation, 3 W. 35th Street, New York, NY 10001-2204, (212) 290-8600.

459

JACKIE ROBINSON FOUNDATION SCHOLARSHIP FUND
Who Can Apply: Minority students who are high school seniors and have demonstrated high academic achievements, financial need, and leadership

potential. Students must have been accepted to an accredited four-year institution. Deadline April 1.
How Much Money Can I Get: Varies
Whom Do I Contact: The Jackie Robinson Scholarship, The Jackie Robinson Foundation, 3 W. 35th Street, New York, NY 10001-2204, (212) 290-8600.

460
JACKSON STATE UNIVERSITY
Hearin-Hess Scholarship Fund
Who Can Apply: Computer Science majors.
How Much Money Can I Get: $5,000
Whom Do I Contact: Dr. Maria Luisa Alvarez Harvey, Dean, W. E. B. DuBois Honors College, Jackson State University, Jackson, MS 39217, (601) 968-2107.

461
JAMES ARCHITECTS & ENGINEERS MINORITY SCHOLARSHIP FOR THE STUDY OF ARCHITECTURE
Who Can Apply: To be eligible for the scholarship, the student must be black, be a high school senior in Indiana, rank in the upper one-quarter of the graduating class (or be recommended by the principal), have been accepted to study architecture or architectural engineering at an accredited institution, and demonstrate financial need. Deadline February.
How Much Money Can I Get: $1,000 up to five years
Whom Do I Contact: James Architects & Engineers, Inc., 120 Monument Circle, Suite 122, Indianapolis, IN 46204, (317) 631-0880.

462
KANSAS NEWMAN COLLEGE
Minority Grant
Who Can Apply: Granted to minority student with 2.25 GPA who has been active in high school, church, and/or community. Letter of reference and special application required. Deadline August 1.
How Much Money Can I Get: Up to $1,000
Whom Do I Contact: Kansas Newman College, Attn.: Director of Financial Aid, 3100 McCormick Avenue, Wichita, KS 67213-2097, (316) 942-4291.

463
KANSAS STATE UNIVERSITY
Academic Achievement and Leadership Scholarship
Who Can Apply: Undergraduate minority students who are Asian American,

African American, Hispanic American, or Native American Indian. Applicants must demonstrate outstanding academic and leadership accomplishments. First-year, transfer, or returning students are eligible for awards. Applicants must submit a description of activities and goals and have a 3.0 GPA. Deadline February 1.
How Much Money Can I Get: $400 to $1,000
Whom Do I Contact: Academic Achievement & Leadership Awards Committee, Office of Admissions, Anderson Hall, Kansas State University, Manhattan, KS 66505, (913) 532-6250 in Kansas, (800) 432-8270 outside.

464
KANSAS STATE UNIVERSITY
Minority Engineering Education Effort
Who Can Apply: Candidate must demonstrate financial need and be majoring in one of the following engineering areas: chemical, electrical, mechanical, civil, industrial, nuclear, or agricultural.
How Much Money Can I Get: $250 to $2,500
Whom Do I Contact: Kansas State University, Department of Engineering, Manhattan, KS 66502, (212) 867-1100.

465
UNIVERSITY OF KANSAS
Who Can Apply: Scholarships available for students majoring in Nursing.
How Much Money Can I Get: Varies
Whom Do I Contact: Dean, School of Nursing, University of Kansas Medical School, Kansas City, KS 66045, (913) 588-1600.

466
UNIVERSITY OF KANSAS
Who Can Apply: Scholarships are available for minorities majoring in Journalism.
How Much Money Can I Get: Varies
Whom Do I Contact: Dean, School of Students, University of Kansas, 200 Stauffer Flint School of Journalism, Lawrence, KS 66045, (913) 864-4755.

467
UNIVERSITY OF KANSAS
Who Can Apply: Scholarships available for students majoring in Pharmacy studies.
How Much Money Can I Get: Varies
Whom Do I Contact: Dean of School of Pharmacy, University of Kansas, 2056 Malott School of Pharmacy, Lawrence, KS 66045, (913) 864-3591.

468

UNIVERSITY OF KANSAS

Who Can Apply: All students of color.
How Much Money Can I Get: Varies
Whom Do I Contact: Office of the Dean, University of Kansas, College of Liberal Arts and Science, Lawrence, KS 66045, (913) 864-3661.

469

KAPPA ALPHA PSI FRATERNITY

Who Can Apply: The fraternity's national service program "Guide Right" mandates each of its approximately 520 chapters to administer scholarships.
How Much Money Can I Get: Varies
Whom Do I Contact: Kappa Alpha Psi Fraternity, Inc., 2320 N. Broad Street, Philadelphia, PA 19132, (215) 228-7184.

470

KELLOGG COMMUNITY COLLEGE

Upjohn Quality Control Minority Scholarship
Who Can Apply: Black students pursuing an associate's degree in chemical technology or a related field; each participant is assigned an Upjohn Company mentor.
How Much Money Can I Get: Tuition, book expenses, and a summer intern program
Whom Do I Contact: Kellogg Community College, North Avenue, Battle Creek, MI 49017, (616) 965-3931.

471

KENDALL COLLEGE OF ART & DESIGN

Who Can Apply: Scholarships are awarded to black U.S. citizens with a 2.7 GPA. Renewable providing recipient meets established criteria and funds are available. Deadline March 15.
How Much Money Can I Get: $800
Whom Do I Contact: Kendall College of Art and Design, 111 Division Avenue, North Grand Rapids, MI 49503, (616) 451-2787.

472

KENT STATE UNIVERSITY

Goebel Family Endowed Founders Scholarship
Who Can Apply: Incoming freshman, underrepresented minority student, preference for African American. Other criteria include 3.25 GPA, national test scores, competitive exam in senior year. Semifinalists selected to participate in the competition held in February. Deadline December 1.

How Much Money Can I Get: $3,100, renewable
Whom Do I Contact: Student Financial Aid, P.O. Box 5190, Kent State University, Kent, OH 44242-0001.

473
KENT STATE UNIVERSITY
Minority Incentive Scholarship
Who Can Apply: Incoming freshman or freshman transfer with minimum 2.75 college GPA and no more than 12 transfer credits. Full-time enrollment is required, as is financial need as determined by FAFSA. Renewal for three years contingent upon GPA requirement and completion of required financial aid forms. Deadline March 1.
How Much Money Can I Get: $2,000 to $3,500, renewable
Whom Do I Contact: Student Financial Aid, P.O. Box 5190, Kent State University, Kent, OH 44242-0001.

474
KENT STATE UNIVERSITY
Minority Uplift Scholarship
Who Can Apply: African-American, Native American Indian, Alaskan Native, Hispanic, Asian, or Pacific Islander Ashtabula Campus students. Candidates must possess a 2.5 high school GPA or be in the top 30 percent of their high school class. Students with GED must have composite of 250, standard score of 50 and transfers must have 3.0 GPA. Continuing student must have 3.0 GPA minimum. Deadline July 15.
How Much Money Can I Get: $1,000— 10 awards, renewable
Whom Do I Contact: Student Financial Aid, P.O. Box 5190, Kent State University, Kent, OH 44242-0001.

475
KENT STATE UNIVERSITY
Oscar Ritchie Memorial Scholarship
Who Can Apply: Academically talented black, Hispanic, and Native American Indian high school juniors. Awards of full tuition plus room and board costs are made based on an examination. Applicants must have a 3.25 GPA, show leadership qualities, and participate in extracurricular activities. In 1947, Oscar Ritchie was the first black appointed to a faculty position at any state university in Ohio when he joined Kent State's sociology department.
Whom Do I Contact: Linda Lanier, Assistant Director of Admissions, Kent State University, Kent, OH 44242-0001, (216) 672-2444.

476

UNIVERSITY OF KENTUCKY

Who Can Apply: Open to black residents of Kentucky. Awards include the Journalism Award and the King Scholarship Fund.
How Much Money Can I Get: Varies
Whom Do I Contact: Office of Admissions, University of Kentucky, Lexington, KY 40506, (606) 257-7148.

477

KNTV MINORITY SCHOLARSHIP

Who Can Apply: Awarded to a full-time student majoring in radio/TV broadcasting at a four-year California institution. Must show interest in television, need, involvement in the community, academics, and career aspirations. Deadline April 14.
How Much Money Can I Get: $1,000
Whom Do I Contact: KNTV Channel 11, Attn.: Scholarship Board, 645 Park Avenue, San Jose, CA 9110, (408) 286-1111.

478

KOPPERS INDUSTRY

Who Can Apply: Grants for minority and female engineering students in chemical, mechanical, or electrical engineering. Koppers awards funds to engineering departments and leaves the selection process to the college.
How Much Money Can I Get: Varies
Whom Do I Contact: Koppers Industry, 436 7th Avenue, Pittsburgh, PA 15219, (412) 227-2001.

479

KRAFT, INC.-NATIONAL URBAN LEAGUE SCHOLARSHIP PROGRAM

Who Can Apply: Minority undergraduate students who are classified as juniors and who are pursuing full-time studies in engineering, sales, marketing, manufacturing operations, or finance and business administration are eligible. Students must be in the top 25 percent of their class.
How Much Money Can I Get: Varies
Whom Do I Contact: Northern Virginia Urban League, 901 N. Washington Street, Suite 202, Alexandria, VA 22314.

480

LA ROCHE COLLEGE, SISTERS OF THE DIVINE PROVIDENCE

Who Can Apply: Awarded to a minority student with a 3.0 GPA. Must

submit a typewritten essay describing activities participated in the past two years. Deadline May 1.
How Much Money Can I Get: $6,000
Whom Do I Contact: La Roche College, Attn.: Financial Aid Director, 9000 Babcock Boulevard, Pittsburgh, PA 15237-5898, (412) 367-9300.

481

LA SALLE UNIVERSITY
Community Academic Opportunity Grant
Who Can Apply: Awarded to minority students in the upper fifth of their graduating class. Contact high school counselor for application. Deadline February 15.
How Much Money Can I Get: Up to tuition
Whom Do I Contact: La Salle University, Attn.: Academic Discovery Program, 20th Street and Olney Avenue, Philadelphia, PA 19141, (215) 951-1084.

482

LAKE ERIE COLLEGE
Minority Scholarship
Who Can Apply: Awarded to outstanding minority students with a 2.75 GPA who show promise of distinction in their field. Deadline March 1.
How Much Money Can I Get: $1,000
Whom Do I Contact: Lake Erie College, Attn.: Director of Financial Aid, 391 W. Washington Street, Box 360, Painesville, OH 44077, (800) 533-4996.

483

LAWRENCE TECHNOLOGICAL UNIVERSITY
Who Can Apply: Must be majoring in Electrical or Mechanical Engineering. Financial need required. Deadline June 1.
How Much Money Can I Get: $250 to $2,500
Whom Do I Contact: Engineering Department Chairman, Lawrence Technological University, 21000 W. Ten Mile Road, Southfield, MI 48075, (313) 356-0200.

484

LE MOYNE COLLEGE
Urban League Scholarship
Who Can Apply: Entering black freshmen. Award will meet student's full need. No self-help is required in freshman year. Financial need required. Deadline February 15.

How Much Money Can I Get: Varies
Whom Do I Contact: Le Moyne College, Office of Financial Aid, Le Moyne Heights, Syracuse, NY 13214, (315) 445-4400.

485
LEE ELDER SCHOLARSHIP FUND
Who Can Apply: The Lee Elder Scholarships are awarded to minorities who show financial need. Also taken into consideration are achievements and career goals.
How Much Money Can I Get: Varies
Whom Do I Contact: Lee Elder Scholarship Fund, 1725 K Street, NW, Suite 1201, Washington, DC 20006.

486
LINCOLN NATIONAL LIFE INSURANCE
Thomas A. Watson Scholarship
Who Can Apply: Applicant must be a minority student from an Allen County high school. Scholarships must be used at an approved and accredited school in Indiana or a state bordering Indiana (Kentucky, Illinois, Michigan, or Ohio). Must be majoring in one of the following: business administration/management, mathematics, insurance, accounting, computer science/data processing, finance, or actuarial science.
How Much Money Can I Get: Varies
Whom Do I Contact: Scholarship Chairman, Lincoln National Life Insurance, 1300 S. Clinton Street, P.O. Box 1110, Fort Wayne, IN 46801.

487
LINCOLN UNIVERSITY
21st Century Scholarship
Who Can Apply: Students with a minimum1200 SAT score (27 ACT) and 3.7 GPA. Renewable with a 3.5 GPA.
How Much Money Can I Get: Tuition + fees + room & board
Whom Do I Contact: Lincoln University, Office of Admissions, MSC 147, P.O. Box 179, Lincoln University, PA 19352, (800) 790-0191.

488
LINCOLN UNIVERSITY
Alumni Endowed Scholarship
Who Can Apply: Students with a minimum 900 SAT score (19 ACT) and 3.0 GPA. Non-renewable.
How Much Money Can I Get: $2,500
Whom Do I Contact: Lincoln University, Office of Admissions, MSC 147, P.O. Box 179, Lincoln University, PA 19352, (800) 790-0191.

489

LINCOLN UNIVERSITY

International Scholars Scholarship

Who Can Apply: International students with a minimum 1000 SAT score (21 ACT) and 3.3 GPA. Renewable with a 3.5 GPA.

How Much Money Can I Get: Tuition & Fees

Whom Do I Contact: Lincoln University, Office of Admissions, MSC 147, P.O. Box 179, Lincoln University, PA 19352, (800) 790-0191.

490

LINCOLN UNIVERSITY

The KTVI Scholarship

Who Can Apply: Minority students or women who live within an 85-mile radius of St. Louis and are majoring in Radio/TV or Mass Communications. Deadline April 1.

How Much Money Can I Get: Varies

Whom Do I Contact: Financial Aid Director, Lincoln University, 820 Chestnut, Jefferson City, MO 65101, (314) 681-5599.

491

LINCOLN UNIVERSITY

Presidential Scholarship

Who Can Apply: Students with a minimum 1100 SAT score (24 ACT) and 3.5 GPA.

How Much Money Can I Get: Tuition + Room & Board

Whom Do I Contact: Lincoln University, Office of Admissions, MSC 147, P.O. Box 179, Lincoln University, PA 19352, (800) 790-0191.

492

LINCOLN UNIVERSITY

University Scholarship

Who Can Apply:. Students with a minimum 1000 SAT score (21 ACT) and 3.3 GPA. Renewable with a 3.5 GPA.

How Much Money Can I Get: Tuition + Fees.

Whom Do I Contact: Lincoln University, Office of Admissions, MSC 147, P.O. Box 179, Lincoln University, PA 19352, (800) 790-0191.

493

LIVINGSTONE COLLEGE

Who Can Apply: Scholarships available for black males interested in teaching careers. Candidates must agree to teach in North Carolina for four years.

How Much Money Can I Get: Full tuition for four years
Whom Do I Contact: Livingstone College, W. Monroe Street, Salisbury, NC 28144, (704) 638-5562.

494
LONG ISLAND UNIVERSITY
Martin Luther King, Jr., Scholarship
Who Can Apply: Black candidates who have financial need. Minimum combined 900 SAT score and a 3.0 GPA required. Deadline May 15.
How Much Money Can I Get: Varies
Whom Do I Contact: Director of Admissions, Long Island University, Brooklyn Center, University Plaza, Brooklyn, NY 11201-9926, (212) 834-6000.

495
LORAS COLLEGE
Diversity Scholarship
Who Can Apply: Full-time minority students.
How Much Money Can I Get: $600 to $2,500
Whom Do I Contact: Loras College, Attn.: Office of Financial Planning, 1450 Alta Vista Street, Dubuque, IA 52004-0178, (319) 588-7136.

496
LORAS COLLEGE
Enrichment Award
Who Can Apply: Selection is based on participation in on-campus college activities. The award is renewable.
How Much Money Can I Get: $400 to $800
Whom Do I Contact: Financial Aid Director, Loras College, P.O. Box 178, 1450 Alta Vista Street, Dubuque, IA 52004-0178, (313) 588-7136.

497
LOUISIANA STATE UNIVERSITY
New York Times **Multicultural Scholarship**
Who Can Apply: Minority student majoring in Journalism or Mass Communications with a 2.0 GPA and a combined 850 SAT score (20 ACT). Deadline March 1.
How Much Money Can I Get: Varies
Whom Do I Contact: Louisiana State University, Manship School of Mass Communications, Attn.: Scholarship Coordinator, Baton Rouge, LA 70803-7202, (504) 388-2336.

498

LOYOLA COLLEGE

Claver Scholarship
Who Can Apply: Awarded to minority students on the basis of academic achievement. Applicants must be U.S. citizens and graduate in the top fifth of their high school class. Deadline February 1.
How Much Money Can I Get: Varies
Whom Do I Contact: Loyola College, Attn.: Director of Financial Aid, 4501 N. Charles Street, Baltimore, MD 21210-2699, (410) 617-2576.

499

LOYOLA MARYMOUNT UNIVERSITY

Minority Engineering Effort
Who Can Apply: Candidate must be majoring in one of the following engineering areas: chemical, mechanical, or civil. Financial need required.
How Much Money Can I Get: $250 to $2,500
Whom Do I Contact: Financial Aid Director, Loyola Marymount University, Loyola Boulevard at West 80th, Los Angeles, CA 90045, (213) 642-2753.

500

LOYOLA UNIVERSITY NEW ORLEANS

Louis Twomey Scholarship
Who Can Apply: Entering black freshmen from the New Orleans area who have a minimum SAT combined score of 770 (17 ACT) and a 3.0 GPA. Applicants must submit a recommendation from a counselor. Deadline February 1.
How Much Money Can I Get: $4,000
Whom Do I Contact: Loyola University, 6363 St. Charles Avenue, New Orleans, LA 70118, (504) 865-3240.

501

LEAGUE OF UNITED
LATIN AMERICAN CITIZENS

National Scholarship Fund
Who Can Apply: Minority students accepted to a two- or four-year U.S. institution. ACT test required. Applicants must be U.S. citizens or legal residents.
How Much Money Can I Get: $200 to $1,000
Whom Do I Contact: Laura Benso, National Scholarship Coordinator, LULAC National Scholarship Foundation, 400 First Street, NW, Suite 716, Washington, DC 20001, (202) 347-1652.

502

LUTHERAN CHURCH WOMEN

Who Can Apply: Awards annual stipends to minority women who wish to pursue postsecondary education. Applicants must be members of the Lutheran Church of America.

How Much Money Can I Get: $1,000

Whom Do I Contact: Lutheran Church Women, 2900 Queen Lane, Philadelphia, PA 19144, (215) 848-3418.

503

LUTHERAN CHURCH WOMEN
KEMP SCHOLARSHIP

Who Can Apply: To those interested in continuing education through undergraduate, graduate, professional, or vocational study and are members of the Lutheran Church of America. They may be women in their teens who are going directly to college from high school. Deadline February.

How Much Money Can I Get: $1,500

Whom Do I Contact: Lutheran Church Women, 2900 Queen Lane, Philadelphia, PA 19144, (215) 848-3418.

504

LYNCHBURG COLLEGE

The Black Leadership Grant

Who Can Apply: Black students who have completed 16 years in school. Deadline June 1.

How Much Money Can I Get: Up to $3,000

Whom Do I Contact: Director of Admissions, Lynchburg College, Admissions Office, Lynchburg, VA 24501, (804) 522-8300.

505

MANSFIELD UNIVERSITY

The Martin Luther King, Jr., Scholarship

Who Can Apply: Incoming black college freshman. Deadline April 3.

How Much Money Can I Get: $1,000

Whom Do I Contact: Mansfield University, Mansfield, PA 16933, (717) 662-4243.

506

MARVIN C. ZANDERS SCHOLARSHIP

Who Can Apply: Awarded to a black, full-time student with a 2.5 GPA who is a resident of Florida. Applicants must demonstrate strong academics, need, and submit an essay and recommendations. Deadline May 1.

How Much Money Can I Get: $500
Whom Do I Contact: Marvin C. Zanders Scholarship, c/o Mrs. Betty Baker, P.O. Box 993, Apopka, FL 32703.

507

MARY BALDWIN COLLEGE

Baldwin Scholarship
Who Can Apply: Minority female students with a 3.0 GPA in the upper fifth of their class. Deadline March 1.
How Much Money Can I Get: $2,000 to $6,000
Whom Do I Contact: Mary Baldwin College, Attn.: Director of Admissions, Staunton, VA 24401-9983, (703) 887-7022.

508

MARYCREST COLLEGE

Honors Award/Minority Student Achievement
Who Can Apply: Granted to minorities who are U.S. citizens and show outstanding academic or personal achievement. Students must apply for admission to Marycrest and submit the Honors Award application form along with high school transcripts, ACT/SAT scores, and letters of recommendation. Awards are renewable based on academic performance. Deadline March 15.
How Much Money Can I Get: $2,000 annually
Whom Do I Contact: Financial Aid Director, Marycrest College, 1607 W. 12th Street, Davenport, IA 52804, (319) 326-9512.

509

MARYLAND STATE BOARD OF HIGHER EDUCATION

Graduate/Professional Program
Who Can Apply: The program is intended to encourage the enrollment of students from races other than the predominant one on the student's campus. Applicants must be residents of Maryland. State public colleges administer this program.
How Much Money Can I Get: $500
Whom Do I Contact: State Board of Higher Education, The Jeffrey Building, 16 Francis Street, Suite 219, Annapolis, MD 21401, (301) 974-5370.

510

UNIVERSITY OF MARYLAND

Who Can Apply: Applicants must be black, Hispanic, or American Indian and U.S. citizens or permanent residents enrolled in a full-time

undergraduate engineering program. Must have at least a 2.5 GPA. Deadline
May 1.
How Much Money Can I Get: $500 to $1,500
Whom Do I Contact: Director, Center for Minorities in Science and
Engineering, University of Maryland, College Park, MD 20742, (301) 405-
3880.

511
UNIVERSITY OF MARYLAND
ALCOA Engineering Scholarship
Who Can Apply: Minority students enrolled in engineering programs.
Deadline March 31.
How Much Money Can I Get: $250
Whom Do I Contact: University of Maryland, Center for Minority in
Science and Engineering, College Park, MD 20742, (301) 454-0100.

512
UNIVERSITY OF MARYLAND
The Alpha Wives—Montgomery County Scholarship
Who Can Apply: Black woman with a minimum 2.8 GPA. Must show
financial need and be a single parent. Deadline March 6.
How Much Money Can I Get: $500
Whom Do I Contact: Office of Human Relations, University of Maryland,
Black Women's Council, Room 1107, Hornbake Library, College Park, MD
20742, (301) 454-4124.

513
UNIVERSITY OF MARYLAND
The *Baltimore Sun* Papers Minority Journalism Scholarship
Who Can Apply: All Maryland high school graduates based on need,
scholarship, and interest. Renewable with a maintained C average and
continued work toward a journalism major or minor. The student must work
every summer as a paid intern at the *Sun* to continue to receive scholarship.
Write before October 1 to *Baltimore Sun* Papers, Calvert & Centre Streets,
Baltimore, MD 21201. Applications should be sent to the *Baltimore Sun*
before December 31.
How Much Money Can I Get: Grant covers full tuition, room, board, and
books
Whom Do I Contact: University of Maryland, College of Journalism,
College Park, MD 20742, (301) 454-2228.

514

UNIVERSITY OF MARYLAND

The Benjamin Banneker Scholarship

Who Can Apply: Entering black freshman students based on academic achievement. The award pays in-state tuition and fees for four years provided the recipient maintains a minimum 2.5 GPA and 12 credits/semester.

How Much Money Can I Get: In-state tuition

Whom Do I Contact: University of Maryland, North Administration Building, Room 0102B, College Park, MD 20742, (301) 454-4008.

515

UNIVERSITY OF MARYLAND

George Phillips Scholarship Fund

Who Can Apply:. Awarded to a full-time minority student with a 3.0 GPA who demonstrates financial need. Deadline May 1.

How Much Money Can I Get: Varies

Whom Do I Contact: University of Maryland, Attn.: Scholarship Coordinator, 0102 Lee Building, College Park, MD 20742, (301) 314-8313.

516

UNIVERSITY OF MARYLAND

NUS Corporation Scholarship

Who Can Apply: Black undergraduate students majoring in Engineering. Must have a 3.0 GPA.

How Much Money Can I Get: Varies

Whom Do I Contact: University of Maryland, College of Engineering, College Park, MD 20742, (301) 454-0100.

517

UNIVERSITY OF MARYLAND

The Volkswagen of America Scholarship

Who Can Apply: Minority students majoring in Computer Science. Deadline March 1.

How Much Money Can I Get: $1,200

Whom Do I Contact: University of Maryland, Office of the Provost, College Park, MD 20742, (301) 454-0100.

518

UNIVERSITY OF MARYLAND

Westinghouse Ramsey Scholarship

Who Can Apply: This renewable award is available to a minority student majoring in Engineering or Computer Science.

How Much Money Can I Get: $1,500
Whom Do I Contact: Assistant Dean of Engineering, University of Maryland, Engineering Classroom Building, Room 1131L, College Park, MD 20742, (301) 454-4048.

519
UNIVERSITY OF MARYLAND, BALTIMORE
Graduate Minority Fellowship
Who Can Apply: This fellowship can be renewed for one additional year. Applicants are selected for the award based on professional and academic achievements in addition to recommendations from the faculty of University of Maryland, Baltimore.
How Much Money Can I Get: $10,000
Whom Do I Contact: University of Maryland, 5401 Wilkins Avenue, Baltimore, MD 21228, (410) 455-1000.

520
UNIVERSITY OF MARYLAND, BALTIMORE
Meyerhoff Scholarship
Who Can Apply: Black students with a 3.0 GPA majoring in Architecture or Engineering.
How Much Money Can I Get: Tuition and fees
Whom Do I Contact: University of Maryland, Baltimore County, Attn.: Office of the President, 5401 Wilkens Avenue, Baltimore, MD 21228-5398, (410) 455-2291.

521
UNIVERSITY OF MARYLAND, BALTIMORE
Scholastic Achievement Award
Who Can Apply:. Awarded to minority student with a 3.0 GPA. Deadline March 1.
How Much Money Can I Get: $2,500
Whom Do I Contact: University of Maryland, Attn.: Director of Financial Aid, Baltimore County, 5401 Wilkins Avenue, Baltimore, MD 21228, (410) 455-2387.

522
MARY WASHINGTON COLLEGE
Who Can Apply: Student must be a black U.S. citizen attending Mary Washington.
How Much Money Can I Get: Varies
Whom Do I Contact: Financial Aid Director, Mary Washington College, Fredericksburg, VA 22401-5358, (703) 899-4684.

523

MARYVILLE COLLEGE

Ethnic Minority Scholarship
Who Can Apply: Incoming freshmen demonstrating good academic
promise and personal achievement. Must have a 2.5 GPA.
How Much Money Can I Get: Varies
Whom Do I Contact: Maryville College, Attn.: Office of Financial Aid, 502
E. Lamar Alexander Highway, Maryville, TN 37801, (615) 981-8100.

524

MAXWELL HOUSE COFFEE

Minority Scholarship
Who Can Apply: Applicants must be minority high school students or
graduates from New York, Philadelphia, Detroit, Chicago, St. Louis,
Baltimore, or Newark. Applicants must be willing to attend one of the black
colleges participating in their local black college fairs.
How Much Money Can I Get: $3,000
Whom Do I Contact: Maxwell House Coffee, 250 North Street, White
Plains, NY 10625, (914) 335-2500.

525

MCKENDREE COLLEGE

Capital Cities Scholarship
Who Can Apply: Qualified minority students based on guidelines.
How Much Money Can I Get: Varies
Whom Do I Contact: Financial Aid Director, McKendree College, 701
College Road, Lebanon, IL 62254, (618) 537-4481.

526

MCKENDREE COLLEGE

The Eddie Hall Scholarship
Who Can Apply: Academically qualified minority students. Must have a 3.0
GPA.
How Much Money Can I Get: Varies
Whom Do I Contact: Financial Aid Director, McKendree College, Lebanon,
IL 62254, (618) 537-4481.

527

MEDICAL LIBRARY ASSOCIATION

Minority Scholarship
Who Can Apply: Applicants must be members of a minority group and be
entering an ALA accredited graduate library school or have at least one half

of his or her academic requirements to complete during the first year following the granting of the scholarship. Deadline February 1.
How Much Money Can I Get: $2,000
Whom Do I Contact: Medical Library Association, 919 N. Michigan Avenue, Suite 3208, Chicago, IL 60611, (312) 266-2456.

528
MEMPHIS STATE UNIVERSITY
The Edward J. Meeman Minority Scholarship
Who Can Apply: Students who demonstrate financial need, interest, and ability.
How Much Money Can I Get: Tuition for one year, renewable
Whom Do I Contact: Memphis State University, Department of Journalism, Memphis, TN 38152, (901) 678-2401.

529
MEMPHIS STATE UNIVERSITY
Minority Scholarship
Who Can Apply: Must maintain a 2.8 GPA and 30 hour per semester service requirement. Deadline March 1.
How Much Money Can I Get: Registration fees/books
Whom Do I Contact: Scholarship Office/Student Aid, Memphis State University, Scates Hall, Memphis, TN 38152, (901) 678-2303.

530
MEMPHIS STATE UNIVERSITY
Nonresident Minority Scholarship
Who Can Apply: Must maintain a 3.2 GPA and 30 hour per semester service requirement. Deadline is March 1.
How Much Money Can I Get: Varies
Whom Do I Contact: Scholarship Office/Student Aid, Memphis State University, Scates Hall, Memphis, TN 38152, (901) 678-2303.

531
MERCER COUNTY COMMUNITY COLLEGE
Dental Assisting Conference Award
Who Can Apply: Two annual awards to dental assisting certificate students with the highest GPAs completing the first semester of the program. At least one award is reserved for a minority student.
Whom Do I Contact: Financial Aid Director, Mercer County Community College, P.O. Box 8, Trenton, NJ 08690, (609) 586-4800.

532

MERCER COUNTY COMMUNITY COLLEGE
The Forum for Minority Concerns Award
Who Can Apply: Black students for academic excellence, community service, and special achievements.
Whom Do I Contact: Mercer County Community College, P.O. Box 8, Trenton, NJ 08690, (609) 586-4800.

533

MERCYHURST COLLEGE
Bishop Meyers Scholarship
Who Can Apply: Awarded to minority student in the top fifth of their high school class with a minimum combined 800 SAT score. Deadline March 15.
How Much Money Can I Get: $2,500 to $5,000
Whom Do I Contact: Mercyhurst College, Attn.: Director of Admissions, Glenwood Hills, Erie, PA 16546, (814) 825-0200.

534

MERCYHURST COLLEGE
Dr. Charles Richard Drew Scholarship
Who Can Apply: Black students with a 2.5 GPA and in the top half of their class.
How Much Money Can I Get: $2,000
Whom Do I Contact: Director of Admissions, Mercyhurst College, Glenwood Hills, Erie, PA 16546, (814) 825-0200.

535

MERRIMACK COLLEGE
Technical Training Foundation Scholarship
Who Can Apply: Awards are renewable provided that the recipient maintains satisfactory academic progress. Must be majoring or plan to major in computer science or electrical engineering.
How Much Money Can I Get: Varies
Whom Do I Contact: Director of Financial Aid, Merrimack College, Office of Financial Aid, North Andover, MA 01845, (617) 683-7111.

536

MESSIAH COLLEGE
Minority Student Grant
Who Can Apply: Full-time, non-Caucasian U.S. citizens, with priority given to students with the greatest demonstrated financial need.
How Much Money Can I Get: $3,000

Whom Do I Contact: Financial Aid Director, Messiah College, Grantham, PA 17027, (717) 766-2511.

537

MIAMI UNIVERSITY, OHIO

Who Can Apply: Students demonstrating financial need. FAF and FA application required. Two-thirds gift and one-third self-help.
How Much Money Can I Get: $200 to $7,600
Whom Do I Contact: Miami University, Ohio, Edwards House, Oxford, OH 45056, (513) 529-5757.

538

MIAMI UNIVERSITY, OHIO

Black Scholars Program
Who Can Apply: Black students with a 2.5 GPA and a combined 1000 SAT score (20 ACT). Deadline January 31.
How Much Money Can I Get: $1,600 to $3,000
Whom Do I Contact: Miami University, Ohio, Attn.: Office of Financial Aid, Edwards House, Oxford, OH 45056, (513) 529-4734.

539

MIAMI UNIVERSITY, OHIO

Black Student Achievement Grant
Who Can Apply: Applicant must have a 21 ACT score and demonstrate financial need. Deadline January 31.
How Much Money Can I Get: Up to $2,000
Whom Do I Contact: Miami University, Ohio, Attn.: Office of Financial Aid, Edwards House, Oxford, OH 45056, (513) 529-4734.

540

MIAMI UNIVERSITY, OHIO

Minority Scholars Program
Who Can Apply: Awarded to a non-black minority students with a minimum 2.5 GPA and a combined 1000 SAT score (26 ACT). Deadline January 31.
How Much Money Can I Get: $1,000
Whom Do I Contact: Miami University, Ohio, Attn.: Office of Financial Aid, Edwards House, Oxford, OH 45056, (513) 529-4734.

541

MICHIGAN STATE UNIVERSITY

Distinguished Minority Freshman
Who Can Apply: Awarded to a minority freshman in the upper fifth of his or

her high school graduating class. Deadline January 1.
How Much Money Can I Get: $4,000 to $10,000
Whom Do I Contact: Michigan State University, Attn.: Office of Financial Aid, 252 Student Services Building, East Lansing, MI 48824-1113, (517) 353-5940.

542

MICHIGAN STATE UNIVERSITY

Mowbray Scholarship
Who Can Apply: Highest-ranked minority students admitted to the university. Provides programs and social events with faculty and visiting scholars, mentoring relationships between students and faculty, and support for research and/or international study opportunities during the junior and senior years.
How Much Money Can I Get: Tuition
Whom Do I Contact: Office of Admissions and Scholarships, 250 Administration Building, Michigan State University, East Lansing, MI 48824, (517) 355-8332.

543

UNIVERSITY OF MICHIGAN

Who Can Apply: Applicants must be U.S. citizens, major in engineering, and have a 3.0 GPA. Deadline December 4.
How Much Money Can I Get: $1,000, four years
Whom Do I Contact: Financial Aid Office, University of Michigan, College of Engineering, 2417 EECS Building, Ann Arbor, MI 48109-2116, (313) 763-5050.

544

UNIVERSITY OF MICHIGAN

Rackham Merit Fellowship for Historically Underrepresented Groups
Who Can Apply: University of Michigan graduate students entering Rackham master's and doctoral programs who are members of racial and ethnic groups historically underrepresented in graduate education in the United States. Programs is for U.S. citizens and permanent residents only. Applicants must be nominated by the department to which they are admitted. Deadline February 21.
How Much Money Can I Get: Tuition, insurance, and $1,000 per month stipend
Whom Do I Contact: Respective departments at the University of Michigan, Ann Arbor, MI 48109-0406, (313) 764-1817.

545

UNIVERSITY OF MICHIGAN CENTER FOR HUMAN GROWTH AND DEVELOPMENT

Minority International Research Training Program
Who Can Apply: Underrepresented minority groups including African Americans, Hispanic Americans, Native American Indians, and Pacific Islanders who are U.S. citizens or permanent residents pursuing degrees and conducting research in the biomedical or behavioral sciences; focus of research must be on child health and development in developing countries. Deadline December 1.
How Much Money Can I Get: Stipend, travel arrangements, and research expenses
Whom Do I Contact: Center for Human Growth and Development, 300 N. Ingalls Building, University of Michigan, Ann Arbor, MI 48109-0406, (313) 674-2443.

546

MILWAUKEE INSTITUTE OF ART AND DESIGN

Who Can Apply: Awarded to a full-time fine or applied arts or design major at MIAD through a portfolio competition. Deadline February 1.
How Much Money Can I Get: $3,500
Whom Do I Contact: Milwaukee Institute of Art and Design, Attn.: Financial Aid Officer, 273 E. Erie Street, Milwaukee, WI 53202, (414) 276-7889.

547

MINORITY BIOMEDICAL RESEARCH SUPPORT (MBRS) PROGRAM

Who Can Apply: Program is aimed toward ensuring minority groups an equal opportunity to pursue careers in biomedical research. The program provides for academic year and summer salaries and wages for faculty, students, and support personnel needed to conduct a research project.
How Much Money Can I Get: Varies
Whom Do I Contact: Program Administrator, National Institutes of Health, Division of Research Resources, Building 31, Room 5B35, Bethesda, MD 20892, (301) 496-6745.

548

MINORITY EDUCATION FUND

Who Can Apply: Minority students admitted to a college who are members of an RCA church or enrolled in an RCA college.
How Much Money Can I Get: Varies

Whom Do I Contact: Reformed Church of America (RCA), 475 Riverside Drive, Room 1819, New York, NY 10027, (212) 870-3071.

549

MINORITY LEADERS FELLOWSHIP PROGRAM
The Washington Center's Minority Leaders Fellowship Program
Who Can Apply: Outstanding college students who will spend ten weeks in Washington, DC as part of the program. Students explore the field of leadership not only as a theoretical concept but also as a daily reality. Applicants must be nominated by the president of their college or university.
How Much Money Can I Get: Varies
Whom Do I Contact: The Washington Public Affairs Center, 512 Tenth Street, NW, Suite 600, Washington, DC 20004, (202) 638-4949.

550

MINORITY PRESENCE/NORTH CAROLINA DOCTORAL/LAW/VETERINARY MEDICINE PROGRAM
Who Can Apply: Black North Carolinians enrolled full-time in a doctoral degree program at East Carolina University, North Carolina State University, the University of North Carolina at Chapel Hill, the University of North Carolina at Greensboro, the Law School at the University of North Carolina at Chapel Hill, or the School of Veterinary Medicine at North Carolina State University. Applications are available at each school.
How Much Money Can I Get: $4,000
Whom Do I Contact: North Carolina State Education Assistance Program, P.O. Box 2688, Chapel Hill, NC 27515-2688, (919) 549-8614.

551

MISSISSIPPI STATE UNIVERSITY
Minority Engineering Effort
Who Can Apply: Financial need required. Must be majoring in agriculture or one of the following engineering areas: electrical, biomedical, civil, nuclear, aerospace, chemical, industrial, or petroleum.
How Much Money Can I Get: Varies
Whom Do I Contact: Institutional Research Office, Mississippi State University, Drawer EY, Mississippi State, MS 39762, (601) 325-3221.

552

UNIVERSITY OF MISSISSIPPI
Minority Engineering Effort
Who Can Apply: Those majoring in Engineering. Financial need required. Deadline August 15.

How Much Money Can I Get: $250 to $2,500
Whom Do I Contact: Financial Aid Director, University of Mississippi, University, MS 38677, (601) 232-8411.

553
UNIVERSITY OF MISSOURI
Who Can Apply: The Knight Foundation Office of Minority Recruiting and Retention offers scholarships to outstanding minority students interested in majoring in journalism who have a high school GPA of at least 2.75 (on a 4.0 scale) and have been admitted to the University of Missouri. Deadline April 15.
How Much Money Can I Get: $2,000 maximum
Whom Do I Contact: Gail Baker Woods, Director, Knight Foundation Office of Minority Recruiting and Retention, University of Missouri, P.O. Box 838, Columbia, MO 65205, (314) 882-4079.

554
UNIVERSITY OF MISSOURI
George Washington Carver Graduate Assistantship
Who Can Apply: Minority students of forestry, fisheries, wildlife, agricultural economics, rural sociology, animal sciences, plant sciences, biochemistry, and food service and engineering. Applicants must be U.S. citizens. Program offers graduate research assistantship for two years on M.S. degrees and three years on Ph.D. degrees.
How Much Money Can I Get: Stipend set annually by the program in which the student is studying; all units have 12-month stipends in excess of $8,000 for M.S. and $10,000 for Ph.D. students; tuition is waived in addition to providing the stipend.
Whom Do I Contact: University of Missouri, College of Agriculture, Agriculture Building 2-60, Columbia, MO 65211, (314) 882-3846.

555
UNIVERSITY OF MISSOURI
The *St. Louis Post-Dispatch* Scholarship
Who Can Apply: Minority students who are seniors in an accredited high school or junior college in Jefferson, St. Charles, or St. Louis Counties or the city of St. Louis, Missouri or Madison or St. Clair Counties in Illinois. Deadline April 1.
How Much Money Can I Get: $1,800 renewable
Whom Do I Contact: University of Missouri, School of Journalism, Columbia, MO 65205, (314) 882-4821.

556

UNIVERSITY OF MISSOURI-KANSAS CITY
Minority Doctoral Fellowship
Who Can Apply: Minority doctoral student (Ph.D./D.M.A.) who is a U.S. citizen. Fellowship is based on merit. Apply to academic department by mid-March. Interdisciplinary Ph.D. students apply through School of Graduate Studies.
How Much Money Can I Get: Maximum academic year amount of $1,200 stipend plus nine hours graduate educational fee plus full nonresident fee differential, if applicable. Up to four awards yearly.
Whom Do I Contact: School of Graduate Studies, University of Missouri-Kansas City, Kansas City, MO 64110-2499, (816) 235-1111, E-mail, Admit@UMKC.EDU.

557

UNIVERSITY OF MISSOURI-KANSAS CITY
Minority Master's Student Fellowship
Who Can Apply: Master's degree student, U.S. citizen, based on merit. Deadline mid-March.
How Much Money Can I Get: $600 maximum academic year amount applicable to fees; renewable for second year.
Whom Do I Contact: School of Graduate Studies, University of Missouri-Kansas City, Kansas City, MO 64110-2499, (816) 235-1111, E-mail, Admit@UMKC.EDU.

558

UNIVERSITY OF MISSOURI-ROLLA
Minority Engineering Program (MEP)
Who Can Apply: The program awards scholarships and free summer sessions to Native American Indian, African-American, and Hispanic American entering freshmen and transfers in selected technological fields. Deadline December 31.
How Much Money Can I Get: Approximately $8,500 freshmen; $500 transfer students
Whom Do I Contact: Student Financial Aid Office, University of Missouri-Rolla, G-1 Parker Hall, 1870 Miner Circle, Rolla, MO 65409-1060, (573) 341-4282, (800) 522-0938, fax: (573) 341-4274.

559

UNIVERSITY OF MISSOURI-ST. LOUIS
Inroads/St. Louis, Inc. Scholarship
Who Can Apply: First-time freshmen enrolled in the Inroads/St. Louis College Component and be admitted to UM-St. Louis. Preference is given to

minority students. Candidate must complete the pre-engineering curriculum at UM-St. Louis. A cumulative GPA of 2.75 required in all engineering courses. Deadline March 31.

How Much Money Can I Get: $1,000 per semester, renewable

Whom Do I Contact: University of Missouri-St. Louis, Financial Aid Office, Saint Louis, MO 63121-4499, (314) 516-5526.

560

UNIVERSITY OF MISSOURI-ST. LOUIS

Interco Scholarship

Who Can Apply: Minority student with high academic achievement in high school. Deadline March 31.

How Much Money Can I Get: Full educational fees and books, renewable

Whom Do I Contact: University of Missouri-St. Louis, Financial Aid Office, St. Louis, MO 63121-4499, (314) 516-5526.

561

UNIVERSITY OF MISSOURI-ST. LOUIS

Mark Twain Bancshares Scholarship

Who Can Apply: First-time freshmen, minority, with high school cumulative 3.0 GPA. Candidates must be living in the St. Louis metropolitan area. Preference is given to students who wish to major in Business Administration. Deadline March 31.

How Much Money Can I Get: $3,000, renewable up to 10 semesters

Whom Do I Contact: University of Missouri-St. Louis, Financial Aid Office, St. Louis, MO 63121-4499, (314) 516-5526.

562

UNIVERSITY OF MISSOURI-ST. LOUIS

Missouri Minority Teacher Scholarship

Who Can Apply: Missouri minority residents in top 25 percent of high school class and who scored at or above the 75 percentile on the ACT or SAT and will complete teacher training at a four year college.

How Much Money Can I Get: $3,000 per academic year, renewable up to four years

Whom Do I Contact: University of Missouri-St. Louis, Financial Aid Office, St. Louis, MO 63121-4499, (314) 516-5526.

563

UNIVERSITY OF MISSOURI-ST. LOUIS

Monsanto Minority Math/Science Scholarship

Who Can Apply: Students who have successfully completed the Bridge Program or minority or economically disadvantaged students with a major in math, computer science, biology, chemistry, engineering, or physics and a minimum cumulative 2.4 GPA.

How Much Money Can I Get: Tuition, fees, and campus housing, renewable

Whom Do I Contact: University of Missouri-St. Louis, Financial Aid Office, St. Louis, MO 63121-4499, (314) 516-5526.

564

MONMOUTH COLLEGE

Margaret Doxey Memorial Scholarship

Who Can Apply: Promising female students who demonstrate financial need. Deadline February 1.

How Much Money Can I Get: Varies

Whom Do I Contact: Monmouth College, Attn.: Director of Admissions, Office of Admissions, West Long Branch, NJ 07764-1898, (908) 571-3456.

565

MONTGOMERY COUNTY COMMUNITY COLLEGE

The Leonard Jones Memorial Scholarship

Who Can Apply: The book scholarship is open to a black freshman or sophomore student in satisfactory standing. Financial need required. Deadline May 1.

How Much Money Can I Get: $50

Whom Do I Contact: Financial Aid Director, Montgomery County Community College, 340 DeKalb Pike, Blue Bell, PA 19422, (215) 641-6566.

566

MONTGOMERY COLLEGE

ORI, Incorporated Scholarship

Who Can Apply: Applicants must be full-time minority students who have completed a minimum of 24 credits with a 3.0 GPA. Must be a U.S. citizen majoring in one of the following areas: mathematics, physics, computer science/data processing, or engineering. Financial need required. Deadline June 15.

How Much Money Can I Get: $1,140

Whom Do I Contact: Financial Aid Director, Montgomery College, Rockville, MD 20850, (301) 279-5000.

567

MOORHEAD STATE UNIVERSITY

Minority Scholarship

Who Can Apply: African Americans, Native American Indians, Latinos, and Asian Americans who have a minimum 2.5 GPA.

How Much Money Can I Get: $300 to $1,500
Whom Do I Contact: Financial Aid & Scholarship Office, 107 Owens Hall, Moorhead State University, Moorhead, MN 56563, (218) 236-2251, (800) 59DRAGON.

568
MOREHOUSE COLLEGE
Who Can Apply: The United Negro College Fund awards scholarships to black entering freshman. Must have a strong academic background. Apply early.
How Much Money Can I Get: $100 to $2,000
Whom Do I Contact: Morehouse College, 233 Chestnut Street, SW, Atlanta, GA 30314, (404) 681-2800.

569
MOUNT MARY COLLEGE
The Tona Diebels Minority Scholarship
Who Can Apply: Minority freshmen graduating in the upper 20 percent of their class with a 3.0 GPA. Applicants are to submit an essay demonstrating leadership qualities through involvement in a variety of extracurricular activities. The award is renewable. Deadline February 15.
How Much Money Can I Get: $500
Whom Do I Contact: Financial Aid Director, Mount Mary College, 2900 N. Menomonee River Parkway, Milwaukee, WI 53222, (414) 259-9220.

570
MOUNT ST. MARY'S COLLEGE
Funston V. Collins Grant
Who Can Apply: Entering black students are eligible. These are renewable based on satisfactory progress. Although need is not a prerequisite, all recipients are required to file a FAF each year and apply for any state or private assistance for which they may be eligible. Deadline January 1.
How Much Money Can I Get: $500 to $3,000
Whom Do I Contact: Financial Aid Director, Mount St. Mary's College, Financial Aid Office, Emmitsburg, MD 21727, (301) 447-5207.

571
MOUNT UNION COLLEGE SCHOLARSHIPS
Who Can Apply: Scholarships are awarded to minority students in the upper fifth of their class. Must have a 3.0 GPA. Based on merit.
How Much Money Can I Get: $2,000
Whom Do I Contact: Office of Admissions, Mount Union College, 1972 Clark Avenue, Alliance, OH 44601, (216) 823-6050.

572

MUNSON INSTITUTE OF
AMERICAN MARITIME STUDIES

Paul Cuffe Memorial Fellowship for the Study of Minorities in American Maritime History

Who Can Apply: Applicants must send a full description of the proposed project, a preliminary bibliography, brief project budget, resume, and references. The fellowships are offered to encourage research that considers the participation of minorities in the maritime activities of New England. Deadline June 15.

How Much Money Can I Get: Up to $2,400

Whom Do I Contact: Director, Munson Institute of American Maritime Studies, Mystic Seaport Museum, P.O. Box 6000, Mystic, CT 06355-0990, (203) 572-5359, fax: (203) 572-5329.

573

MUSIC ASSISTANCE FUND

Scholarship Fund

Who Can Apply: Minority students who need financial help to attend conservatories and schools of music, if they are interested in playing orchestral instruments.

How Much Money Can I Get: $250 to $1,000

Whom Do I Contact: The Music Assistance Fund, New York Philharmonic, Avery Fisher Hall, Broadway at 65th Street, New York, NY 10023, (212) 580-8700.

574

MUSIC ASSISTANCE FUND

Who Can Apply: Applicants must intend to pursue a career in orchestral playing. Voice, piano, and conducting students not eligible. Audition is required. Deadline November 1.

How Much Money Can I Get: $500 to $2,000

Whom Do I Contact: Music Assistance Fund, Avery Fisher Hall, Lincoln Center, Broadway at 65th Street, New York, NY 10023, (212) 580-8700.

575

MUSIC ASSISTANCE FUND

Who Can Apply: Financial aid to students who intend to pursue a professional career in symphony orchestra. Applicant must be a U.S. citizen. Deadline January 14.

How Much Money Can I Get: Up to $2,500

Whom Do I Contact: Music Assistance Fund, Attn.: Awards Officer,

American Symphony Orchestra League, 777 14th Street, NW, Suite 500, Washington, DC 20005-3201, (202) 628-0099.

576

NAACP ACT-SO ACADEMIC, CULTURAL, TECHNOLOGICAL AND SCIENTIFIC OLYMPICS SCHOLARSHIPS

Who Can Apply: Scholarships are offered to black students who are winners in local NAACP competitions. Students also earn an expense-paid trip to the national competition usually held in June. Categories include the performing arts, humanities, visual arts, and sciences. Deadline is usually two weeks before the national convention of ACT-SO.

How Much Money Can I Get: $500 to $1,000

Whom Do I Contact: Whom Do I Contact a local NAACP branch.

577

NAACP AGNES JONES JACKSON SCHOLARSHIP

Who Can Apply: Awarded to full-time students under age 25 based on need, academic achievement, and NAACP involvement. High school seniors must have a 2.5 GPA. College undergraduates must have a 2.0 GPA. Deadline April 30.

How Much Money Can I Get: $1,500

Whom Do I Contact: NAACP, Attn.: Education Department, 4805 Mount Hope Drive, Baltimore, MD 21215-3297, (410) 358-8900.

578

NAACP ROY WILKINS EDUCATION SCHOLARSHIP PROGRAM

Who Can Apply: Awarded to a black student with a 2.5 GPA, letters of recommendation, financial and grade transcripts, and need. Deadline April 30.

How Much Money Can I Get: $1,000

Whom Do I Contact: NAACP, Attn.: Education Department, 4805 Mount Hope Drive, Baltimore, MD 21215-3297, (410) 358-8900.

579

NAACP SCHOLARSHIP PROGRAM

Who Can Apply: Applicants must be members of the NAACP who are majoring in the fields of engineering, science, computer science, mathematics, or environmental science. Applicants must be U.S. citizens and be enrolled or accepted at an accredited college or university in the U.S. and

are graduating high school seniors who rank in the top third of their class with a 3.0 GPA. Deadline April 30.
How Much Money Can I Get: Varies
Whom Do I Contact: Director of Education, NAACP, 4805 Mount Hope Drive, Baltimore, MD 21215, (410) 486-9135.

580
NAACP SUTTON EDUCATION SCHOLARSHIP
Who Can Apply: Awarded to a black U.S. citizen with a 3.0 GPA. Applicants must be majoring in education, be active in the NAACP, and show financial need. Deadline April 30.
How Much Money Can I Get: $1,000 to $2,000 renewable
Whom Do I Contact: Education Department, NAACP, 4805 Mt. Hope Drive, Baltimore, MD 21215-3297, (301) 358-8900.

581
NAACP WILLEMS SCHOLARSHIP
The Willems Scholarship
Who Can Apply: Awarded to a black U.S. citizen with a 3.0 GPA. Applicants must be majoring in Mathematics, Physics, Engineering, or Chemistry, and be active in the NAACP.
How Much Money Can I Get: $2,000 to $3,000, renewable
Whom Do I Contact: Education Department, NAACP, 4805 Mt. Hope Road, Baltimore, MD 21215-3297, (301) 358-8900.

582
NATIONAL ACHIEVEMENT SCHOLARSHIP PROGRAM FOR OUTSTANDING NEGRO STUDENTS
Who Can Apply: Black students who plan to earn a bachelor's degree. PSAT/NMSQT must be taken. Application, transcript, and recommendations required.
How Much Money Can I Get: Varies
Whom Do I Contact: NASP for Outstanding Negro Students, One Rotary Center, Evanston, IL 60201, (847) 866-05100.

583
NATIONAL ACTION COUNCIL FOR MINORITIES IN ENGINEERING, INC.
Incentive Grant Program
Who Can Apply: Needy minorities enrolled full-time in an undergraduate engineering program. Also for entering freshmen and transfer students with at least a 2.5 GPA.

How Much Money Can I Get: Varies
Whom Do I Contact: NACME, 3 W. 35th Street, New York, NY 10001, (212) 279-2626.

584
NATIONAL ASSOCIATION
OF BLACK ACCOUNTANTS
Who Can Apply: The annual scholarship is awarded to a black student with a 3.5 GPA majoring in accounting. Recipient must attend annual convention, expenses paid. Deadline March 31.
How Much Money Can I Get: $2,500
Whom Do I Contact: Executive Director, National Association of Black Accountants, 300 I Street, NE, Suite 107, Washington, DC 20002, (202) 543-6656.

585
NATIONAL ASSOCIATION
OF BLACK JOURNALISTS
Who Can Apply: These scholarship program awards are for majors in Journalism, Photography, and Radio/TV Broadcasting enrolled in accredited four-year colleges. A 500 to 800-word article and three samples of work must be submitted. Apply late fall.
How Much Money Can I Get: $2,500
Whom Do I Contact: Executive Director, National Association of Black Journalists Scholarship Program, 11600 Sunrise Valley Drive, Reston, VA 22091, (703) 648-1283.

586
NATIONAL ASSOCIATION OF
BLACK JOURNALISTS SCHOLARSHIP PROGRAM
Who Can Apply: Applicants must have participated in the annual St. Louis Minority Journalism Workshop, be black college students majoring in journalism, and live in the St. Louis area.
How Much Money Can I Get: $1,000
Whom Do I Contact: National Association of Black Journalists, Greater St. Louis Area Chapter, 2953 Dr. Martin Luther King Drive, St. Louis, MO 63106, (314) 535-5185.

587
NATIONAL ASSOCIATION OF
BLACK WOMEN ATTORNEYS
Who Can Apply: Black women law students are eligible to enter this essay contest. The subject of the essay changes each year but always focuses on an

issue of contemporary concern. Applicants must have completed 16 years in school.
How Much Money Can I Get: $1,000
Whom Do I Contact: National Association of Black Women Attorneys, 724 9th Street, NW, Suite 206, Washington, DC 20001, (202) 637-3570.

588
NATIONAL ASSOCIATION OF BLACKS IN CRIMINAL JUSTICE
Thurgood Marshall Scholarship
Who Can Apply: Students who are graduating from high school with a B average or better and who plan to major in criminal justice and demonstrate financial need.
How Much Money Can I Get: Varies
Whom Do I Contact: National Association of Blacks in Criminal Justice, North Carolina Central University, 106 Criminal Justice Building, P.O. Box 19788 Durham, NC 27707.

589
NATIONAL ASSOCIATION OF COLORED WOMEN'S CLUBS
Hallie Q. Brown Scholarship Fund
Who Can Apply: Minority students who are U.S. citizens with financial need and have applied to an accredited college or university.
How Much Money Can I Get: Up to $1,000
Whom Do I Contact: National Association of Colored Women's Clubs, 5808 16th Street, NW, Washington, DC 20011, (202) 726-2044.

590
NATIONAL ASSOCIATION OF MEDIA WOMEN
Atlanta Daily World Scholarship/Internship
Who Can Apply: Minority female undergraduate majoring in Mass Communications. Applicants must attend a Georgia college.
How Much Money Can I Get: Varies
Whom Do I Contact: *Atlanta Daily World*, 145 Auburn Avenue, NW, Atlanta, GA 30335, (404) 659-1110.

591
NATIONAL ASSOCIATION OF MEDIA WOMEN, ATLANTA CHAPTER
Who Can Apply: Scholarship awarded to an undergraduate female minority student majoring in Mass Communications and attending an institution in Georgia.

How Much Money Can I Get: $5,000
Whom Do I Contact: National Association of Media Women—Atlanta Chapter, Attn.: Chairperson, 1185 Niskey Lane Road, SW, Atlanta, GA 30331, (404) 344-5862.

592

NATIONAL ASSOCIATION OF NEGRO MUSICIANS, INC.

Who Can Apply: Awards for minority students, ages 18 to 30, for instrumental and vocal music. Applicants must be sponsored by a local branch of the organization, and compete and win local, regional, and national competitions. Deadline July 1.
How Much Money Can I Get: $250 to $1,500
Whom Do I Contact: National Association of Negro Musicians, Inc., P.O. Box S-011, Chicago, IL 60628.

593

NATIONAL BLACK CAUCUS OF LIBRARIANS
Charlemae Hill Rollins Scholarship
Who Can Apply: Black college graduates who have an excellent academic record and have completed no more than 12 semester hours toward the graduate degree in librarianship if they are legal residents of the Chicago area. Recipients may attend any library school accredited by the American Library Association. Deadline March 1.
How Much Money Can I Get: $300
Whom Do I Contact: Chairman, Rollins Scholarship Committee, Chicago Chapter, National Black Caucus of Librarians, 6914 S. Morgan, Chicago, IL 60621, (773) 874-7534.

594

NATIONAL BLACK MBA ASSOCIATION, INC.
MBA Scholarship
Who Can Apply: Minority students enrolled in a full-time graduate or doctoral business program. Deadline March 31.
How Much Money Can I Get: $3,000 for master's, $5,000 to $10,000 for doctorate
Whom Do I Contact: MBA Scholarships, National Black MBA Association, Inc., 180 N. Michigan Avenue, Chicago, IL 60601, (312) 236-2622.

595

NATIONAL BLACK NURSES' ASSOCIATION
Ambi-Nicholas Laboratories Scholarship
Who Can Apply: Awarded to black American nursing students belonging to

a chapter of the National Black Nurses' Association and who are enrolled in a current program. Applicants must demonstrate academic excellence, professional commitment, personal integrity, active involvement in the black community, and financial need. Deadline May.
How Much Money Can I Get: Varies
Whom Do I Contact: National Black Nurses' Association, Inc., P.O. Box 18358, Boston, MA 02118, (617) 266-9703.

596

NATIONAL BLACK NURSES' ASSOCIATION
Lauranne Sams Scholarship Award
Who Can Apply: Black nursing students who belong to a local chapter of the National Black Nurses' Association and who demonstrate academic excellence, professional commitment, personal integrity, and financial need. Deadline May.
How Much Money Can I Get: Varies
Whom Do I Contact: National Black Nurses' Association, Inc., P.O. Box 18358, Boston, MA 02118, (617) 266-9703.

597

NATIONAL BLACK NURSES' ASSOCIATION
March of Dimes Birth Defect Award
Who Can Apply: Black nursing student with the best essay addressing the "Prevention of Teenage Pregnancy and Decrease in Infant Mortality Rates." Entrants must be members of the National Black Nurses' Association and must be enrolled in an LPN/LVN program, associate's degree program, diploma program, or baccalaureate program. Essays are judged on the basis of the statement of the problem, proposal for dealing with the problem, clarity and innovation of the approach, grammar, style, clarity, and format (under 2,500 words). The competition is held annually and is cosponsored by the March of Dimes Birth Defects Foundation. Deadline May.
How Much Money Can I Get: $1,000
Whom Do I Contact: National Black Nurses' Association, Inc., P.O. Box 18358, Boston, MA 02118, (617) 266-9703.

598

NATIONAL BLACK POLICE ASSOCIATION
Who Can Apply: Must be a black U.S. citizen in the upper three-fifths of his or her class, have a 2.5 GPA, and major in law enforcement/police administration. Financial need required.
How Much Money Can I Get: $500
Whom Do I Contact: National Black Police Association, 1100 17th Street, NW, Suite 1000, Washington, DC 20036, (202) 457-0563.

599

NATIONAL CANCER INSTITUTE
Comprehensive Minority Biomedical Program
Who Can Apply: This program is for minority scientists developing careers in cancer research.
How Much Money Can I Get: Varies
Whom Do I Contact: CMBP Program Director, National Cancer Institute, Division of Examural Activities, Building 31, Room 10A04, Bethesda, MD 20892, (301) 496-7344.

600

NATIONAL CENTER FOR ATMOSPHERIC RESEARCH
Summer Employment Program
Who Can Apply: Minority undergraduate students interested in the sciences and engineering. Applicants must be undergraduates with at least 60 hours of course work and be studying physics, math, computer science, meteorology, electrical engineering, chemistry, technical writing, or other physical sciences. Deadline March.
How Much Money Can I Get: Varies
Whom Do I Contact: NCAR, Human Resources Administrator, P.O. Box 3000, Boulder, CO 80307, (303) 497-8717.

601

NATIONAL GEM CENTER
Fellowship Program
Who Can Apply: Minority students in master's or Ph.D. programs in engineering or natural sciences at GEM-member universities. Deadline December 1.
How Much Money Can I Get: Full-tuition+
Whom Do I Contact: Fellowship Programs, The National GEM Center, P.O. Box 537, Notre Dame, IN 46556, (219) 631-5000.

602

NATIONAL HEART, LUNG & BLOOD INSTITUTE
Minority School Faculty Development Award
Who Can Apply: This program is intended to encourage the development of faculty investigators at minority schools in areas relevant to cardiovascular, pulmonary, and hematological diseases and resources. Candidates should be minority school faculty members who are U.S. citizens, non-citizen nationals or permanent residents, with a doctoral degree or equivalent in a biomedical science.

How Much Money Can I Get: Varies
Whom Do I Contact: Program Administrator, National Heart, Lung & Blood Institute, National Institutes of Health, Federal Building, Room 3C02, Bethesda, MD 20892, (301) 496-1724.

603

NATIONAL HEART, LUNG & BLOOD INSTITUTE
Minority Summer Program in Pulmonary Research Program
Who Can Apply: Qualified minority school faculty and graduate students interested in develop skills in research in pulmonary diseases at established (minority) pulmonary training centers.
How Much Money Can I Get: Varies
Whom Do I Contact: Program Administrator, National Heart, Lung & Blood Institute, Research Training & Development, Westwood Building, Room 640, Bethesda, MD 20892, (301) 496-7668.

604

NATIONAL INSTITUTES OF HEALTH
Marc Faculty Fellowship Program
Who Can Apply: Faculty members of a public or private nonprofit university, four-year college, or other institution offering undergraduate, graduate, or health professional degrees with a substantial minority student enrollment. Institutions nominate faculty members for these fellowships, which support either a period of advanced study in research training leading to a graduate degree or a period of postdoctoral research training in the biomedical sciences. Stipends, based on the applicant's current salary, are not to exceed $25,000 per year. Support is available for periods of up to three years at the end of which time the fellow is expected to return to his or her institution. Deadline January 10, September 10, and May 1.
How Much Money Can I Get: Varies
Whom Do I Contact: National Institution of General Medical Services, Attn.: Dr. Adolphus Toliver, Building 45, Suite SA-37, 45 Center Drive, MSC 6200, Bethesda, MD 20892, (301) 594-3900.

605

NATIONAL INSTITUTES OF HEALTH
The Minority Biomedical Research Support Program
Who Can Apply: The program provides for academic year and summer salaries and wages for faculty, students, and support personnel needed to conduct a research project. Majors in health science also eligible.
The program is aimed toward ensuring ethnic minority groups an equal opportunity to pursue careers in biomedical research.
How Much Money Can I Get: Varies

Whom Do I Contact: National Institutes of Health, Division of Research Resources, Building 31, Room 5B35, Bethesda, MD 20892, (301) 496-6745.

606
NATIONAL INSTITUTES OF HEALTH
Research Apprentice Program for Minority High School Students
Who Can Apply: Program is designed to stimulate interest among minority high school students in science careers and to establish individualized working relationships between these students and active researchers. Apprentices are paid a salary equivalent to the minimum wage.
How Much Money Can I Get: Varies
Whom Do I Contact: Program Administrator, National Institutes of Health, Division of Research Resources, Building 31, Room 5B23, Bethesda, MD 20892, (301) 496-6743.

607
NATIONAL INSTITUTES OF HEALTH/
NATIONAL INSTIUTE OF INFECTIOUS DISEASES
Minority Research Enhancement Award
Who Can Apply: The National Institute of Allergy and Infectious Diseases provides support for underrepresented minority researchers. Must be majoring in biomedical research.
How Much Money Can I Get: Varies
Whom Do I Contact: Chief, Research Manpower Development, National Institutes of Health, Westwood Building, Room 7A03, NIAID, Bethesda, MD 20892, (301) 496-3461.

608
NATIONAL MEDICAL FELLOWSHIPS
Who Can Apply: First- or second-year students studying at an American medical school toward an MD or DO degree. Candidates must be a U.S. citizen and black, Hispanic, or Native American Indian with financial need. Deadline August 31.
How Much Money Can I Get: Varies
Whom Do I Contact: National Medical Fellowships, Inc., 254 W. 31st Street, Seventh Floor, New York, NY 10001-2813, (212)714-0933.

609
NATIONAL NEWSPAPER
PUBLISHERS SCHOLARSHIPS
Who Can Apply: Minority college students who wish to pursue careers in journalism.
How Much Money Can I Get: $600

Whom Do I Contact: National Newspaper Publishers Association, c/o *The Louisville Defender*, 1720 Dixie Highway, Louisville, KY 40210, (502) 772-2591.

610
NATIONAL PHARMACEUTICAL FOUNDATION, INC. ETHNIC MINORITY PHARMACY SCHOLARSHIPS

Who Can Apply: Applicants must be U.S. citizens majoring in Pharmacy. Submission of ACT, SAT, or CEEB scores required.
How Much Money Can I Get: $500 to $1,000
Whom Do I Contact: President, National Pharmaceutical Foundation, Inc., 1728 17th Street, NE, Washington, DC 20002, (202) 829-5008.

611
NATIONAL PHYSICAL SCIENCE CONSORTIUM

Who Can Apply: The National Physical Science Consortium offers a six-year doctoral fellowship program for women and minorities in the physical sciences for U. S. citizens who are African American, Hispanic, American Indian, and/or female, have a 3.0 GPA, and are eligible to pursue graduate study at a participating NPSC member university. Deadline November 15.
How Much Money Can I Get: Each fellowship is worth from $150,000 up to $180,000.
Whom Do I Contact: L. N. Snow, Executive Director, National Physical Science Consortium, New Mexico State University, Box 30001, Department 3NPS, Las Cruces, NM 88003-8001, (800) 952-4118.

612
NATIONAL PRESS PHOTOGRAPHERS ASSOCIATION

Joseph Ehrenreich Scholarship
Who Can Apply: Students enrolled in a recognized four-year college or university studying photojournalism. Financial need required.
How Much Money Can I Get: $1,000
Whom Do I Contact: National Press Photographers Association, P.O. Box 1146, Durham, NC 27702, (919) 489-3700.

613
NATIONAL SCHOLARSHIP SERVICE AND FUND FOR MINORITY STUDENTS

Who Can Apply: Awards based on need and designed to supplement the resources of students who have received other aid.
How Much Money Can I Get: $200 to $600

Whom Do I Contact: National Scholarship Service and Fund for Minority Students, 322 Eighth Avenue, New York, NY 10001.

614

NATIONAL SCIENCE FOUNDATION
Minority Graduate Fellowships
Who Can Apply: Applicant must be a member of a minority group. Eligibility is limited to those who have not completed more than 20 semester/30 quarter hours, or equivalent, of study in any of the qualifying fields, following completion of their undergraduate degree. No student will be eligible for more than three years of any NSF graduate fellowship support. Recipient will be required to enroll in full-time programs leading to graduate degrees in one of the following majors: mathematics, biology, social science, physical science, science, engineering, or humanities. Must be a U.S. citizen.
How Much Money Can I Get: $12,550
Whom Do I Contact: National Research Council, The Fellowship Office, 2101 Constitution Avenue, Washington, DC 20418, (202) 334-2872.

615

NATIONAL SCIENCE FOUNDATION
Postdoctoral Fellowships
Who Can Apply: Scientists and engineers usually initiate research proposals that are submitted by their employing organizations. Before formal submission, the proposal may be discussed with NSF staff. The foundation considers proposals for support of research in any field of science. The foundation normally will not support clinical research, including research on the etiology, diagnosis, or treatment of physical or mental diseases, abnormality, or malfunction in human beings or animals. Proposals may be submitted by individuals or groups for support of research or research equipment. Research proposals may be submitted at any time. Applicants should allow six to nine months for review and processing. Whom Do I Contact the foundation for additional information. Applicants must be female and majoring in one of the following: science, atmospheric sciences, chemistry, earth sciences, oceanography, social science, astronomy, biology, computer science/data processing, engineering, materials management/ marketing/handling, or physics. Deadline is November 5.
How Much Money Can I Get: Varies
Whom Do I Contact: Data Support Services Section, National Science Foundation, Nato Postdoctoral Fellowship Directorate for Science/ Engineering Education, Washington, DC 20550, (703) 308-5282.

616

NATIONAL SECURITY AGENCY
UNDERGRADUATE TRAINING PROGRAM

Who Can Apply: Any student, particularly a minority student, who chooses a full-time college major in electrical or computer engineering, computer science, mathematics, or Asian, Middle Eastern, or Slavic languages. Students must attend classes full-time and work at NSA during summers. Students must maintain a 3.0 GPA. After graduation, the student must work for NSA for at least one and half times the length of study.
How Much Money Can I Get: Full tuition+
Whom Do I Contact: NSA, Undergraduate Training Program, Manager, Attn.: M322 (UTP), Fort Meade, MD 20755-6000, (800) 962-9398.

617

NATIONAL SOCIETY OF PROFESSIONAL
ENGINEERS RACIAL MINORITY GRANTS

Who Can Apply: Minority or female high school seniors who rank in the top quarter of their class, with plans to major in engineering. Financial need required.
How Much Money Can I Get: $1,000
Whom Do I Contact: National Society of Professional Engineers Education Foundation, 2029 K Street, NW, Washington, DC 20006, (202) 463-2300.

618

NATIONAL STUDENT NURSES ASSOCIATION

Who Can Apply: Nine scholarships for undergraduate minority students interested in nursing and demonstrating financial need. Deadline February 1. Applications available in September.
How Much Money Can I Get: $1,000 to $2,500
Whom Do I Contact: National Student Nurses Association, 555 W. 57th Street, New York, NY 10019, (212) 581-2211.

619

NATIONAL STUDENT NURSES ASSOCIATION
Breakthrough to Nursing Scholarship

Who Can Apply: Minority undergraduate students interested in studying for nursing careers. Financial need is a requirement.
How Much Money Can I Get: $2,000
Whom Do I Contact: National Student Nurses Association, 10 Columbus Circle, New York, NY 10019, (212) 581-2211.

620

NATIONAL TECHNICAL ASSOCIATION

Who Can Apply: Award is for minority students pursuing degrees in finance and engineering. Deadline March 31.
How Much Money Can I Get: 50 percent of tuition
Whom Do I Contact: Scholarship Officer, National Technical Association, P.O. Box 27787, Washington, DC 20038, (202) 829-6100.

621

NATIONAL URBAN LEAGUE

Dart & Kraft/National Urban League Scholarship
Who Can Apply: Awarded to minorities in good scholastic standing. Applicants must be full-time undergraduate juniors pursuing bachelor's degrees in engineering, marketing, manufacturing operations, finance, or business administration at an accredited institution. Deadline April.
How Much Money Can I Get: $1,000 to $10,000
Whom Do I Contact: Director of Education, National Urban League, 500 E. 62nd Street, New York, NY 10021, (212) 310-9000.

622

NAVAL RESERVE OFFICERS TRAINING CORPS (NROTC) SCHOLARSHIP PROGRAM

Who Can Apply: Applicants must be U.S. citizens and meet age, physical, personal, and educational requirements outlined by NROTC standards.
How Much Money Can I Get: Varies
Whom Do I Contact: NROTC, Chief of Naval Education and Training, N21, 250 Dallas Street, Pensacola, FL 32508, (800) NAV-ROTC.

623

NCR FOUNDATION MINORITY SCHOLARSHIP PROGRAM

Paul Laurence Dunbar Memorial Scholarship
Who Can Apply: Students should be graduating high school seniors or enrolled in a college-level program. Applicants must be studying accounting, finance, business, computer science, engineering, or a related field.
How Much Money Can I Get: $5,000 a year up to four years
Whom Do I Contact: College Relations Manager, NCR Corporation, World Headquarters, 1700 S. Patterson Boulevard, Dayton, OH 45479, (513) 445-1337.

624

NEBRASKA STUDENT LOAN PROGRAM

Who Can Apply: Applicants must show financial need and be enrolled in an eligible school approved by NSLP. Applicants must meet other eligibility criteria; details in the NSLP application.

How Much Money Can I Get: Varies

Whom Do I Contact: NSLP, P.O. Box 82507, Lincoln, NE 68501-2507, (402) 475-8686.

625

UNIVERSITY OF NEBRASKA

Rick Davis Scholarship

Who Can Apply: This is awarded to a minority student. Student must take ACT, file FFS, and submit UNO Scholarship Application by December 1. This scholarship is three years renewable and includes room and board.

How Much Money Can I Get: Full tuition

Whom Do I Contact: University of Nebraska at Omaha, Office of Financial Aid, 60th & Dodge Street, Omaha, NE 68182, (402) 554-2327.

626

UNIVERSITY OF NEBRASKA, OMAHA

Isaacson Early Entry Tuition Grant

Who Can Apply: Omaha high school students. The award has been established to encourage ethnic minority student participation in the UNO Early Entry Program.

How Much Money Can I Get: Full tuition costs for three credit hours per semester.

Whom Do I Contact: University of Nebraska at Omaha, Office of Financial Aid, Omaha, NE 68182, (402) 554-2327.

627

NEGRO EDUCATIONAL
EMERGENCY DRIVE (NEED)

Who Can Apply: Black students attending high school in Pennsylvania and accepted at a college in that state. Geared toward the average student rather than the top achiever.

How Much Money Can I Get: $100 to $500

Whom Do I Contact: Negro Educational Emergency Drive, 2003 Law & Finance Building, 429 Fourth Avenue, Pittsburgh, PA 15219, (412) 566-2760.

628

NELLIE MAE EXCEL EDUCATION LOANS
FOR STUDENTS AND FAMILIES

Who Can Apply: Borrower can be a parent, spouse, student, or other responsible person and must be a U.S. citizen or permanent resident and live in the U.S. EXCEL loans are available to students at any accredited institution.

How Much Money Can I Get: Loan How Much Money Can I Gets of $2,000 to $20,000 a year

Whom Do I Contact: Nellie Mae, Credit Department, 50 Braintree Hill Park, Suite 300, Braintree, MA 02184, (800) 634-9308.

629

NELLIE MAE GRADEXCEL EDUCATION LOANS
FOR STUDENTS AND FAMILIES

Who Can Apply: GradEXCEL loans are for graduate and professional students, and eligibility is based on future earning potential. A student may borrow on his or her own or choose to have a co-borrower who must have a satisfactory credit history and demonstrate sufficient current income. The student or co-borrower must be a U.S. citizen or permanent resident living in the U.S.

How Much Money Can I Get: Loan amount of $2,000 to $20,000 a year

Whom Do I Contact: Nellie Mae, Credit Department, 50 Braintree Hill Park, Suite 300, Braintree, MA 02184, (800) 634-9308.

630

NELLIE MAE GRADSHARE EDUCATION LOANS
FOR STUDENTS AND FAMILIES

Who Can Apply: GradSHARE loans are for graduate and professional students and eligibility is based on future earning potential. Loans may be used at any graduate school belonging to the Consortium on Financing Higher Education (see entry 629). A student may borrow on his or her own or have a co-borrower who must have a satisfactory credit history and demonstrate sufficient current income. The student or co-borrower must be a U.S. citizen or permanent resident living in the U.S.

How Much Money Can I Get: Loan amount of $2,000 to $15,000 a year

Whom Do I Contact: Nellie Mae, Credit Department, 50 Braintree Hill Park, Suite 300, Braintree, MA 02184, (800) 634-9308.

631

NELLIE MAE SHARE EDUCATION LOANS FOR STUDENTS AND FAMILIES

Who Can Apply: Borrower can be a parent, spouse, student, or other responsible person and must be a U.S. citizen or permanent resident and live in the U.S. SHARE loans may be used at any one of the 32 colleges and universities belonging to the Consortium on Financing Higher Education (COFHE): Amherst, Barnard, Brown, Bryn Mawr, Carleton, Columbia, Cornell, Dartmouth, Duke, Georgetown, Harvard, Johns Hopkins, MIT, Mount Holyoke, Northwestern, Oberlin, Pomona, Princeton, Radcliffe, Rice, Smith, Stanford, Swarthmore, Trinity, University of Chicago, University of Pennsylvania, University of Rochester, Washington University, Wellesley, Wesleyan, Williams College, and Yale.
How Much Money Can I Get: Loan amount of $2,000 to $20,000 a year
Whom Do I Contact: Nellie Mae, Credit Department, 50 Braintree Hill Park, Suite 300, Braintree, MA 02184, (800) 634-9308.

632

NEW MEXICO INSTITUTE OF MINING AND TECHNOLOGY

Technical Community Minority Scholarship
Who Can Apply: Applicant must be a minority majoring in Technical Communications. Deadline March 1.
How Much Money Can I Get: $500
Whom Do I Contact: Financial Aid Director, New Mexico Institute of Mining and Technology, Campus Station, Box M, Socorro, NM 87801, (505) 835-5333.

633

NEW MEXICO STATE UNIVERSITY

Who Can Apply: Designated academic opportunity is available to incoming freshman women and minority students. Must be a U.S. citizen, have a 3.0 GPA and major in engineering.
How Much Money Can I Get: Varies
Whom Do I Contact: Financial Aid Director, New Mexico State University, Box 5100, Las Cruces, NM 88003, (505) 646-4105.

634

NEW MEXICO STATE UNIVERSITY

Minorities Access to Research
Who Can Apply: Awarded to undergraduates to prepare for pursuit of a Ph.D. Applicants must have 3.0 GPA and be majoring in Biology,

Chemistry, or Medicine. Deadline March 1.
How Much Money Can I Get: Varies
Whom Do I Contact: New Mexico State University, Box 30001, Department of Biology, Las Cruces, NM 88003-0001, (505) 646-2001.

635
NEW MEXICO STATE UNIVERSITY
National Action Council Award
Who Can Apply: Students must be majoring in Engineering. Award may be renewed until graduation provided the recipient maintains academic requirements. Deadline March 1.
How Much Money Can I Get: $600 to $800
Whom Do I Contact: Dean of Engineering, New Mexico State University, Box 30001, Las Cruces, NM 88003-0001, (505) 646-3547.

636
NEW MEXICO STATE UNIVERSITY
The Rockwell International Scholarship
Who Can Apply: Female or minority students of junior standing. The recipient is chosen by the company on the basis of career potential, scholastic achievement and need. The award is renewable if the recipient continues to meet the requirements. Must be majoring in one of the following engineering areas: electrical, chemical, or mechanical. Must have a 2.8 GPA. Deadline is March 1.
How Much Money Can I Get: $800
Whom Do I Contact: Dean of Engineering, New Mexico State University, Box 3Z, Las Cruces, NM 88003, (505) 646-0111.

637
NEW MEXICO STATE UNIVERSITY
The TRW Scholarship
Who Can Apply: Junior or senior minority students with a 3.0 GPA and majoring in Electrical Engineering.
How Much Money Can I Get: Varies
Whom Do I Contact: Dean of Engineering, New Mexico State University, Las Cruces, NM 88003, (505) 646-0111.

638
NEWSDAY SCHOLARSHIP COMMITTEE
FOR MINORITIES
Who Can Apply: Minority student graduating from a high school in Nassau or Suffolk County, New York. Must attend college in the United States. Deadline March 15.

How Much Money Can I Get: $5,000
Whom Do I Contact: *Newsday*, 1096 Front Street, Uniondale, NY 11747, (516) 454-2183.

639

THE NEWSPAPER FUND SCHOLARSHIP/ INTERNSHIP CONTEST

Who Can Apply: Gives minority college seniors studying journalism a paid internship at a newspaper or news service specified by the Newspaper Fund. Further, a cash award may be applied to graduate school or to repay undergraduate debt.
How Much Money Can I Get: Varies
Whom Do I Contact: The Newspaper Fund, P.O. Box 300, Princeton, NJ 08540, (609) 452-2820.

640

NEW YORK ALLIANCE OF BLACK SCHOOL EDUCATORS

Gwendolyn Calvert Baker Scholarship
Who Can Apply: Outstanding African-American high school seniors who plan to pursue a career in education.
How Much Money Can I Get: $5,000
Whom Do I Contact: Fund for Educational Excellence, c/o NYABSE, Attn.: Dr. Gwendolyn C. Baker Humanitarian Scholarship Award, P.O. Box 604, Bronx, NY 10462.

641

NEW YORK STATE DEPARTMENT OF EDUCATION

Regents Professional Opportunity Scholarship
Who Can Apply: Priority given to disadvantaged and underrepresented populations. Must be majoring in one of the following areas: chiropractic medicine, optometry, podiatry, veterinary medicine, dental hygiene, physical therapy, or medical technology. Financial need required.
How Much Money Can I Get: $1,000 to $5,000
Whom Do I Contact: Professional Opportunity Scholarship Administration, New York State Department of Education, Professional Education Testing Bureau, Cultural Education Center, Albany, NY 12230, (518) 474-6394.

642

NEW YORK UNIVERSITY

AEJ/NYU Summer Intern Program for Minorities in Journalism
Who Can Apply: This is a 10-week internship program in which students are

placed in entry-level positions at magazines, newspapers, book publishers, broadcasting stations, and corporate public relations departments. Interns work 35 hours per week and are paid minimum weekly salaries of $175 to $200. Interns participate in the two-credit course "Journalism and Minorities" and on-site visits. Housing is available on the New York University campus for a fee. Deadline December 17.

How Much Money Can I Get: Varies.

Whom Do I Contact: Institute of Afro-American Affairs, New York University, 269 Mercer Street, Suite 601, New York, NY 10003, (212) 598-7095.

643

NEW YORK UNIVERSITY

Martin Luther King, Jr., Scholarship Program

Who Can Apply: Minority or economically disadvantaged students who exemplify the ideals of Martin Luther King, Jr., and who have demonstrated significant academic excellence and achievement. Applicants should show evidence of a commitment to community service, humanitarianism, and social progress. Apply for admission by February 1, and file a financial aid form with college scholarship service by February 15.

How Much Money Can I Get: Full-tuition for four years

Whom Do I Contact: Office of Admissions, New York University, P.O. Box 909, Cooper Station, New York, NY 10276, (212) 998-4544.

644

NICHOLLS STATE UNIVERSITY

Clarence "C. J." James Memorial Minority Scholarship

Who Can Apply: First-time freshmen minority students with a 3.0 GPA and a minimum 20 ACT score.

How Much Money Can I Get: $1,000 per academic year for a maximum of four years; includes the option for regular student employment on campus worth more than $6,000 of earned income over a four-year period

Whom Do I Contact: Nicholls State University, P.O. Box 2009-NSU, Thibodaux, LA 70310, (504) 448-4929.

645

NISSAN SCHOLARSHIP PROGRAM

Who Can Apply: An innovative college scholarship program to help minority students in automotive careers. Applicants must attend universities participating in the program: Northwood University, Midland University, University of Michigan, and Xavier University, New Orleans.

How Much Money Can I Get: $10,000

Whom Do I Contact: Paul Strawhecker, Northwood University, (313) 837-4200; Clarence Jupiter, Xavier University, (504) 486-7411; or Nissan Division, Public Relations Department, P.O. Box 191, Gardena, CA 90248-0191, (310) 719-5631.

646

NORFOLK STATE UNIVERSITY

Agnes Moore Jennings Scholarship
Who Can Apply: Full-time students majoring in Elementary Education. Minimum 2.5 GPA required. Deadline is March 1.
How Much Money Can I Get: Varies
Whom Do I Contact: Norfolk State University, Admissions Office, Norfolk, VA, 23504, (804) 623-8396.

647

NORFOLK STATE UNIVERSITY

Alice Lee Sams Scholarship
Who Can Apply: Juniors with the highest GPA will be chosen. Deadline is March 1.
How Much Money Can I Get: Varies
Who Do I Contact: Norfolk State University, Admissions Office, Norfolk, VA, 23504, (804) 623-8396.

648

NORFOLK STATE UNIVERSITY

Allied Health Scholarship
Who Can Apply: Juniors with the highest GPA will be chosen. Deadline is March 1.
How Much Money Can I Get: $250 annually
Who Do I Contact: Norfolk State University, Admissions Office, Norfolk, VA, 23504, (804) 623-8396.

649

NORFOLK STATE UNIVERSITY

The Delta Sigma Theta—Chesapeake Chapter Scholarship
Who Can Apply: Local black entering students with a 3.0 GPA. This award is renewable for three years.
How Much Money Can I Get: $1,000
Whom Do I Contact: Norfolk State University, Delta Sigma Theta—Chesapeake Chapter, Norfolk, VA 23504, (804) 623-8229.

650

NORFOLK STATE UNIVERSITY
Dozoretz National Institute Minority in Science Award
Who Can Apply: Student must be majoring in one of the following:
computer science, science, or chemistry. Full tuition and a computer
awarded to minorities to increase the number of minority doctors and
scientists. This award is renewable for four years.
How Much Money Can I Get: Varies
Whom Do I Contact: Norfolk State University, Admissions Office, Norfolk,
VA 23504, (804) 623-8396.

651

NORTH CAROLINA CENTRAL UNIVERSITY
National Alumni Scholarship
Who Can Apply: Though the majority of the National Alumni Scholarship
awards made annually will be to incoming freshman students, applications are
acceptable from any student regardless of classification or academic interest. All
alumni scholars are required to carry a full class load. The deadline for receiving
all application materials is March 15th. Notices of initial awards will be made
by April 15th of each year.
How Much Money Can I Get: Varies
Whom Do I Contact: North Carolina Central University c/o Scholarships
and Student Aid Office P.O. Box 19496, Durham, NC 27707, (919) 530-
6180.

652

NORTH CAROLINA CENTRAL UNIVERSITY
North Carolina Central University Scholarship
Who Can Apply: Open to all students
How Much Money Can I Get: Tuition
Whom Do I Contact: North Carolina Central University c/o Scholarships
and Student Aid Office P.O. Box 19496, Durham, NC 27707, (919) 530-
6180.

653

NORTH CAROLINA COMMUNITY COLLEGE
SCHOLARSHIP PROGRAM
Who Can Apply: Each school selects its own recipients from applicants.
Student must be a North Carolina resident enrolled at least part-time at one
of the 58 institutions in the community college system. Financial need
required. Minority students enrolled in college transferable curriculum
programs, persons seeking new job skills, women in nontraditional curricula,

and students who participated in an ABE, GED, or H.S. diploma program are eligible.
How Much Money Can I Get: $400
Whom Do I Contact: Scholarship Administrator, Department of Community Colleges, 177 Education Building, Raleigh, NC 27603, (919) 733-3652.

654

NORTH CAROLINA STATE
EDUCATION ASSISTANCE AUTHORITY
Who Can Apply: Dental and medical students from economically disadvantaged backgrounds are eligible for the Board of Governors (University of North Carolina) awards. Candidates must be North Carolina residents and attend a North Carolina medical or dental school.
How Much Money Can I Get: $5,000 plus tuition and fees
Whom Do I Contact: North Carolina State Education Assistance Authority, P.O. Box 2688, Chapel Hill, NC 27515-2688, (919) 549-8614.

655

UNIVERSITY OF NORTH CAROLINA
Alexander Morisey Minority Scholarship
Who Can Apply: Entering freshmen majoring in journalism.
How Much Money Can I Get: $1,000, two awards
Whom Do I Contact: University of North Carolina, School of Journalism & Mass Communications, CB 3365 Howell Hall, Chapel Hill, NC 27599-3365.

656

UNIVERSITY OF NORTH CAROLINA
Board of Governors' Medical Scholarship
Who Can Apply: Student must be nominated by the medical school and plan to practice in North Carolina. Financial need is required.
How Much Money Can I Get: $5,000 +
Whom Do I Contact: Financial Aid Office, University of North Carolina, 300 Vance Hall, 057A, Chapel Hill, NC 27599, (919) 962-8396.

657

UNIVERSITY OF NORTH CAROLINA
AT CHAPEL HILL
Pogue Scholarship
Who Can Apply: Outstanding students in the state of North Carolina. Special emphasis is given to minority applicants while considering students from all ethnic backgrounds. Applicants must demonstrate and value academic achievement, have strong leadership potential, eagerly identify

ways to implement positive change, show commitment to local community, display maturity and wisdom, and submit one letter of recommendation.
How Much Money Can I Get: $6,750 per year to students from North Carolina, renewable for three years
Whom Do I Contact: The Office of Undergraduate Admission, University of North Carolina at Chapel Hill, Monogram Building, CB 2200, Chapel Hill, NC 27599-2200, (919) 966-3621.

658
UNIVERSITY OF NORTH FLORIDA
The Clayton Hawkins Scholarship
Who Can Apply: Entering black freshman on the basis of outstanding academic and leadership achievement. Must be in the upper fifth percent of class.
How Much Money Can I Get: $1,000
Whom Do I Contact: University of North Florida, 4567 St. Johns Bluff Road, South Jacksonville, FL 32216, (904) 646-2604.

659
UNIVERSITY OF NORTH FLORIDA
The Eartha M. M. White Scholarship
Who Can Apply: The top entering black students who have a minimum 3.0 GPA and rank in the top 15 percent of their high school class. Students who have a minimum 1000 SAT score (23 ACT) and have a 3.0 GPA are encouraged to apply. Applicants must submit at least one letter of recommendation from a teacher or counselor and a one-page essay explaining why they want a college education. Deadline March 1.
How Much Money Can I Get: $1,000
Whom Do I Contact: University of North Florida, Attn.: Scholarship Coordinator, 4567 Street Johns Bluff Road, South Jacksonville, FL 32216, (904) 646-2604.

660
NORTHEASTERN UNIVERSITY
Minority Engineering Education Effort
Who Can Apply: Must be majoring in one of the following engineering areas: chemical, electrical, mechanical, civil, or industrial. Financial need required. Deadline May 1.
How Much Money Can I Get: $250 to $2,500
Whom Do I Contact: Financial Aid Director, Northeastern University, 360 Huntington Avenue, Boston, MA 02115, (617) 437-2200.

661

NORTHEASTERN UNIVERSITY

The Ralph J. Bunche Scholarship

Who Can Apply: Eligibility is based on academic achievement as determined by the applicant's high school record, class rank, college board examination scores, and letters of recommendation from guidance counselors and teachers.

How Much Money Can I Get: Scholarship is awarded for five years and totals full tuition for the first year and half tuition for the remaining four years.

Whom Do I Contact: Northeastern University, 360 Huntington Avenue, Boston, MA 02115, (617) 437-2200.

662

NORTHEASTERN STATE UNIVERSITY

W. W. Keeler Scholarship

Who Can Apply: Junior year minority students are nominated by the university's faculty and employees. Selection is based on academic achievement. Selected students get summer employment opportunities with Phillips Petroleum Company. Applicants must have a 3.0 GPA and be majoring in accounting, journalism, marketing/sales/retailing, or science.

How Much Money Can I Get: Award is $500 for the junior year and $750 for the senior year if satisfactory academic progress in maintained

Whom Do I Contact: Dean of Student Affairs, Northeastern State University, Tahlequah, OK 74464, (918) 456-5511.

663

NORTHERN VIRGINIA BRANCH WASHINGTON URBAN LEAGUE, ESSAY

Who Can Apply: This essay contest is open to residents of the northern Virginia area. Participants must be entering college freshmen who will be attending an accredited institution of higher learning in the fall following high school graduation. Awards are payable to the school. Essays must be between 500 and 1,000 words; be typewritten and double-spaced or legibly handwritten; be accompanied by entry blank, letter of acceptance from the college or university, high school transcript, and activity form. Essays will be judged for content, originality, organization, style, grammar, spelling, and neatness. Academic standing is also given consideration. Contact the below address for the assigned topic and additional information.

How Much Money Can I Get: $1,000

Whom Do I Contact: Deputy Director, Northern Virginia Branch, Washington Urban League, Inc., 901 N. Washington Street, #202, Alexandria, VA 22314.

664

NORTHSIDE ASSOCIATION FOR EDUCATIONAL ADVANCEMENT SCHOLARSHIP

Who Can Apply: While no requirement is made regarding major or career plans, it is expected that the applicants will be goal directed and able to discuss their goals during the interview portion of the requirements. These awards are for minority students in Kalamazoo County schools. They are automatically renewed annually if the recipient maintains grades. Contact the high school guidance/counseling office for more information. Must have a 2.0 GPA and financial need. Deadline April 15.

How Much Money Can I Get: $1,300

Whom Do I Contact: Local High School Counselors, Northside Association for Educational Advancement, Kalamazoo, MI 49008, (616) 775-0960.

665

NORTHWEST MISSOURI STATE UNIVERSITY

Martin Luther King, Jr., Scholarship

Who Can Apply: Full-time minority students who have a 3.25 GPA.

How Much Money Can I Get: Varies

Whom Do I Contact: Northwest Missouri State University, Attn.: Scholarship Committee, 800 University Drive, Maryville, MO 64468-6001, (800) 633-1175.

666

NORTHWEST MISSOURI STATE UNIVERSITY

Minority Achievement Scholarship

Who Can Apply: Awarded to minority student with a 2.0 GPA, in the upper two-fifths of their class, and a 21 ACT score. Deadline May 1.

How Much Money Can I Get: $1,000 to $1,250

Whom Do I Contact: Northwest Missouri State University, Attn.: Scholarship Committee, 800 University Drive, Maryville, MO 64468-6001, (800) 633-1175.

667

NORTHWEST MISSOURI STATE UNIVERSITY

Minority Transfer Scholarship

Who Can Apply: Awarded to a full-time minority transfer student with a 2.7 GPA.

How Much Money Can I Get: $1,000 to $1,250

Whom Do I Contact: Northwest Missouri State University, Attn.: Scholarship Committee, 800 University Drive, Maryville, MO 64468-6001, (800) 633-1175.

668

NORTHWOOD INSTITUTE

Chrysler Corporation Minority Scholarship

Who Can Apply: Applicants must be majoring in Automotive Industry, have a 3.0 GPA, and show financial need. Relatives of dealers/employees of Chrysler are ineligible.

How Much Money Can I Get: $5,000

Whom Do I Contact: Private Donor Scholarship Office, Northwood Institute, 3225 Cook Road, Midland, MI 48640-2398, (517) 832-4279.

669

UNIVERSITY OF NOTRE DAME

Who Can Apply: Available scholarships include the Martin Luther King Scholarship Program to assist minority students in financial need.

How Much Money Can I Get: $500 to $1,900

Whom Do I Contact: Office of Admissions, University of Notre Dame, Notre Dame, IN 46556, (219) 239-6011.

670

NOVA UNIVERSITY

Nova College Honors Award

Who Can Apply: For day program freshmen with combined 1000 SAT score (22 ACT) and transfer and minority students with a 3.0 GPA and 15 or more semester credits from a regionally accredited institution.

How Much Money Can I Get: Varies

Whom Do I Contact: Financial Planning Counselor, Nova University, 3301 College Avenue, Ft. Lauderdale, FL 33314, (305) 475-7411.

671

NOVA UNIVERSITY

The School of Psychology Scholarship

Who Can Apply: New, continuing and minority M.S., Ph.D., Psy.D. levels with financial need and minimum 3.0 GPA.

How Much Money Can I Get: $1,500 to $2,000

Whom Do I Contact: Financial Planning Counselor, Nova University, 3301 College Avenue, Ft. Lauderdale, FL 33314, (305) 475-7411.

672

NURSES' EDUCATIONAL FUND

The Estelle Massey Osborne Scholarship and the M. Elizabeth Carnegie Scholarship.

Who Can Apply: Black registered nurses pursuing a master's or doctoral

degree program, must attend a National League for Nursing program, and must be a member of a professional nursing program. Deadline February.
How Much Money Can I Get: $2,500 to $10,000
Whom Do I Contact: Nurses' Educational Fund, 555 W. 57 Street, New York, NY 10019, (212) 582-8820.

673

NYACK COLLEGE
The Tom Skinner Associates Scholarship
Who Can Apply: Black entering freshmen who have a 3.0 GPA and financial need. Deadline March 1.
How Much Money Can I Get: Varies
Whom Do I Contact: Nyack College, South Boulevard, Nyack, NY 10960, (914) 358-1710.

674

OAK RIDGE ASSOCIATED UNIVERSITIES
Historically Black Colleges and Universities Nuclear Energy Training Program for Undergraduates
Who Can Apply:. Applicants must be undergraduate students seeking degrees in nuclear energy-related areas at designated historically black colleges and universities. Applicants must be either U.S. citizens or permanent residents. Deadline February.
How Much Money Can I Get: $6,000+ per year
Whom Do I Contact: Oak Ridge Associated Universities, P.O. Box 117, Oak Ridge, TN 37831-0117, (615) 576-3428.

675

OAKWOOD COLLEGE
Who Can Apply: Must be a black entering freshman and have a strong academic background. Apply early.
How Much Money Can I Get: $1,000 to $2,000
Whom Do I Contact: Oakwood College, Huntsville, AL 35896, (205) 837-1630.

676

OHIO NORTHERN UNIVERSITY
Minority Engineering Scholarship
Who Can Apply: Minority students majoring in one of the following engineering areas: civil, mechanical, or electrical. Deadline August 21.
How Much Money Can I Get: $500 to $2,500
Whom Do I Contact: Financial Aid Director, Ohio Northern University, Ada, OH 45810, (419) 772-2272.

677
OHIO STATE UNIVERSITY GRADUATE SCHOOL
Who Can Apply: One-year and multiple-year competitive fellowships to minority students just beginning graduate work at Ohio State. Deadline February 1.
How Much Money Can I Get: $11,400 stipend (12 months) and fee authorization
Whom Do I Contact: Dean of the Graduate School, Ohio State University, 230 North Oval Mall, 250 University Hall, Columbus, OH 43210, (614)292-6031.

678
OHIO UNIVERSITY
Opportunity Scholarship
Who Can Apply: Underrepresented students enrolling in communication systems management, interpersonal communication, journalism, telecommunications, or visual communications are eligible for the renewable awards. Deadline April.
How Much Money Can I Get: $1,000
Whom Do I Contact: Ohio University, School of Journalism, Scripps Hall, Athens, OH 45701, (613) 593-2590.

679
OKLAHOMA STATE UNIVERSITY
Who Can Apply: Minority U.S. citizens are eligible for awards if they have the minimum ACT composite score required for admission and a 3.0 GPA or better on a six- or seven-semester transcript. Minority applicants who meet the criteria described for other scholarships will qualify for the highest award.
How Much Money Can I Get: $725
Whom Do I Contact: University Scholarship Director, Oklahoma State University, Hanner/Whitehurst Hall, Student Union, Stillwater, OK 74078, (405) 744-7541.

680
UNIVERSITY OF OKLAHOMA
Graduate Assistantship
Who Can Apply: Awards are from the College of Arts and Sciences Office of Minority Participation. Applicants must be U.S. citizens, hold a bachelor's or master's degree, and must show strong promise of successfully completing a graduate degree program, and be leading to a master's or doctoral degree in the humanities, social sciences, mathematical, physical, or biological sciences, library and information sciences, social work, or history and

philosophy of science. Deadline April.
How Much Money Can I Get: $7,500 to $12,000
Whom Do I Contact: Assistant Dean, College of Arts and Sciences, Room 110C, University of Oklahoma, Norman, OK 73019-0315, (800) 522-0772 in state, (800) 523-7363 out of state.

681

UNIVERSITY OF OKLAHOMA
Minority Achievement Award
Who Can Apply: Entering minority students on the basis of grades, test scores, activities, and leadership skills. Must have a 3.0 GPA.
How Much Money Can I Get: $750
Whom Do I Contact: Financial Aid Director, University of Oklahoma, 731 Elm, Robertson AKK, Norman, OK 73019, (405) 325-2151.

682

OLD DOMINION UNIVERSITY
Alfred B. Rollins, Jr., Scholarship
Who Can Apply: Recipient will be a minority student who is a rising senior with financial need and a 2.5 GPA.
How Much Money Can I Get: $1,000
Whom Do I Contact: Mary Schultz, Office of Student Financial Aid, Old Dominion University, 121 Rollins Hall, Norfolk, VA 23529, (804) 683-3683.

683

OLD DOMINION UNIVERSITY
The Edgar and Kathleen Kovner Scholarship Award
Who Can Apply: Scholarships are based on the student's potential to successfully complete the requirements for a bachelor's degree. All recipients must be full-time students and may be entering freshmen, transfer, or continuing undergraduates. Must be majoring in Engineering or Technology.
How Much Money Can I Get: $500
Whom Do I Contact: Mary Schultz, Office of Student Financial Aid, Old Dominion University, 121 Rollins Hall, Norfolk, VA 23529, (804) 683-3683.

684

OLD DOMINION UNIVERSITY
The Herman E. Valentine Scholarship
Who Can Apply: Qualified recipients must be black graduate students, preferably attending ODU part-time. A minimum of three scholarships is to

be awarded for those majoring in Business Administration/Management, Computer Science, and/or Data Processing and Engineering, for two semesters at six credit hours each semester.
How Much Money Can I Get: Up to $5,000
Whom Do I Contact: Mary Schultz, Office of Student Financial Aid, Old Dominion University, 121 Rollins Hall, Norfolk, VA 23529, (804) 683-3683.

685

OLD DOMINION UNIVERSITY
Holland Dunston Ellis, Jr. Memorial Scholarship
Who Can Apply: Awarded to a minority student who resides in Virginia.
How Much Money Can I Get: Varies
Whom Do I Contact: Old Dominion University, Office of Student Financial Aid, 121 Rollins Hall, Norfolk, VA 23529-0052, (804) 683-3683.

686

OLD DOMINION UNIVERSITY
The Martin Luther King, Jr., Scholarship
Who Can Apply: Open to black student majoring in Engineering, Accounting, or Technology. Financial need is required. Applicants must have completed at least 60 credit hours.
How Much Money Can I Get: $1,000
Whom Do I Contact: Mary Schultz, Office of Student Financial Aid, Old Dominion University, 121 Rollins Hall, Norfolk, VA 23529, (804) 683-3683.

687

OLD DOMINION UNIVERSITY
Special Minority Part-Time Tuition Grant
Who Can Apply: Minority students enrolled in graduate programs for the first time. Grants cover part-time tuition.
How Much Money Can I Get: Part-time tuition
Whom Do I Contact: Mary Schultz, Office of Student Financial Aid, Old Dominion University, 121 Rollins Hall, Norfolk, VA 23529, (804) 683-3683.

688

OLD DOMINION UNIVERSITY
Vice Admiral Samuel L. Gravely Scholarship
Who Can Apply: Entering black students active in ROTC. The recipient will participate in the Hampton Roads NROTC program at ODU but will not

receive a NROTC scholarship for the award year.

How Much Money Can I Get: Varies

Whom Do I Contact: Mary Schultz, Office of Student Financial Aid, Old Dominion University, 121 Rollins Hall, Norfolk, VA 23529, (804) 683-3683.

689

OMEGA PSI PHI FRATERNITY, INC.

Who Can Apply: The chapters nominate a district scholar who is a college senior with at least a 3.0 GPA. The winner receives a matching dollar amount from the Drew Commission. Applicants must be an active member of Omega Psi Phi and demonstrate financial need.

How Much Money Can I Get: Up to $500

Whom Do I Contact: Omega Psi Phi Fraternity, Inc., International Headquarters, 2714 Georgia Avenue, NW, Washington, DC 20001, (202) 667-7158.

690

OMEGA PSI PHI FRATERNITY, INC.

The Creative and Research Fellowship

Who Can Apply: The scholarship is awarded to scholars and creative artists who need financial assistance to complete a work that is already in progress or to publish a manuscript of study that has been completed. This is for black males who have completed their sophomore year majoring in one of the following: humanities, natural sciences, education, physical science, or social science. Must be an active Omega Psi Phi member.

How Much Money Can I Get: $1,000

Whom Do I Contact: Omega Psi Phi Fraternity, Inc., International Headquarters, 2714 Georgia Avenue, NW, Washington, DC 20001, (202) 667-7158.

691

OMEGA PSI PHI FRATERNITY, INC.

Founders' Memorial Scholarship

Who Can Apply: Applicants must be active in the Omega Psi Phi Fraternity, have a 3.0 GPA, and show financial need. Extracurricular activities and community/campus involvement required. Award is not available to freshmen, but this information may be used for planning purposes.

How Much Money Can I Get: $300

Whom Do I Contact: Omega Psi Phi Fraternity, Inc., International Headquarters, 2714 Georgia Avenue, NW, Washington, DC 20001, (202) 667-7158.

692

OMEGA PSI PHI FRATERNITY, INC.

The Graduate and Undergraduate Scholarship Grant
Who Can Apply: Black males active in Omega Psi Phi. Deadlines for undergraduate applications are October 15 and May 15 annually. Deadline for graduate application is May 15 annually.
How Much Money Can I Get: $500
Whom Do I Contact: Omega Psi Phi Fraternity, Inc., International Headquarters, 2714 Georgia Avenue, NW, Washington, DC 20001, (202) 667-7158.

693

OMEGA PSI PHI DADE COUNTY BLACK MALE AWARD

Who Can Apply: Awarded to a black male student entering college with a 2.7 GPA. Applicant must be a resident of Dade County, Florida, and must be nominated by a fraternity member. Deadline February 2.
How Much Money Can I Get: $1,000
Whom Do I Contact: Omega Psi Phi Fraternity, Inc., Attn.: Scholarship Chairman, 13121 NW 18th Avenue, Miami, FL 33167.

694

OMEGA WIVES SCHOLARSHIP

Who Can Apply: Applicants must be black females who are William Penn High seniors and who have maintained an 80 percent average in grades 10-12. A transcript must accompany application. Applicants must have participated in school- and/or community-related activities and be accepted by an accredited school of higher learning. Contact your high school guidance counselor for further information and an application form.
How Much Money Can I Get: Varies
Whom Do I Contact: William Penn High School, Broad and Master Streets, Philadelphia, PA 19122.

695

OTTERBEIN COLLEGE

Ammons-Thomas Minority Scholarship
Who Can Apply: Awarded to a minority student with a 2.5 GPA and in the upper three-fifths of his or her class. Applicant must be a U.S. citizen. Deadline May 1.
How Much Money Can I Get: $1,500
Whom Do I Contact: Otterbein College, Attn.: Financial Aid Director, West College Avenue and Grove Street, Westerville, OH 43081, (614) 823-1500.

696
UNIVERSITY OF THE PACIFIC
Who Can Apply: Must be majoring in one of the following engineering areas: civil, mechanical, computer, electrical, systems, or physics. Financial need required.
How Much Money Can I Get: $250 to $2,500
Whom Do I Contact: Financial Aid Director, University of the Pacific, Stockton, CA 95211, (209) 946-3091.

697
PACIFIC GAS & ELECTRIC COMPANY
Who Can Apply: There are two awards for $1,000 a year for four years and four one-time awards for $1,000. The applicant must be a deserving minority high school senior who has advanced despite economic, cultural, or motivational disadvantages. The applicant must reside or attend school in the Pacific Gas & Electric Company service area. Applications may be obtained from high school guidance counselors. Deadline November 15.
Whom Do I Contact: Pacific Gas & Electric Company, 77 Beale Street, Room F-1500, San Francisco, CA 94106, (415) 972-1338.

698
PATRICIA ROBERTS HARRIS FELLOWSHIP
Who Can Apply: Must plan a career in agricultural education. Must be a minority student with a 3.2 GPA. Financial need required.
How Much Money Can I Get: $8,000
Whom Do I Contact: Chair, Agriculture Education Department, Iowa State University, 201 Curtiss Hall, Ames, IA 50011, (515) 294-0241.

699
PEIRCE JUNIOR COLLEGE
ARA Services Scholarship
Who Can Apply: Second-year minority student majoring in a discipline that would be employable at ARA, Inc. Must have a 3.0 GPA. Awards are based primarily on academic achievement and contribution to Peirce Junior College. Deadline end of spring semester.
How Much Money Can I Get: Varies
Whom Do I Contact: Financial Aid Director, Peirce Junior College, 1420 Pine Street, Philadelphia, PA 19102, (215) 545-6400.

700
UNIVERSITY OF PENNSYLVANIA
Gloria Twine Chisum Scholarship
Who Can Apply: Black full-time students majoring in social work who

shows need and merit.
How Much Money Can I Get: $2,000
Whom Do I Contact: University of Pennsylvania, Attn.: School of Social Work, Admissions Office, 3701 Locust Walk, Philadelphia, PA 19104-6214, (215) 898-5539.

701

UNIVERSITY OF PENNSYLVANIA
Louise P. Shoemaker Award
Who Can Apply: Full-time minority students majoring in social work.
How Much Money Can I Get: $2,000
Whom Do I Contact: University of Pennsylvania, Attn.: School of Social Work, Admissions Office, 3701 Locust Walk, Philadelphia, PA 19104-6214, (215) 898-5539.

702

UNIVERSITY OF PENNSYLVANIA
Minority Scholarship Fund
Who Can Apply: Awarded to full-time minority students who are majoring in social work and who show need and merit.
How Much Money Can I Get: $1,000 to $8,000
Whom Do I Contact: University of Pennsylvania, Attn.: School of Social Work, Admissions Office, 3701 Locust Walk, Philadelphia, PA 19104-6214, (215) 898-5539.

703

PEPPERDINE UNIVERSITY
The Earl D. Baker-Scripps-Howard Scholarship
Who Can Apply: Minority students planning a career in journalism. Deadline May 1.
How Much Money Can I Get: $1,000
Whom Do I Contact: Pepperdine University, Division of Communications, 24255 Pacific Coast Highway, Malibu, CA 90263, (213) 456-4211.

704

PEPPERDINE UNIVERSITY
Getty Scholarship
Who Can Apply: Black students preparing for elementary education positions in predominantly minority schools.
How Much Money Can I Get: Varies
Whom Do I Contact: Office of Admissions, Pepperdine University, Los Angeles, CA 90044, (213) 456-4391.

705

PHI BETA SIGMA FRATERNITY

Who Can Apply: Scholarships, employment referrals, and other programs are available to college-bound black high school students.
How Much Money Can I Get: Varies
Whom Do I Contact: Phi Beta Sigma Fraternity, Inc., 1327 R Street, NW, Washington, DC 20011, (202) 726-5434.

706

PHI DELTA KAPPA

Who Can Apply: Scholarships available to minority high school seniors who are planning a career in teaching. Deadline January 31.
How Much Money Can I Get: Varies
Whom Do I Contact: Howard D. Hill, Director of Chapter Programs, Phi Delta Kappa, P.O. Box 789, Bloomington, IN 47402-0789, (812) 339-1156.

707

PHILANDER SMITH COLLEGE

Athletic Grant
Who Can Apply: Selected participants on intercollegiate athletic teams.
How Much Money Can I Get: Varies
Whom Do I Contact: Philander Smith College Financial Aid Office, One Trudie Kibbe Reed Drive, Little Rock, AR 72202, (501) 370-5350.

708

PHILANDER SMITH COLLEGE

Collegiate Choir Scholarship
Who Can Apply: Members of the collegiate choir.
How Much Money Can I Get: Varies
Whom Do I Contact: Philander Smith College Financial Aid Office, One Trudie Kibbe Reed Drive, Little Rock, AR 72202, (501) 370-5350.

709

PHILANDER SMITH COLLEGE

Honors Scholarship
Who Can Apply: Entering freshmen with high SAT scores and honors-level high school grade point averages.
How Much Money Can I Get: $8,000 per year.
Whom Do I Contact: Philander Smith College Financial Aid Office, One Trudie Kibbe Reed Drive, Little Rock, AR 72202, (501) 370-5350.

710

PHILANDER SMITH COLLEGE
Institutional Scholarship
W ho Can Apply: New and continuing Philander Smith students are eligible. Award is based on financial need and academic performance.
How Much Money Can I Get: Tuition
Whom Do I Contact: Philander Smith College Financial Aid Office, One Trudie Kibbe Reed Drive, Little Rock, AR 72202, (501) 370-5350.

711

PINE MANOR COLLEGE
The Massachusetts Minority Scholarship
Who Can Apply: Minority residents of Massachusetts on the basis of academic ability and record, commitment to a liberal arts education, recommendations from three adults, and a personal interview with one or more faculty members at the college. The award provides full tuition. Deadline March 1.
How Much Money Can I Get: Varies
Whom Do I Contact: Financial Aid Director, Pine Manor College, 400 Heath Street, Chestnut Hill, MA 02107, (617) 731-7000.

712

UNIVERSITY OF PITTSBURGH
The Challenge Scholarship
Who Can Apply: Black students on basis of high school academics/entrance exams. Applicants must be in the upper two-fifths of their class, have a minimum 3.0 GPA, and show financial need. Must be majoring in liberal arts or humanities.
How Much Money Can I Get: $1,000 to $4,000
Whom Do I Contact: University of Pittsburgh, Financial Aid Office, Third Floor, Bruce Hall, Pittsburgh, PA 15260, (412) 624-7488.

713

UNIVERSITY OF PITTSBURGH
General Studies Grants
Who Can Apply: Minority and disadvantaged students entering the School of General Studies.
How Much Money Can I Get: Maximum cost of tuition
Whom Do I Contact: Office of Admissions, University of Pittsburgh, Pittsburgh, PA 15260-0001, (412) 624-4141.

714

UNIVERSITY OF PITTSBURGH

Mellon Grant for NSSFMS Students
Who Can Apply: Students who have already received aid from the National Scholarship Service and Fund for Minority Students.
How Much Money Can I Get: Varies
Whom Do I Contact: Office of Admissions, University of Pittsburgh, Pittsburgh, PA 15260-0001, (412) 624-4141.

715

PORTLAND STATE UNIVERSITY

The Martin Luther King, Jr., Scholarship Fund of Oregon
Who Can Apply: Minority students with high grade point averages studying at any Oregon college.
How Much Money Can I Get: Varies
Whom Do I Contact: Martin Luther King, Jr., Scholarship Fund of Oregon, Portland State University, P.O. Box 751, Portland, OR 97207.

716

UNIVERSITY OF PORTLAND

King-Kennedy Scholarship
Who Can Apply: Minority students.
How Much Money Can I Get: Varies
Whom Do I Contact: Office of Admissions, University of Portland, 5000 N. Willamette Boulevard, Portland, OR 97203-5798, (503) 283-7911.

717

POTOMAC VALLEY ALUMNAE CHAPTER

Alum-Delta Sigma Theta Scholarship
Who Can Apply: This is for an entering black student demonstrating financial need. This scholarship is renewable for four years. Students may be recommended by their high school. Deadline March 31.
How Much Money Can I Get: $2,000
Whom Do I Contact: Potomac Valley Alumnae Chapter, Delta Sigma Theta Sorority, Inc., Attn.: Scholarship Committee, 9913 Sorrel Avenue, Potomac, MD 20854, (301) 299-8011.

718

PROFESSIONAL OPPORTUNITY SCHOLARSHIP

Who Can Apply: Applicants must have completed undergraduate work with assistance from HEOP, EOP SEEK, or College Discovery Opportunity

Program. Must major in physical therapy. Financial need required. Deadline June 1.
How Much Money Can I Get: Up to $5,000
Whom Do I Contact: State Education Department, Cultural Education Center, Empire State Plaza, Albany, NY 12230.

719

PROVIDENCE COLLEGE
The Martin de Porres Scholarship
Who Can Apply: Qualified minority applicants who demonstrate outstanding academic achievement.
How Much Money Can I Get: Tuition, room and board, renewable
Whom Do I Contact: Providence College, 549 River Avenue, Providence, RI 02918-0001, (401) 456-8234.

720

PROVIDENCE COLLEGE
The Martin Luther King Scholarship
Who Can Apply: Qualified undergraduate minority students on the basis of need and academic potential.
How Much Money Can I Get: Varies
Whom Do I Contact: Dr. Stephen J. Mecca, Director, Martin Luther King Program, Providence College, 549 River Avenue, Providence, RI 02918-0001, (401) 865-2164.

721

PROVIDENCE COLLEGE
The Mary J. Benson Scholarship
Who Can Apply: Deserving black students who can show financial need.
How Much Money Can I Get: Varies
Whom Do I Contact: Financial Aid Director, Providence College, Providence, RI 02918-0001, (401) 865-2286.

722

PURDUE UNIVERSITY
Merit Award for Minorities
Who Can Apply: Freshmen admitted to the school of engineering and have a strong academic background, particularly in math and science.
How Much Money Can I Get: Varies
Whom Do I Contact: Office of Admissions, Purdue University, West Lafayette, IN 47907, (317) 749-2681.

723

QUEENS COLLEGE

Outstanding Minority Award
Who Can Apply: Awarded to minority students attending Queens College.
Deadline February 1.
How Much Money Can I Get: Varies
Whom Do I Contact: Queens College, Attn.: Director of Scholarships, 1900
Selwyn Avenue, Charlotte, NC 28774, (704) 337-2225.

724

QUINNIPIAC COLLEGE

Minority Scholarship
Who Can Apply: Minority students who indicate unusual potential are
eligible for this award. This award is renewable with a 2.5 GPA. Deadline
March 1.
How Much Money Can I Get: $3,500
Whom Do I Contact: Financial Aid Director, Quinnipiac College, Mount
Carmel Avenue, Hamden, CT 06518-0569, (203) 281-8750.

725

RACINE ENVIRONMENT COMMITTEE
EDUCATIONAL ASSISTANCE PROGRAM

Who Can Apply: Minority group members and low-income youths who are
residents of Racine and/or graduates of a local high school.
How Much Money Can I Get: $100 to $1,000
Whom Do I Contact: Racine Environment Committee Educational Fund,
316 Fifth Street, Racine, WI 53403, (414) 637-8893.

726

RACINE ENVIRONMENT COMMITTEE
EDUCATIONAL FUND

Who Can Apply: Award is given to a minority and low-income student from
Racine. Must have a 2.0 GPA. Financial need required. Deadline June 30.
How Much Money Can I Get: $1,200
Whom Do I Contact: Scholarship Officer, Racine Environment Committee,
310 Fifth Street, Room 101, Racine, WI 53403, (414) 631-5600.

727

RANDOLPH-MACON COLLEGE

Who Can Apply: Offers scholarships ranging from $5,000 to full tuition to
outstanding entering black freshman and transfer students. Scholarships,
awarded without regard to need, are renewable annually as long as the
student maintains the required academic average. Superior academic

performance, evidence of strong leadership qualities, and general merit are among the criteria. Recipients may participate in the Honors Program, which features special topic courses, students and faculty support groups, organized trips, and exclusive use of Pannill (Honors) House.

Whom Do I Contact: Office of Admissions, Randolph-Macon College, Ashland, VA 23005, (804) 846-7392.

728

RANDOLPH-MACON WOMAN'S COLLEGE
M. Landis Minority Scholarship

Who Can Apply: Incoming freshmen minority student on the basis of academic record and personal qualities. The award is renewable each year based on committee review. No application is required.

How Much Money Can I Get: $2,500

Whom Do I Contact: Financial Aid Director, Randolph Macon Woman's College, Lynchburg, VA 24503, (804) 846-7392.

729

RANDOLPH-MACON WOMAN'S COLLEGE
The Robert A. and Martha Crocker Spivey Scholarship

Who Can Apply: Entering minority students who are deserving by virtue of academic record and personal qualities. The award is renewable based on committee review. No application is required.

How Much Money Can I Get: $2,500

Whom Do I Contact: Financial Aid Director, Randolph-Macon Woman's College, Lynchburg, VA 24503, (804) 846-7392.

730

REFORMED CHURCH OF AMERICA
Minority Education Fund

Who Can Apply: Minority students admitted to college and RCA members. Financial need required. Deadline May 15.

How Much Money Can I Get: Varies

Whom Do I Contact: Reformed Church of America, Office of Human Resources, 475 Riverside Drive, Room 1819, New York, NY 10027, (212) 870-3071.

731

REGISTERED NURSE FELLOWSHIP PROGRAM FOR ETHNIC/RACIAL MINORITIES

Who Can Apply: Fellowship program is for careers in behavioral science research. Applicants must be American citizens or permanent residents. Deadline January 15.

Whom Do I Contact: Director, American Nurses Association, Minority Fellowship Programs, 1030 15th Street, NW, Suite 716, Washington, DC 20005, (202) 789-1334.

732

RENSSELAER POLYTECHNIC INSTITUTE
International Paper Scholarship for Minorities
Who Can Apply: Freshmen minority or female students each year for up to four years who maintain a satisfactory grade point average.
How Much Money Can I Get: $2,500 a year
Whom Do I Contact: Rensselaer Polytechnic Institute, Office of Minority Student Affairs, Troy, NY 12180-3590, (518) 276-6531.

733

RHODES COLLEGE
The National Achievement Scholarship
Who Can Apply: Entering freshmen who are finalists in the National Achievement Scholarship program for outstanding Negro students, who have indicated Rhodes College as their first choice college, and who have not been selected as winners of other National Achievement Scholarships.
How Much Money Can I Get: $500 to $2,000 dependent upon financial need
Whom Do I Contact: Rhodes College, 2000 North Parkway, Memphis, TN 38112, (901) 274-1800.

734

RICE UNIVERSITY
Rice Minority Scholarship Program
Who Can Apply: Minority students seeking enrollment at Rice University are eligible. Applicants must exhibit outstanding qualifications and ability academically and non-academically. Deadline January 15.
How Much Money Can I Get: Varies
Whom Do I Contact: Ron Moss, Director of Admissions, Rice University, P.O. Box 1892, Houston, TX 77251, (800) 527-6957.

735

RIDER COLLEGE
Who Can Apply: Offers full-tuition minority scholarships. Up to 25 scholarships are given each year to students who demonstrate academic excellence as evidenced by grades, strength of academic program, SAT scores, and rank in class.
Whom Do I Contact: Barry Taylor, Assistant Director of Admissions, 2083 Lawrenceville Road, Lawrenceville, NJ 08648-3099, (609) 896-5041.

736

RIDER COLLEGE
Minority Transfer Scholarship Program
Who Can Apply: Awarded to minority transfer students based on interview, essay, academic record, and motivation. Deadline August 1.
How Much Money Can I Get: Varies
Whom Do I Contact: Rider College, Attn.: Office of Admissions and Financial Aid, 2083 Lawrenceville Road, Lawrenceville, NJ 08648-3099, (609) 896-5041.

737

ROANOKE-CHOWAN COMMUNITY COLLEGE
The Intern Program
Who Can Apply: Black sophomores with a GPA of 2.0. Financial need is required.
How Much Money Can I Get: $100
Whom Do I Contact: Roanoke-Chowan Community College, Route 2, Box 46-A, Ahoskie, NC 27910, (919) 332-5921.

738

ROBERT WOOD JOHNSON FOUNDATION
Who Can Apply: The foundation funds will be used for need-based scholarships to first- and second-year medical students.
How Much Money Can I Get: $1,000 to $5,000
Whom Do I Contact: The Robert Wood Johnson Foundation, College Road, P.O. Box 2316, Princeton, NJ 08543-2316, (609) 452-8701.

739

ROBERTS WESLEYAN COLLEGE
Minority Student Scholarship
Who Can Apply: Full-time minority students who are U.S. citizens or permanent residents with financial need and who exhibit academic achievement and leadership qualities. Must have a 3.0 GPA. Deadline May 1.
How Much Money Can I Get: $500
Whom Do I Contact: Director of Financial Aid, Roberts Wesleyan College, 2301 Westside Drive, Rochester, NY 14624-1997, (716) 594-9471.

740

ROCKHURST COLLEGE
Special Minority Scholarship
Who Can Apply: Awarded to talented black, Hispanic, and other minority men and women based on merit and not on need.

How Much Money Can I Get: Varies
Whom Do I Contact: Rockhurst College, 5225 Troost Avenue, Kansas City, MO 64110-2599, (816) 926-4100.

741

ROLLINS COLLEGE

The William Randolph Hearst Scholarship
Who Can Apply: Entering minority freshman. No application required.
How Much Money Can I Get: $1,500
Whom Do I Contact: Financial Aid Director, Rollins College, Campus Box 2721, Winter Park, FL 32789, (305) 646-2173.

742

ROLLINS COLLEGE MINORITY STUDENT SCHOLARSHIPS

The Martin Luther King, Jr., Scholarship
Who Can Apply: This scholarship competition requires a separate application and essay.
How Much Money Can I Get: $3,000 annually
Whom Do I Contact: Office/Student Financial Planning, Rollins College, Campus Box 2721, Winter Park, FL 32789-4499, (407) 646-2395.

743

ROSEMONT COLLEGE

Opportunity Grant
Who Can Apply: Awarded to minority students who have overcome significant historical, educational, and economic hardship to pursue higher education. Must be a female and a U.S. citizen or permanent resident. Deadline February 1.
How Much Money Can I Get: $7,500
Whom Do I Contact: Rosemont College, Attn.: Director of Admissions, Rosemont, PA 19010, (610) 527-9721.

744

ROSS UNIVERSITY SCHOOL OF MEDICINE AND SCHOOL OF VETERINARY MEDICINE IN THE WEST INDIES

Who Can Apply: Offers partial scholarships to qualified applicants who want to pursue careers in medicine or veterinary science.
How Much Money Can I Get: Varies
Whom Do I Contact: Dr. Robert Ross, Chairman of the Board of Trustees, Ross University, 460 W. 34th Street, 12th Floor, New York, NY 10001, (212) 279-5500.

745

RUTGERS UNIVERSITY
James Dickson Carr Minority Merit Scholarship
Who Can Apply: Black and Hispanic students in the top 40 percent of their high school class who have a minimum combined 1100 SAT score. In the three previous years, 125 students have received the awards, worth $5,000 this year. Carr, in 1886, was the first African American graduate of Rutgers, the eighth oldest college in the country.
How Much Money Can I Get: Room, board, tuition, and fees total $6,094 for New Jersey residents and $9,500 for out-of-state students.
Whom Do I Contact: James Ruffin, c/o Office of Undergraduate Admissions, Davidson Road, Rutgers University, Piscataway/New Brunswick, NJ 08854, (908) 445-3777.

746

SACHS FOUNDATION
UNDERGRADUATE SCHOLARSHIP
Who Can Apply: Black Colorado residents with at least a 3.6 GPA. Applicants must show community involvement. Deadline March 1.
How Much Money Can I Get: $3,000 to $4,000, renewable
Whom Do I Contact: Sachs Foundation, 90 S. Cascade Avenue, Suite 1410, Colorado Springs, CO 80903.

747

SAGINAW VALLEY STATE COLLEGE
Minority Scholarship
Who Can Apply: Students with high academic performance. Award renewable by maintaining a 3.0 GPA. Deadline March 1.
How Much Money Can I Get: $1,000
Whom Do I Contact: Director of Admissions, Saginaw Valley State College, 2250 Pierce Road, University Center, MI 48710, (517) 790-4000.

748

SAN FRANCISCO STATE UNIVERSITY
Scholarships for Underrepresented Minority Students
Who Can Apply: Offered to students at the undergraduate and MBA level in the College of Business.
How Much Money Can I Get: Varies
Whom Do I Contact: Sharon Collins, Assistant Dean, College of Business, San Francisco State University, 1600 Holloway Avenue, San Francisco, CA 94132, (415) 338-6363, fax: (415) 338-6237.

749

UNIVERSITY OF SAN FRANCISCO
Bank of America Scholarship
Who Can Apply: Minority undergraduate students majoring in Business.
How Much Money Can I Get: Varies
Whom Do I Contact: Financial Aid Director, University of San Francisco, Champion Hall, Ignatian Heights, San Francisco, CA 94117-1080, (415) 666-6886.

750

SAN JOAQUIN DELTA COLLEGE
The Links Incorporated Scholarship
Who Can Apply: Black females in their freshman or sophomore year. This is available to students who have completed at least one semester as a full-time student with a minimum 3.0 GPA.
How Much Money Can I Get: Varies
Whom Do I Contact: San Joaquin Delta College, 5151 Pacific Avenue, Goleman 125, Stockton, CA 95207, (209) 474-5114.

751

SAN JOAQUIN DELTA COLLEGE
The Minority Improvement Scholarship
Who Can Apply: Student who shows academic improvement and financial need. A 2.0 GPA is required.
How Much Money Can I Get: Varies
Whom Do I Contact: Financial Aid Director, San Joaquin Delta College, 5151 Pacific Avenue, Goleman 125, Stockton, CA 95207, (209) 474-5114.

752

SANGAMON STATE UNIVERSITY
Illinois Association Community Action Scholarship
Who Can Apply: Minority students planning a career in public affairs on the basis of need.
How Much Money Can I Get: $300
Whom Do I Contact: Sangamon State University, Springfield, IL 62708, (217) 786-6600.

753

SANGAMON STATE UNIVERSITY
The Otis Morgan Memorial Scholarship
Who Can Apply: Minority student who plans to pursue a career in teaching. Financial need required. Deadline April 1.

How Much Money Can I Get: $250
Whom Do I Contact: Financial Aid Director, Sangamon State University, Springfield, IL 62708, (217) 786-6600.

754
SANGAMON STATE UNIVERSITY
The William Ferris Cummings Award
Who Can Apply: Undergraduate or graduate students who are member of a minority group and interested in community service. The recipient should be in good academic standing and have demonstrated financial need. Majors: social science, education, social work, and political science. Deadline April 1.
How Much Money Can I Get: $100 to $200
Whom Do I Contact: Financial Aid Director, Sangamon State University, Springfield, IL 62708, (217) 786-6600.

755
SCHOMBURG CENTER FOR RESEARCH IN BLACK CULTURE
Scholars-in-Residence Program
Who Can Apply: Open to scholars in the humanities studying black history and culture and to professionals in fields related to the Schomburg Center's collections and program activities. Fellows funded by the program will spend six months or one year in residence at the Schomburg Center. Deadline January 15.
How Much Money Can I Get: Varies
Whom Do I Contact: Scholars-in-Residence Program, Schomburg Center for Research in Black Culture, 515 Malcolm X Boulevard, New York, NY 10037-1801, (212) 491-2203.

756
SCRIPPS HOWARD FOUNDATION SCHOLARSHIP
Who Can Apply: Students who are in good academic standing, demonstrate an interest in journalism, and have financial need. Request an application during November.
How Much Money Can I Get: $500 to $3,000
Whom Do I Contact: Scripps Howard Foundation Scholarship, P.O. Box 5380, Cincinnati, OH 45201.

757
SENIOR ADULT SCHOLARSHIP PROGRAM
Who Can Apply: Senior citizens (persons aged 60 or over)
How Much Money Can I Get: Varies

Whom Do I Contact: Financial aid office at any public two-year post secondary educational institution in Alabama. For additional information, contact the Alabama Department of Education, Administrative and Financial Services Division, Gordon Persons Building, 50 North Ripley, Montgomery, AL 36130, (334) 242-9742.

758

SHERMAN COLLEGE

Minority Scholarship
Who Can Apply: Student must submit an essay on why he or she chose a career in chiropractic medicine. Students may write to the financial aid office for information about other scholarships available to SCSC students. Financial need required. The FAF is required. Deadline August 15.
How Much Money Can I Get: Varies
Whom Do I Contact: Financial Aid Officer, Sherman College, SC, P.O. Box 1452, Spartanburg, SC 29304, (803) 578-8770.

759

SIERRA COMMUNITY COLLEGE

The Observer McDonald's Scholarship
Who Can Apply: Black students who have completed 6 to 23 units and enroll full-time the following fall semester.
How Much Money Can I Get: $50
Whom Do I Contact: Sierra Community College, 5000 Rocklin Road, Rocklin, CA 95677, (916) 624-3333.

760

SIGMA GAMMA RHO SORORITY
NATIONAL EDUCATION FUND, INC.

Who Can Apply: Students with a sincere interest in achieving a higher education. Applicants must be enrolled in or qualified for admission to an institution for higher education and must demonstrate need and scholastic ability.
How Much Money Can I Get: Varies
Whom Do I Contact: Dr. Jimmie C. Jackson, Scholarship Chairperson, 7135 8th Street, NW, Washington, DC 20012.

761

SIMMONS COLLEGE

Dorothy Ferebee Scholarship
Who Can Apply: AHANA students who have distinguished themselves throughout high school.

How Much Money Can I Get: $3,000 a year for four years
Whom Do I Contact: Simmons College Admissions Office, Simmons College, 300 The Fenway, Boston, MA 02115, (617) 738-2107.

762
SIOUX FALLS COLLEGE

Who Can Apply: Entering freshmen must have a minimum ACT composite score of 19 or graduate in the upper half of their high school class. Limited funds are available to upper-class students with a 2.0 GPA. Deadline May 1.
How Much Money Can I Get: Varies
Whom Do I Contact: Director of Admissions, Sioux Falls College, 150 S. Prairie, Sioux Falls, SD 57105-1699, (605) 331-6600.

763
SOCIETY OF ACTUARIES

Who Can Apply: Applicants must have taken the advanced mathematics test of the Graduate Record Examination (GRE) or first actuarial exam. Deadline May 1.
How Much Money Can I Get: Varies
Whom Do I Contact: Scholarship Committee, Society of Actuaries, 500 Park Boulevard, Itasca, IL 60143, (630) 773-3010.

764
SOCIETY OF ACTUARIES
Minority Student Scholarship

Who Can Apply: Applicants must have taken the SAT or ACT, have a 3.3 GPA, and be majoring in one of the following: insurance, actuarial science, or mathematics. Deadline May 1.
How Much Money Can I Get: $2,500
Whom Do I Contact: Scholarship Committee, Society of Actuaries, 500 Park Boulevard, Itasca, IL 60143, (630) 773-3010.

765
SOCIETY OF PROFESSIONAL JOURNALISTS, LOS ANGELES
Ken Inouye Memorial Scholarship

Who Can Apply: Those eligible to apply must be currently enrolled in Los Angeles chapter schools. Selection is based on proven ability in journalism, potential, and financial need. Deadline March.
How Much Money Can I Get: $1,000
Whom Do I Contact: Society of Professional Journalists/L.A., c/o Greater

Los Angeles Press Club, 600 N. Vermont, Los Angeles, CA 90004, (213) 469-8180.

766

SOUTH CAROLINA STATE UNIVERSITY
The A.I. Mose Scholarship
Who Can Apply: Students who are majoring in Elementary Education. Selection is based on a 2.8 GPA and active membership in the Arnett Club, demonstration of intellectual curiosity in the classroom and faculty vote.
How Much Money Can I Get: $500
Whom Do I Contact: South Carolina State University, 300 College Street, NE, P.O. Box 7386, Orangeburg, SC 29117, (803) 536-7042.

767

SOUTH CAROLINA STATE UNIVERSITY
Amelia S. Roberts Scholarship
Who Can Apply: Freshmen students who made significant academic achievements during their initial semester at South Carolina State University. Selection is based on a 2.8 GPA, active membership in the Arnett Club, demonstration of intellectual curiosity in and outside the classroom, demonstration of a college reading level and faculty vote.
How Much Money Can I Get: $500
Whom Do I Contact: South Carolina State University, 300 College Street, NE, P.O. Box 7386, Orangeburg, SC 29117, (803) 536-7042.

768

SOUTH CAROLINA STATE UNIVERSITY
Atlanta, Ga. Alumni Chapter Scholarship
Who Can Apply: Candidates must meet selection criteria as set by chapter.
How Much Money Can I Get: $500
Whom Do I Contact: South Carolina State University, 300 College Street, NE, P.O. Box 7386, Orangeburg, SC 29117, (803) 536-7042.

769

SOUTH CAROLINA STATE UNIVERSITY
Beaufort Alumni Chapter Scholarship
Who Can Apply: Candidates must meet selection criteria as set by chapter.
How Much Money Can I Get: $500
Whom Do I Contact: South Carolina State University, 300 College Street, NE, P.O. Box 7386, Orangeburg, SC 29117, (803) 536-7042.

770

SOUTH CAROLINA STATE UNIVERSITY
Burrell E. Workman, Jr., Memorial Scholarship
Who Can Apply: Senior pre-medical students matriculating at South
Carolina State University.
How Much Money Can I Get: $500
Whom Do I Contact: South Carolina State University, 300 College Street,
NE, P.O. Box 7386, Orangeburg, SC 29117, (803) 536-7042.

771

SOUTH CAROLINA STATE UNIVERSITY
Central Florida Alumni Chapter Scholarship
Who Can Apply: Candidates must meet selection criteria as set by chapter.
How Much Money Can I Get: $500
Whom Do I Contact: South Carolina State University, 300 College Street,
NE, P.O. Box 7386, Orangeburg, SC 29117, (803) 536-7042.

772

SOUTH CAROLINA STATE UNIVERSITY
The Class of 1953 Scholarship
Who Can Apply: Recipients must exhibit academic ability and demonstrate
a high standard of self-discipline, initiative and stability. Students must also
possess outstanding leadership qualities, good moral character, enthusiasm
and intellectual curiosity.
How Much Money Can I Get: $300-$500
Whom Do I Contact: South Carolina State University, 300 College Street,
NE, P.O. Box 7386, Orangeburg, SC 29117, (803) 536-7042.

773

SOUTH CAROLINA STATE UNIVERSITY
Dick Horne Foundation Scholarship
Who Can Apply: Recipients must be in upper two-thirds of class
scholastically, must have demonstrated outstanding leadership qualities and
require financial assistance towards achieving an education. Parents or
guardians must reside in Orangeburg County.
How Much Money Can I Get: $1,000
Whom Do I Contact: South Carolina State University, 300 College Street,
NE, P.O. Box 7386, Orangeburg, SC 29117, (803) 536-7042.

774

SOUTH CAROLINA STATE UNIVERSITY
Dwight David Eisenhower Transportation Fellowship
Who Can Apply: The applicant must be a U.S. citizen or a legal permanent resident, a full-time undergraduate student majoring in a designated transportation related discipline, and be within the final 40 credit hours of the bachelor's degree at the time the fellowship becomes effective. Candidates must have a minimum 3.0 cumulative and have plans for a career in a transportation-related profession.
How Much Money Can I Get: $8,500
Whom Do I Contact: South Carolina State University, 300 College Street, NE, P.O. Box 7386, Orangeburg, SC 29117, (803) 536-7042.

775

SOUTH CAROLINA STATE UNIVERSITY
Eliza T. Hampton Scholarship
Who Can Apply: Upper class student who demonstrates leadership and genuine commitment to the nursing profession.
How Much Money Can I Get: $500
Whom Do I Contact: South Carolina State University, 300 College Street, NE, P.O. Box 7386, Orangeburg, SC 29117, (803) 536-7042.

776

SOUTH CAROLINA STATE UNIVERSITY
Florida Gulf Coast Alumni Chapter Scholarship
Who Can Apply: Candidates must meet selection criteria as set by chapter.
How Much Money Can I Get: $500
Whom Do I Contact: South Carolina State University, 300 College Street, NE, P.O. Box 7386, Orangeburg, SC 29117, (803) 536-7042.

777

SOUTH CAROLINA STATE UNIVERSITY
The Gibert Spears Scholarship
Who Can Apply: Award is based of academic merit and financial need.
How Much Money Can I Get: $500
Whom Do I Contact: South Carolina State University, 300 College Street, NE, P.O. Box 7386, Orangeburg, SC 29117, (803) 536-7042.

778

SOUTH CAROLINA STATE UNIVERSITY
Greenwood Alumni Chapter Scholarship
Who Can Apply: Candidates must be selection criteria as set by chapter.

How Much Money Can I Get: $500
Whom Do I Contact: South Carolina State University, 300 College Street, NE, P.O. Box 7386, Orangeburg, SC 29117, (803) 536-7042.

779
SOUTH CAROLINA STATE UNIVERSITY
Greenville Alumni Chapter Scholarship
Who Can Apply: Candidates must meet selection criteria as set by chapter.
How Much Money Can I Get: $500
Whom Do I Contact: South Carolina State University, 300 College Street, NE, P.O. Box 7386, Orangeburg, SC 29117, (803) 536-7042.

780
SOUTH CAROLINA STATE UNIVERSITY
Helen T. Bankhead Memorial Scholarship
Who Can Apply: Students of high academic standing who has demonstrated outstanding qualities of leadership.
How Much Money Can I Get: $500
Whom Do I Contact: South Carolina State University, 300 College Street, NE, P.O. Box 7386, Orangeburg, SC 29117, (803) 536-7042.

781
SOUTH CAROLINA STATE UNIVERSITY
The Helen Wilkinson Sheffield Memorial Scholarship
Who Can Apply: Young women who have earned at least forty-five hours with a minimum 3.0 GPA. Applicants should also be industrious, a good citizen of character exemplifying finer womanhood.
How Much Money Can I Get: $600
Whom Do I Contact: South Carolina State University, 300 College Street, NE, P.O. Box 7386, Orangeburg, SC 29117, (803) 536-7042.

782
SOUTH CAROLINA STATE UNIVERSITY
Henderson-Davis Players' Performance Scholarship
Who Can Apply: Sophomore or junior Dramatic Art majors at South Carolina State University who have demonstrated a serious intent to pursue a degree in either educational or professional theater. Students must have at least a 2.5 GPA and a 3.0 average in his or her major field. In addition, the student must also demonstrate an interest in the total theater program at South Carolina State University and openly support its functions and projects through active involvement.
How Much Money Can I Get: $500

Whom Do I Contact: South Carolina State University, 300 College Street, NE, P.O. Box 7386, Orangeburg, SC 29117, (803) 536-7042.

783
SOUTH CAROLINA STATE UNIVERSITY
The James R. Washington and Family Scholarship
Who Can Apply: Students majoring in Education with priority given to Health and/or Physical Education majors entering their professional clinical experiences and providing evidence of financial need.
How Much Money Can I Get: $500
Whom Do I Contact: South Carolina State University, 300 College Street, NE, P.O. Box 7386, Orangeburg, SC 29117, (803) 536-7042.

784
SOUTH CAROLINA STATE UNIVERSITY
M. Maceo Nance, Jr., School of Nursing
Who Can Apply: Students must meet specific criteria and submit an application to the Department of Nursing annually for consideration of the award.
How Much Money Can I Get: Varies
Whom Do I Contact: South Carolina State University, 300 College Street, NE, P.O. Box 7386, Orangeburg, SC 29117, (803) 536-7042.

785
SOUTH CAROLINA STATE UNIVERSITY
Mobile Oil Foundation Scholarship
Who Can Apply: Students enrolled in South Carolina's State University's School of Business.
How Much Money Can I Get: $3,000
Whom Do I Contact: South Carolina State University, 300 College Street, NE, P.O. Box 7386, Orangeburg, SC 29117, (803) 536-7042.

786
SOUTH CAROLINA STATE UNIVERSITY
National Alumni Association Scholarship Award
Who Can Apply: Talented student who will be entering in the fall as freshman.
How Much Money Can I Get: $1,000
Whom Do I Contact: South Carolina State University, 300 College Street, NE, P.O. Box 7386, Orangeburg, SC 29117, (803) 536-7042.

787

SOUTH CAROLINA STATE UNIVERSITY
New York Alumni Chapter Scholarship
Who Can Apply: Candidates must meet selection criteria as set by chapter.
How Much Money Can I Get: $500
Whom Do I Contact: South Carolina State University, 300 College Street, NE, P.O. Box 7386, Orangeburg, SC 29117, (803) 536-7042.

788

SOUTH CAROLINA STATE UNIVERSITY
Oliver C. Dawson Scholarship
Who Can Apply: Full-time students at South Carolina State University in the junior class with a 3.0 GPA. Candidates must exhibit dedication toward the discipline of physical education and must possess the qualities of maturity, initiative, stability, enthusiasm, and high morals.
How Much Money Can I Get: $1,000
Whom Do I Contact: South Carolina State University, 300 College Street, NE, P.O. Box 7386, Orangeburg, SC 29117, (803) 536-7042.

789

SOUTH CAROLINA STATE UNIVERSITY
Orangeburg Alumni Chapter Scholarship
Who Can Apply: Candidates must meet selection criteria as set by chapter.
How Much Money Can I Get: $500
Whom Do I Contact: South Carolina State University, 300 College Street, NE, P.O. Box 7386, Orangeburg, SC 29117, (803) 536-7042.

790

SOUTH CAROLINA STATE UNIVERSITY
Presidential Scholarship
Who Can Apply: Students must be in upper one fifth of high school graduating class, have demonstrated outstanding leadership qualities and present a minimum score of 1000 SAT score. Applicants must also present at least two letters of recommendation (one from a former high school teacher and one from an adult of the applicant's community) and exhibit worthy educational goals and manifest outstanding personal qualities.
How Much Money Can I Get: $6,000
Whom Do I Contact: South Carolina State University, 300 College Street, NE, P.O. Box 7386, Orangeburg, SC 29117, (803) 536-7042.

791

SOUTH CAROLINA STATE UNIVERSITY
Robert Shaw Evan's Endowment Scholarship
Who Can Apply: Candidates must be freshmen students accepted for admission with a minimum 3.0 high school GPA and enrolled in s full-time program.
How Much Money Can I Get: $700 per year
Whom Do I Contact: South Carolina State University, 300 College Street, NE, P.O. Box 7386, Orangeburg, SC 29117, (803) 536-7042.

792

SOUTH CAROLINA STATE UNIVERSITY
Smith-Hammond-Middleton Memorial Scholarship
Who Can Apply: Students who demonstrate financial need.
How Much Money Can I Get: $635
Whom Do I Contact: South Carolina State University, 300 College Street, NE, P.O. Box 7386, Orangeburg, SC 29117, (803) 536-7042.

793

SOUTH CAROLINA STATE UNIVERSITY
South Carolina State Alumni Scholarship Fund
Who Can Apply: Nursing students enrolled in clinical nursing courses or accepted for progression into the upper division of the curriculum.
How Much Money Can I Get: Varies
Whom Do I Contact: South Carolina State University, 300 College Street, NE, P.O. Box 7386, Orangeburg, SC 29117, (803) 536-7042.

794

SOUTH CAROLINA STATE UNIVERSITY
Spartanburg Alumni Chapter Scholarship
Who Can Apply: Candidates must meet selection criteria as set by chapter.
How Much Money Can I Get: $500
Whom Do I Contact: South Carolina State University, 300 College Street, NE, P.O. Box 7386, Orangeburg, SC 29117, (803) 536-7042.

795

SOUTH CAROLINA STATE UNIVERSITY
USDA/1890 National Scholars Program
Who Can Apply: Students pursuing a bachelor degree at South Carolina State University in any field of study in agriculture, food, or natural resource sciences.

How Much Money Can I Get: Tuition, employment, employee benefits, fees, books, personal computer and software and room and board each year
Whom Do I Contact: South Carolina State University, 300 College Street, NE, P.O. Box 7386, Orangeburg, SC 29117, (803) 536-7042.

796
SOUTH CAROLINA STATE UNIVERSITY
Wal-Mart Competitive Edge Scholarship
Who Can Apply: Each applicant must demonstrate high academic achievement, community service, leadership, and must declare a major in an approved competitive edge field.
How Much Money Can I Get: $5,000 for 4 years
Whom Do I Contact: South Carolina State University, 300 College Street, NE, P.O. Box 7386, Orangeburg, SC 29117, (803) 536-7042.

797
SOUTH CAROLINA STATE UNIVERSITY
Washington, D.C., Alumni Chapter Memorial Scholarship
Who Can Apply: Candidates must meet selection criteria as set by chapter.
How Much Money Can I Get: $500
Whom Do I Contact: South Carolina State University, 300 College Street, NE, P.O. Box 7386, Orangeburg, SC 29117, (803) 536-7042.

798
SOUTH CAROLINA STATE UNIVERSITY
The Wilhelmina Funchess Scholarship Award
Who Can Apply: Students must have a minimum 2.8 GPA and be in good standing at the University. The recipient is selected by the University Fellowship and Scholarship Committee.
How Much Money Can I Get: $500
Whom Do I Contact: South Carolina State University, 300 College Street, NE, P.O. Box 7386, Orangeburg, SC 29117, (803) 536-7042.

799
UNIVERSITY OF SOUTH DAKOTA
SCHOOL OF LAW
The Mary Hanson Scholarship
Who Can Apply: First-, second- and third-year minority students.
How Much Money Can I Get: Varies
Whom Do I Contact: University of South Dakota, School of Law, 414 E. Clark Street, Vermillion, SD 57069, (605) 677-5443.

800

UNIVERSITY OF SOUTH FLORIDA
The Richard Pride Research Fellowship
Who Can Apply: Minority students pursuing a Ph.D. at the University of South Florida in anthropology, biology, chemistry, English, marine science, mathematics, psychology, or communications. Applicants must be U.S. citizens. Deadline January 15.
How Much Money Can I Get: $15,000 + tuition
Whom Do I Contact: University of South Florida, Attn.: Institute on Black Life, 4202 E. Fowler Avenue, SVC 1087, Tampa, FL 33260-6911, (813) 974-4727.

801

SOUTHERN ILLINOIS UNIVERSITY
James M. & Aune P. Nelson Scholarship
Who Can Apply: Awarded to minority graduates of Alton Secondary Schools who have at least a 2.0 cumulative GPA in high school and a 2.5 GPA in college. Deadline March 1.
How Much Money Can I Get: Varies
Whom Do I Contact: Southern Illinois University, Attn.: Office of Student Financial Aid, Rendleman Building, Box 1060, Edwardsville, IL 62026-1060, (618) 692-2562.

802

SOUTHERN ILLINOIS UNIVERSITY AT EDWARDSVILLE
Minority Scholarship Program
Who Can Apply: Applicants must have a cumulative 3.5 (on a 5.0) GPA or equivalent, enroll in and satisfactorily complete 12 hours each quarter, and maintain a 3.5 GPA each quarter. Applicants must complete the ACT Family Financial Statement by April 1.
How Much Money Can I Get: Varies
Whom Do I Contact: Dr. Janet McReynolds, Assistant to the Provost and Vice President for Academic Affairs, Box 1021, SIUE, Edwardsville, IL 62026-1021, (618) 692-3778.

803

UNIVERSITY OF SOUTHERN MAINE SCHOOL OF LAW
Who Can Apply: Three minority students are offered three-year awards using Federal Affirmative Action standards, which include blacks, Hispanics, Asians, and Native American Indians.

How Much Money Can I Get: Full tuition
Whom Do I Contact: University of Southern Maine, School of Law, 246 Deering Avenue, Portland, ME 04102, (207) 780-4345.

804
SOUTHERN METHODIST UNIVERSITY
SCHOOL OF LAW
Diversity Scholarship
Who Can Apply: Students from minority groups.
How Much Money Can I Get: Full and partial tuition
Whom Do I Contact: Southern Methodist University, School of Law, Office of Admissions, Dallas, TX 75275-0116, (214)692-2549.

805
SOUTHERN METHODIST UNIVERSITY
SCHOOL OF LAW
Sarah T. Hughes Fellowship
Who Can Apply: Outstanding minority students regardless of financial need. Established by the Dallas Bar Association and underwritten by the Dallas Bar Foundation, the Hughes Fellowship enables minority men and women to obtain an SMU legal education in preparation for entry to the legal profession.
How Much Money Can I Get: Full tuition, fees, and additional amount for books and living expenses
Whom Do I Contact: Southern Methodist University, School of Law, Office of Admissions, Dallas, TX 75275-0116, (214) 692-2549.

806
SOUTHWEST TEXAS STATE UNIVERSITY
Graduate Minority Scholarship
Who Can Apply: Qualified minority candidates who are citizens of the United States and accepted to the graduate school. Candidate must also be in good academic standing and must demonstrate academic and intellectual promise and leadership. Award designed to encourage minority graduate students with intellectual promise and leadership to complete a master's degree at SWT. Deadline February 1.
How Much Money Can I Get: Annual scholarships of $1,500 (awarded in $500 increments per semester), renewable for a second year
Whom Do I Contact: Chair, Graduate Minority Scholarship Committee, The Graduate School, Southwest Texas State University, 601 University Drive, San Marcos, TX 78666-4605.

807

SOUTHWESTERN UNIVERSITY
Presidential Scholar Award
Who Can Apply: Black and Hispanic students ranking in the top 10 percent of their high school class with at least a 3.5 GPA and 1150 SAT combined score (25 ACT).
How Much Money Can I Get: Tuition
Whom Do I Contact: Director of Admissions, Office of Admissions, Southwestern University, Georgetown, TX 78626, (512) 863-6511 or (800) 252-3166.

808

SOUTHWESTERN UNIVERSITY SCHOOL OF LAW
Who Can Apply: Available to black students on the basis of community service, scholastic achievement, and financial need. Application forms are available in late November and selections are usually made in March. The money is available for the following academic year. Applicants must have successfully completed their first year of law school and have a 3.0 GPA. Recipients selected by wives of bench and bar. Deadline June 1.
How Much Money Can I Get: Varies
Whom Do I Contact: Southwestern University School of Law, 675 S. Westmoreland Avenue, Los Angeles, CA 90005, (213) 738-6719.

809

SOUTHWESTERN UNIVERSITY SCHOOL OF LAW
The Tom Bradley Scholarship Fund
Who Can Apply: is available to assist needy and deserving students. Must be in top 30 percent of their class. Not for entering students. Preference given to minority applicant in second or third year of law school. Financial need required.
How Much Money Can I Get: $2,500
Whom Do I Contact: Financial Aid Director, Southwestern University School of Law, 675 S. Westmoreland Avenue, Los Angeles, CA 90005, (213) 738-6719.

810

SPECIAL LIBRARIES ASSOCIATION
Minority Stipend Program
Who Can Apply: Applicants must be U.S. citizens or submit evidence of becoming naturalized at the beginning of the award period. Must be majoring in library science, and financial need required. Deadline October 30.

How Much Money Can I Get: $3,000
Whom Do I Contact: Minority Groups Committee, Special Libraries Association, 1700 Eighteenth Street, NW, Washington, DC 20009, (202) 234-4700.

811

SPELMAN COLLEGE

Deans' Scholarship
Who Can Apply: For approximately 65 students annually
How Much Money Can I Get: Partial to full tuition; up to four years
Whom Do I Contact: Spelman College 350 Spelman Lane, Campus Box 771, Atlanta, GA 30314-4399, (404) 270-5212.

812

SPELMAN COLLEGE

Dewitt Wallace Service Scholarship
Who Can Apply: Upper class student who has a minimum 2.5 cumulative GPA, a good citizenship record, and a record of service to her school, college, and/or community.
How Much Money Can I Get: Varies
Whom Do I Contact: Spelman College 350 Spelman Lane, Campus Box 771, Atlanta, GA 30314-4399, (404) 270-5212.

813

SPELMAN COLLEGE

DeWitt Wallace Service Scholarship for International Students
Who Can Apply: Students holding a F1 Visa, with a cumulative GPA of 2.8 or higher, evidence of financial need, record of service to the college, school, or community and who have had no disciplinary action.
How Much Money Can I Get: Varies
Whom Do I Contact: Spelman College 350 Spelman Lane, Campus Box 771, Atlanta, GA 30314-4399, (404) 270-5212.

814

SPELMAN COLLEGE

Hope Scholarship
Who Can Apply: Students who demonstrate academic and extracurricular merit, leadership abilities, and involvement in the community. Georgia residents who graduate from high school with a cumulative GPA of 3.0 or higher and will be enrolled as full-time students are eligible.
How Much Money Can I Get: Tuition
Whom Do I Contact: Spelman College 350 Spelman Lane, Campus Box 771, Atlanta, GA 30314-4399, (404) 270-5212.

815

SPRING GARDEN COLLEGE

The President's Council Scholarship
Who Can Apply: Outstanding minority applicants on the basis of class rank and SAT scores. This award is renewable. Must be in the upper fifth of their class. Deadline March 1.
How Much Money Can I Get: Full tuition
Whom Do I Contact: Financial Aid Director, Spring Garden College, 7500 Germantown Avenue, Philadelphia, PA 19119, (215) 248-7905.

816

ST. AUGUSTINE'S COLLEGE

Alpha Kappa Alpha Scholarship
Who Can Apply: College students of sophomore status or higher, who demonstrate exceptional academic achievement. Applicant must be a full-time student planning on completing degree requirements. Includes the merit scholarship ($1,000), based on academic ability, and the financial assistance scholarship ($1,500), based upon demonstrated financial need.
How Much Money Can I Get: $1,000-1,500
Whom Do I Contact: St. Augustine's College, Office of Financial Aid, Charles Mosee Building, 1315 Oakwood Avenue, Raleigh, NC 27610, (919) 516-4131.

817

ST. AUGUSTINE'S COLLEGE

Ambassadorial Scholarship
Who Can Apply: Students who can speak a language other than English and want to study abroad in the "host" country of that language.
How Much Money Can I Get: $10,000 to $23,000 for a 3 month to full year of study abroad.
Whom Do I Contact: St. Augustine's College, Office of Financial Aid, Charles Mosee Building, 1315 Oakwood Avenue, Raleigh, NC 27610, (919) 516-4131.

818

ST. AUGUSTINE'S COLLEGE

American Institute of Architects Minority Disadvantaged Scholarship
Who Can Apply: Students of color enrolling in architecture programs.
How Much Money Can I Get: $500 to $3,000
Whom Do I Contact: St. Augustine's College, Office of Financial Aid, Charles Mosee Building, 1315 Oakwood Avenue, Raleigh, NC 27610, (919) 516-4131.

819

ST. AUGUSTINE'S COLLEGE

American Institute of Certified Public Accountants Scholarship

Who Can Apply: Undergraduates studying accounting at a U.S. college with at least 30 credits completed.

How Much Money Can I Get: Up to $5,000 with about 300 winners annually.

Whom Do I Contact: St. Augustine's College, Office of Financial Aid, Charles Mosee Building, 1315 Oakwood Avenue, Raleigh, NC 27610, (919) 516-4131.

820

ST. AUGUSTINE'S COLLEGE

ARMY ROTC Scholarship

Who Can Apply: Students interested in learning more about military lifestyle. Awards are awarded on a competitive basis and are available for four years. Candidates must have minimum 920 SAT score (19 ACT).

How Much Money Can I Get: Tuition

Whom Do I Contact: St. Augustine's College, Office of Financial Aid, Charles Mosee Building, 1315 Oakwood Avenue, Raleigh, NC 27610, Phone: (919) 516-4131.

821

ST. AUGUSTINE'S COLLEGE

Arts Recognition and Talent Search Award

Who Can Apply: Students 17 and 18 years of age who show talent in dance, voice, music, art, photography, jazz, visual arts, writing, or other creative areas.

How Much Money Can I Get: $100- $3,000

Whom Do I Contact: St. Augustine's College, Office of Financial Aid, Charles Mosee Building, 1315 Oakwood Avenue, Raleigh, NC 27610, (919) 516-4131.

822

ST. AUGUSTINE'S COLLEGE

Coca-Cola Scholars Scholarship

Who Can Apply: Incoming freshman students with a minimum 3.0 GPA. Coca-Cola also considers such factors as school activities and volunteer activities. Deadline October 31.

How Much Money Can I Get: $4,000 (200), $20,000 (50)

Whom Do I Contact: St. Augustine's College, Office of Financial Aid, Charles Mosee Building, 1315 Oakwood Avenue, Raleigh, NC 27610, (919) 516-4131.

823

ST. AUGUSTINE'S COLLEGE

Developmental Fund for Black Students in Science and Technology Scholarship
Who Can Apply: Science or engineering students at HBCUs.
How Much Money Can I Get: $2,000
Whom Do I Contact: St. Augustine's College, Office of Financial Aid,
Charles Mosee Building, 1315 Oakwood Avenue, Raleigh, NC 27610, (919) 516-4131.

824

ST. AUGUSTINE'S COLLEGE

Gates Millennium Scholarship
Who Can Apply: Candidates must be a U.S. citizen or legal permanent resident or national of the United States and have attained a cumulative 3.3 GPA on a 4.0 scale (unweighted) at the time of nomination. Students must also be entering a U.S. accredited college or university as full-time, degree seeking freshmen in the Fall of the award year. Students must demonstrate leadership abilities through participation in community service, extracurricular or other activities and meet the Federal Pell Grant eligibility criteria.
How Much Money Can I Get: Tuition
Whom Do I Contact: St. Augustine's College, Office of Financial Aid,
Charles Mosee Building, 1315 Oakwood Avenue, Raleigh, NC 27610, Phone: (919) 516-4131

825

ST. AUGUSTINE'S COLLEGE

Hispanic Scholarship Fund
Who Can Apply: Students majoring in Business
How Much Money Can I Get: Varies
Whom Do I Contact: St. Augustine's College, Office of Financial Aid,
Charles Mosee Building, 1315 Oakwood Avenue, Raleigh, NC 27610, (919) 516-4131.

826

ST. AUGUSTINE'S COLLEGE

Jackie Robinson Foundation Scholarship
Who Can Apply: Students who demonstrate academic merit.
How Much Money Can I Get: $6,000
Whom Do I Contact: St. Augustine's College, Office of Financial Aid,
Charles Mosee Building, 1315 Oakwood Avenue, Raleigh, NC 27610, Phone: (919) 516-4131.

827

ST. AUGUSTINE'S COLLEGE

Intel Science—Talent Search

Who Can Apply: Eligible students include high school seniors in the United States and territories, and American students attending school abroad. Students are judged based on their individual research ability, scientific originality and creative thinking. A required research project covers all disciplines of science, including chemistry, physics, mathematics, engineering, social science and biology. All Intel STS entries were reviewed and judged by top scientists from a variety of disciplines. Dr. Andrew Yeager of the University of Pittsburgh Medical Center oversaw the judging process.

How Much Money Can I Get: $1,000 to $100,000.

Whom Do I Contact: St. Augustine's College, Office of Financial Aid, Charles Mosee Building, 1315 Oakwood Avenue, Raleigh, NC 27610, (919) 516-4131.

828

ST. AUGUSTINE'S COLLEGE

Kodak Scholarship

Who Can Apply: Students studying film/cinematography at U.S. colleges.

How Much Money Can I Get: $5,000

Whom Do I Contact: St. Augustine's College, Office of Financial Aid, Charles Mosee Building, 1315 Oakwood Avenue, Raleigh, NC 27610, Phone: (919) 516-4131.

829

ST. AUGUSTINE'S COLLEGE

NACME Scholarship

Who Can Apply: Students majoring in Engineering

How Much Money Can I Get: $20,000

Whom Do I Contact: St. Augustine's College, Office of Financial Aid, Charles Mosee Building, 1315 Oakwood Avenue, Raleigh, NC 27610, Phone: (919) 516-4131.

830

ST. AUGUSTINE'S COLLEGE

National Alliance for Excellence Scholarship

Who Can Apply: Candidates must present recommendations or art portfolios that point to talent and achievement in all areas.

How Much Money Can I Get: Varies

Whom Do I Contact: St. Augustine's College, Office of Financial Aid, Charles Mosee Building, 1315 Oakwood Avenue, Raleigh, NC 27610, (919) 516-4131.

831

ST. AUGUSTINE'S COLLEGE
National Association of Black Journalists Scholarship
Who Can Apply: Students should be attending a four-year university. They must present three letters of recommendation from a school adviser, dean or a faculty member. Also, a 500-800 word article on a Black journalist must be presented. A minimum 3.0 GPA is desirable. Eligible students must be majoring in Journalism-Print, Photography, Radio or Television.
How Much Money Can I Get: $2,500
Whom Do I Contact: St. Augustine's College, Office of Financial Aid, Charles Mosee Building, 1315 Oakwood Avenue, Raleigh, NC 27610, (919) 516-4131.

832

ST. AUGUSTINE'S COLLEGE
National Association of Hispanic Journalists Scholarship
Who Can Apply: Students of Hispanic descent majoring in Journalism. Application is required.
How Much Money Can I Get: $1,000 to $5,000
Whom Do I Contact: St. Augustine's College, Office of Financial Aid, Charles Mosee Building, 1315 Oakwood Avenue, Raleigh, NC 27610, (919) 516-4131.

833

ST. AUGUSTINE'S COLLEGE
NCAA Scholarship
Who Can Apply: Students demonstrating financial need.
How Much Money Can I Get: $3,000 to $12,000
Whom Do I Contact: St. Augustine's College, Office of Financial Aid, Charles Mosee Building, 1315 Oakwood Avenue, Raleigh, NC 27610, (919) 516-4131.

834

ST. AUGUSTINE'S COLLEGE
NSBE Scholarship
Who Can Apply: Students majoring in Engineering.
How Much Money Can I Get: $1,000
Whom Do I Contact: St. Augustine's College, Office of Financial Aid, Charles Mosee Building, 1315 Oakwood Avenue, Raleigh, NC 27610, Phone: (919) 516-4131.

835

ST. AUGUSTINE'S COLLEGE

Project Excellence Scholarship
Who Can Apply: Students who demonstrate academic merit.
How Much Money Can I Get: $6,000
Whom Do I Contact: St. Augustine's College, Office of Financial Aid, Charles Mosee Building, 1315 Oakwood Avenue, Raleigh, NC 27610, Phone: (919) 516-4131.

836

ST. AUGUSTINE'S COLLEGE

Ron Brown Scholarship
Who Can Apply: Students who demonstrate academic merit.
How Much Money Can I Get: Varies
Whom Do I Contact: St. Augustine's College, Office of Financial Aid, Charles Mosee Building, 1315 Oakwood Avenue, Raleigh, NC 27610, Phone: (919) 516-4131.

837

ST. AUGUSTINE'S COLLEGE

Ronald McDonald House Charities and the United Negro College Fund
Who Can Apply: Students must be studying at a HBCU that is a member of the UNCF.
How Much Money Can I Get: $1,000
Whom Do I Contact: St. Augustine's College, Office of Financial Aid, Charles Mosee Building, 1315 Oakwood Avenue, Raleigh, NC 27610, (919) 516-4131.

838

ST. AUGUSTINE'S COLLEGE

Society of Women Engineers Scholarship
Who Can Apply: Women who are majoring in Engineering or Computer science.
How Much Money Can I Get: $200 to $5,000, and at least 90 are granted.
Whom Do I Contact: St. Augustine's College, Office of Financial Aid, Charles Mosee Building, 1315 Oakwood Avenue, Raleigh, NC 27610, (919) 516-4131.

839

ST. AUGUSTINE'S COLLEGE

Xerox Technology Minority Scholarship
Who Can Apply: Students studying chemistry, engineering, physics, and other technical areas.

How Much Money Can I Get: $4,000
Whom Do I Contact: St. Augustine's College, Office of Financial Aid,
Charles Mosee Building, 1315 Oakwood Avenue, Raleigh, NC 27610, (919) 516-4131.

840
ST. JOHN FISHER COLLEGE
Who Can Apply: Minority Student Grants are available to the ten best applicants. Must have a 3.0 GPA and financial need required.
How Much Money Can I Get: Half tuition
Whom Do I Contact: Director of Admissions, St. John Fisher College, 3690 East Avenue, Rochester, NY 14618, (716) 385-8064.

841
ST. JOHN'S UNIVERSITY
Who Can Apply: Library Science Minority Fellowship. These grants are provided by the U.S. Department of Education. Contact the university for details.
How Much Money Can I Get: $4,000
Whom Do I Contact: Library Science Division, St. John's University, Grand Central & Utopia Parkway, Jamaica, NY 11439, (718) 990-6403.

842
ST. LOUIS COMMUNITY COLLEGE
Who Can Apply: The Heartland's Alliance for Minority Participation (HAMP) provides an annual scholarship to qualified minority students who wish to pursue science, mathematics, or engineering studies at St. Louis Community College, then transfer to an HAMP four-year institution to complete a bachelor's degree.
How Much Money Can I Get: Varies, 20 awards
Whom Do I Contact: Dr. Judith Toman, St. Louis Community College, 5600 Oakland Avenue, St. Louis, MO 63110, (314) 644-9772, fax: (314) 644-9992, E-mail: jtoman@goldie.stlcc.cc.mo.us.

843
ST. MARY OF THE WOODS COLLEGE
Who Can Apply: Minority Leadership Award for a full-time female minority student who demonstrates leadership, community service, and commitment to achievement. Deadline August 15.
How Much Money Can I Get: $2,000
Whom Do I Contact: Street Mary of the Woods College, Attn.: Director of Admissions/Financial Aid, Guerin Hall, St. Mary of the Woods, IN 47876, (812) 535-5106.

844

ST. MARY'S COLLEGE OF MARYLAND

Who Can Apply: Offers several scholarship programs: Matthias D'Sousa Scholarships, General Scholarships, Brent Calvert Fellowship Honors Program, and The Waring Award. For example, the Matthias D'Sousa Scholarship is available to entering freshmen who are minority students and residents of Maryland. The award pays up to full tuition, room, and board and is renewable. Deadline February 1.
How Much Money Can I Get: Varies
Whom Do I Contact: Office of Admissions, St. Mary's College of Maryland, St. Mary's City, MD 20686, (800) 492-7181.

845

ST. PAUL'S COLLEGE

Who Can Apply: United Negro College Fund is available to entering black students. Must have a strong academic background. Apply early.
How Much Money Can I Get: $100 to $2,000
Whom Do I Contact: St. Paul's College, 406 Windsor Avenue, Lawrenceville, VA 23868, (804) 848-3111.

846

ST. THOMAS CHURCH

Who Can Apply: The James Townsend Scholarship in Music. Applicant must be a black student enrolled as a freshman or sophomore in a college, university, or school of music. Selection is based on results of competitive auditions. Must be majoring in music or music vocals.
How Much Money Can I Get: $1,000
Whom Do I Contact: Mrs. Parthenia L. Twisdale, 11 Placid Lane, Willingboro, NJ 08046.

847

UNIVERSITY OF ST. THOMAS

Who Can Apply: The Brown Foundation, Inc. Multicultural Scholarship Fund provides resources to enable more qualified minority students to gain access to the University of St. Thomas; applicants must be in the top 25 percent of their high school graduating class. Deadline March 1.
How Much Money Can I Get: Varies, renewable for up to three years
Whom Do I Contact: University of St. Thomas, 3800 Montrose Boulevard, Houston, TX 77006-4694, (713) 525-3500, (800) 856-8565.

848

STATE STUDENT ASSISTANCE COMMISSION OF INDIANA

Minority Teacher Scholarship
Who Can Apply: Applicant must be a black U.S. citizen, have a 2.0 GPA, and major in Education (special and preschool included). Must teach three out of five years in Indiana following certification.
How Much Money Can I Get: $1,000
Whom Do I Contact: State Student Assistance Commission of Indiana, 964 N. Pennsylvania, First Floor, Indiana, IN 46208, (317) 251-1304.

849

STATE UNIVERSITY OF NEW YORK AT ALBANY

Minority Graduate Assistantships in Library Science
Who Can Apply: African Americans, Asian Americans, Hispanic Americans, and Native American Indians.
How Much Money Can I Get: Fellowships of up to $7,500 per year with available full-tuition scholarships. Assistantships offer a stipend of up to $8,000 per academic year. In addition, full-tuition scholarships are available.
Whom Do I Contact: State University of New York at Albany, School of Information Science & Policy, 135 Western Avenue, Albany, NY 12222, (518) 442-5110.

850

STATE UNIVERSITY OF NEW YORK AT ALBANY, SCHOOL OF CRIMINAL JUSTICE

New York State Fellowship and Assistantships for Underrepresented Minority Students
Who Can Apply: Qualified graduate students.
How Much Money Can I Get: $7,500 to $10,000 stipend and a tuition scholarship
Whom Do I Contact: State University of New York at Albany, School of Criminal Justice, 135 Western Avenue, Albany, NY 12222, (518) 442-5214.

851

STATE UNIVERSITY OF NEW YORK AT ONEONTA

Minority Honors Scholarship
Who Can Apply: African American, Hispanic, or Native American Indian students
How Much Money Can I Get: Up to $1,000

Whom Do I Contact: Director of Financial Aid, State University of New York, Netzer Administration Building, Ravine Parkway, Oneonta, NY 13820, (607) 431-2532.

852

STATE UNIVERSITY OF NEW YORK AT ONEONTA

Scott-Jenkins Memorial Grant
Who Can Apply: African American or Hispanic students with a 2.0 GPA, financial need, and who are U.S. citizens.
How Much Money Can I Get: $700
Whom Do I Contact: SUNY, Attn.: Financial Aid Director, Netzer Administration Building, Ravine Parkway, Oneonta, NY 13820, (607) 431-2532.

853

STILLMAN COLLEGE

Who Can Apply: Applicants must be black entering freshmen and have a strong academic background. Apply early.
How Much Money Can I Get: $100 to $2,000
Whom Do I Contact: Stillman College, P.O. Box 1430, Tuscaloosa, AL 35403, (205) 349-4240 or (800) 841-5722.

854

STILLMAN COLLEGE

Harte Honors College Scholarship
Who Can Apply: Applicants must have a minimum 1150 SAT score (25 ACT).
How Much Money Can I Get: Tuition
Whom Do I Contact: Stillman College, Office of Financial Aid, P.O. Box 1430, Tuscaloosa, AL 35403-9990, (205) 366-8844.

855

STILLMAN COLLEGE

Performing Arts Scholarship
Who Can Apply: Students who possess musical talent and who also show academic promise.
How Much Money Can I Get: Tuition
Whom Do I Contact: Stillman College, Office of Financial Aid, P.O. Box 1430, Tuscaloosa, AL 35403-9990, (205) 366-8844.

856

STUDIO ARTS CENTER

Who Can Apply: Various fellowships and awards to ethnic minorities and women studio artists and photographers to study in Florence. Deadline May 1.
How Much Money Can I Get: $1,000 to $17,000
Whom Do I Contact: Studio Arts Center, IIE, 809 United Nations Plaza, New York, NY 10017-3580, (800) 344-9186.

857

STUDENT ASSISTANCE COMMISSION

Minority Teacher Scholarship
Who Can Apply: Applicants must be U.S. citizens, attend an Indiana institution full-time and major in education. Must teach three out of five years in Indiana.
How Much Money Can I Get: $1,000
Whom Do I Contact: Student Assistance Commission, 964 N. Pennsylvania Street, Indianapolis, IN 46204, (317) 232-2350.

858

SYNOD OF THE TRINITY

Who Can Apply: Scholarships for minority students in several designated areas of the presbytery surrounding Pennsylvania who must have been admitted to attend college and who demonstrate financial need.
How Much Money Can I Get: Varies
Whom Do I Contact: Synod of the Trinity, 3040 Market Street, Camp Hill, PA 17011.

859

SYNOD OF THE TRINITY

Minority Scholarship Program
Who Can Apply: Applicants must live in West Virginia (does not include northeastern and southwestern counties in the panhandles). Applicants must demonstrate financial need, submit a narrative of career goals and family situation, file a transcript of grades, register with their financial aid office, and apply for federal (Pell) and state programs. Deadline March 1.
How Much Money Can I Get: $200 to $800
Whom Do I Contact: Minority Scholarship Program, 3040 Market Street, Camp Hill, PA 17011-4591, (717) 737-0421.

860

SYRACUSE HERALD JOURNAL

Who Can Apply: One or more students selected to attend the S. I. Newhouse School of Public Communications at Syracuse University; selected from among participants in the two-semester high school journalism course sponsored annually by the Syracuse Newspapers (*Herald Journal, Post standard, Herald American*). Winners are selected on basis of general academic promise, sincerity of purpose, and specific potential as a journalist. Candidate must maintain enrollment in the newspaper journalism program of the S. I. Newhouse School of Public Communications at Syracuse University.
How Much Money Can I Get: Valued at full expense of attendance at Syracuse University for one year, renewable for four years
Whom Do I Contact: *Syracuse Herald Journal*, Clinton Square, P.O. Box 4915, Syracuse, NY 13221-4915.

861

SYRACUSE UNIVERSITY

WSYR Minority Award
Who Can Apply: Open to candidates from an ethnic minority who wish to study broadcast journalism.
How Much Money Can I Get: $4,000
Whom Do I Contact: Office of Admissions, Syracuse University, Syracuse, NY 13210, (315) 423-1870.

862

TALLADEGA COLLEGE

Alice M. Holman Scholarship Fund
Who Can Apply: Students majoring in Music.
How Much Money Can I Get: Tuition
Whom Do I Contact: Talladega College, Attn.: Office of Financial Aid, 627 West Battle Talladega, AL 35160, (205) 761-6236.

863

TALLADEGA COLLEGE

Alumni Centennial Endowment Fund
Who Can Apply: Students who demonstrate financial need.
How Much Money Can I Get: Tuition
Whom Do I Contact: Talladega College, Attn.: Office of Financial Aid, 627 West Battle Talladega, AL 35160, (205) 761-6236.

864

TALLADEGA COLLEGE

Athletic Award

Who Can Apply: Eligible students who participate in intercollegiate athletics.

How Much Money Can I Get: Tuition

Whom Do I Contact: Talladega College, Attn.: Office of Financial Aid, 627 West Battle Talladega, AL 35160, (205) 761-6236.

865

TALLADEGA COLLEGE

The Fritz Pappenheim Academic Freedom Award

Who Can Apply: Students with above average academic achievement and who have demonstrated concern for people through volunteer service and leadership.

How Much Money Can I Get: Tuition

Whom Do I Contact: Talladega College, Attn.: Office of Financial Aid, 627 West Battle Talladega, AL 35160, (205) 761-6236.

866

TALLADEGA COLLEGE

Grant (A)

Who Can Apply: Candidate must possess a cumulative GPA of 3.20 to 3.40 (on a 4 scale).

How Much Money Can I Get: $2,000 per year

Whom Do I Contact: Talladega College, Attn.: Office of Financial Aid, 627 West Battle Talladega, AL 35160, (205) 761-6236.

867

TALLADEGA COLLEGE

Grant (B)

Who Can Apply: Applicant must possess a cumulative 3.0 GPA.

How Much Money Can I Get: $1,000 per year

Whom Do I Contact: Talladega College, Attn.: Office of Financial Aid, 627 West Battle Talladega, AL 35160, (205) 761-6236.

868

TALLADEGA COLLEGE

John and Huey Cross Scholarship

Who Can Apply: Students who demonstrate financial need.

How Much Money Can I Get: Tuition

Whom Do I Contact: Talladega College, Attn.: Office of Financial Aid, 627 West Battle Talladega, AL 35160, (205) 761-6236.

869

TALLADEGA COLLEGE
Laura G. Hunting Scholarship
Who Can Apply: Students who demonstrate above average academic achievement, concern for people through volunteer service, leadership in activities, and potential for post-graduate success.
How Much Money Can I Get: Tuition
Whom Do I Contact: Talladega College, Attn.: Office of Financial Aid, 627 West Battle Talladega, AL 35160, (205) 761-6236.

870

TALLADEGA COLLEGE
Leonard E. and Bessie B. Dewry Fund
Who Can Apply: Students who demonstrate financial need.
How Much Money Can I Get: Tuition
Whom Do I Contact: Talladega College, Attn.: Office of Financial Aid, 627 West Battle Talladega, AL 35160, (205) 761-6236.

871

TALLADEGA COLLEGE
Monroe Hill Scholarship Fund
Who Can Apply: Students from the Delaware Valley, including New York State. If there is no student from this area, then one is selected from Florida.
How Much Money Can I Get: Tuition
Whom Do I Contact: Talladega College, Attn.: Office of Financial Aid, 627 West Battle Talladega, AL 35160, (205) 761-6236.

872

TALLADEGA COLLEGE
Nettye George Kent Goodard Scholarship
Who Can Apply: Students majoring in English who plans to teach and has a minimum 3.3 GPA.
How Much Money Can I Get: Tuition
Whom Do I Contact: Talladega College, Attn.: Office of Financial Aid, 627 West Battle Talladega, AL 35160, (205) 761-6236.

873

TALLADEGA COLLEGE
The Presidential I Scholarship
Who Can Apply: Students who qualify for consideration are in the top 5 percent of their high school graduating class, possess a GPA of 3.75 to 4 (on a 4 scale), and have a combined SAT score of 1200 (26 ACT).

How Much Money Can I Get: $9,048 per year plus book awards up to $500 each semester.
Whom Do I Contact: Talladega College, Attn.: Office of Financial Aid, 627 West Battle Talladega, AL 35160, (205) 761-6236.

874

TALLADEGA COLLEGE
The Presidential II Scholarship
Who Can Apply: Five students who rank in the top 10 percent of their graduating class. The average GPA of recipients ranges from 3.50 to 3.75 (on a scale). Students who qualify have a combined SAT 1000 score (23 ACT).
How Much Money Can I Get: This scholarship covers tuition up to $5,666 per year.
Whom Do I Contact: Talladega College, Attn.: Office of Financial Aid, 627 West Battle Talladega, AL 35160, (205) 761-6236.

875

TALLADEGA COLLEGE
William R. Harvey Endowed Scholarship
Who Can Apply: Student majoring in either History or Business.
How Much Money Can I Get: Tuition
Whom Do I Contact: Talladega College, Attn.: Office of Financial Aid, 627 West Battle Talladega, AL 35160, (205) 761-6236.

876

TECHNOLOGY SCHOLARSHIP PROGRAM FOR ALABAMA TEACHERS
Who Can Apply: Students who are full-time regularly certified Alabama public school teachers enrolled in approved courses that incorporate new technologies in the curriculum.
How Much Money Can I Get: Tuition
Whom Do I Contact: TSPAT, Alabama Commission on Higher Education, P.O. Box 302000, Montgomery, AL 36130-2000, (800) ALTSPAT.

877

TENNESSEE STATE UNIVERSITY
Who Can Apply: Must be black and have a 3.0 GPA. Deadline April 1.
How Much Money Can I Get: Tuition + room
Whom Do I Contact: Tennessee State University, 3500 John A. Merritt Boulevard, Nashville, TN 37209-1561, (615) 320-3042.

878

TENNESSEE STUDENT ASSISTANCE
Minority Teaching Fellowship
Who Can Apply: Must be a U.S. citizen with a 2.5 GPA and in the upper two-fifths of their class. One-year teaching obligation per year of award. Forgivable loan program. Deadline May 15.
How Much Money Can I Get: $5,000
Whom Do I Contact: Program Administrator, Tennessee Student Assistance, Suite 1950, Parkway Towers, 404 James Robertson Parkway, Nashville, TN 37243, (615) 741-1346.

879

TENNESSEE TECHNOLOGICAL UNIVERSITY
Minority Engineering Effort
Who Can Apply: Financial need required. Must be majoring in one of the following engineering areas: chemical, electrical, industrial, civil, or mechanical.
How Much Money Can I Get: $250 to $2,500
Whom Do I Contact: Financial Aid Director, Tennessee Technological University, P.O. Box 5076, Cookeville, TN 38505, (615) 372-3888.

880

UNIVERSITY OF TENNESSEE
The Minority Engineering Scholarship Program (MESP)
Who Can Apply: Awarded to African American high school students with a minimum 3.0 GPA, 940 SAT score (23 ACT), 3 1/2 units of math, and letters of recommendations from a counselor and math and science teachers. Deadline February.
How Much Money Can I Get: $11,000+
Whom Do I Contact: James T. Pippin, Assistant Dean, College of Engineering, University of Tennessee, 103 Estabrook Hall, Knoxville, TN 37996.

881

UNIVERSITY OF TENNESSEE
Whittle Communications Minority Scholarship
Who Can Apply: Graduating Tennessee minority high school seniors based on scholastic ability and interest in print journalism. Deadline January 1.
How Much Money Can I Get: Award includes $7,050 (full tuition, lodging fees, plus internship with Whittle Communications) renewable for three additional years.
Whom Do I Contact: University of Tennessee, College of Communications, Knoxville, TN 37996-0332, (615) 974-3031.

882

TEXAS A & I UNIVERSITY
The National Action Council-ME Scholarship
Who Can Apply: Freshmen in the top 25 percent of their class who have a competitive ACT/ SAT score and who submit one letter of recommendation. The award is renewable with a 2.5 GPA. Deadline April 15.
How Much Money Can I Get: $1,000
Whom Do I Contact: Texas A & I University, Engineering Dept., Box 188, Kingsville, TX 78363, (512) 595-3907.

883

TEXAS A & I UNIVERSITY
Atlantic Richfield Co. Scholarship
Who Can Apply: Applicant must have a competitive class rank and ACT/ SAT score. The award is renewable with a 2.7 GPA. Must be majoring in Chemical Engineering or Natural Resources. Deadline November 15 and April 1.
How Much Money Can I Get: $500
Whom Do I Contact: Dean, Chemical/Natural Gas, Texas A & I University, Chemical/Natural Gas, Box 193, Kingsville, TX 78363, (512) 595-3907.

884

TEXAS A & I UNIVERSITY
Texas State Ethnic Recruitment
Who Can Apply: Open to non-Hispanic minorities who have financial need, are in the top 33 percent of their class, and have a 2.75 GPA. Applicants must also have a minimum ACT/SAT score of 18/800.
How Much Money Can I Get: $1,000
Whom Do I Contact: Financial Aid Director, Texas A & I University Financial Aid, Box 115, Kingsville, TX 78363, (512) 595-3907.

885

TEXAS A & I UNIVERSITY
The 3M Foundation Scholarship
Who Can Apply: Applicants must have an ACT/SAT score of at least 22/ 950 and submit one letter of recommendation. The award is renewable with at least a 3.0 GPA. Must be a U.S. citizen, show financial need, and be majoring in one of the following engineering areas: electrical, chemical, or mechanical.
How Much Money Can I Get: $1,000
Whom Do I Contact: Director of Admissions, Texas A & I University Engineering, Box 188, Kingsville, TX 78363, (512) 595-2111.

886

TEXAS A & I UNIVERSITY
Larry and Charlotte Franklin Scholarship
Who Can Apply: Applicants must be active on the yearbook staff and majoring in journalism, be in the top half of their class, have a minimum ACT/SAT score of 18/800, a 2.75 GPA, and submit two letters of recommendation. Deadline May 1.
How Much Money Can I Get: $250
Whom Do I Contact: Dean, Communications Department, Texas A & I University Communications, Box 178, Kingsville, TX 78363, (512) 595-3907.

887

TEXAS A & M UNIVERSITY
President's Achievement Award
Who Can Apply: African American and Hispanic students who are U.S. citizens or permanent residents admitted to the university. Approximately 350 non-need-based scholarship offers are made annually. Applicants may compete for other Texas A & M scholarships including an additional $1,000 stipend for those participating in study abroad and awards to those seeking professional degrees at Texas A & M. Academic achievement, SAT or ACT test results and class rank are considered.
How Much Money Can I Get: Stipends of $2,500 yearly for a total of $10,000 for four years of undergraduate study are awarded. On-campus housing is guaranteed to recipients submitting residence applications by June 1.
Whom Do I Contact: Texas A & M University, Office of School Relations, Memorial Student Center, College Station, TX 77843-1265, (409) 845-3741.

888

TEXAS A & M UNIVERSITY
Minority Engineering Education
Who Can Apply: Financial need required. Must be majoring in agriculture or one of the following engineering areas: aerospace, biomedical, civil, industrial, nuclear, chemical, electrical, mechanical, or petroleum. Deadline February 15.
How Much Money Can I Get: $500
Whom Do I Contact: Engineering Department, Texas A & M University, College Station, TX 77843-1252, (409) 845-7200.

889

TEXAS A & M UNIVERSITY
The Minority Merit Fellowship
Who Can Apply: Students who will begin graduate study toward a doctoral
or master's degree in any field of study offered by the Texas A & M
University at the College Station campus. Deadline March 1.
How Much Money Can I Get: $7,800
Whom Do I Contact: Admissions Office, Texas A & M University, College
Station, TX 77843-1252, (409) 845-3631.

890

TEXAS ALLIANCE FOR MINORITIES
IN ENGINEERING
Who Can Apply: The TAME program provides financial assistance and
helps minority students gain admission into engineering programs.
How Much Money Can I Get: Varies
Whom Do I Contact: Texas Alliance for Minorities in Engineering, UTA
Station 19775, Arlington, TX 76019.

891

TEXAS BLACK BAPTIST SCHOLARSHIP
Who Can Apply: Awarded to resident of Texas attending a Texas school
with a minimum GPA of 2.0 (3.0 if a high school senior) and who possesses a
vital interest in the advancement of the Kingdom of God.
How Much Money Can I Get: $800 a year
Whom Do I Contact: Texas Black Baptist Scholarship Committee, Black
Church Relations Section, Attn.: James W. Culp, Sr., 333 N. Washington,
Suite 371, Dallas, TX 74246-1798, (214) 828-5100.

892

TEXAS STATE SCHOLARSHIP PROGRAM
FOR ETHNIC RECRUITMENT
Who Can Apply: Students whose ethnic group comprises less than 40
percent of the enrollment at a particular institution may be eligible for a
scholarship. Entering freshmen must attain an ACT score of at least 18, and
transfer students must have at least a 2.75 GPA.
How Much Money Can I Get: $500 to $1,000
Whom Do I Contact: Texas Higher Education Coordinating Board, P.O.
Box 12788, Capitol Station, Austin, TX 78711, (512) 483-6340.

893

UNIVERSITY OF TEXAS, ARLINGTON

Ethnic Recruitment Scholarship
Who Can Apply: Applicants must be residents of Texas. Entering freshmen must rank in the upper third of their high school graduating class or have a minimum SAT combined score of 800 (18 ACT). Entering transfer students must have a GPA of at least 2.75 at the college they last attended.
How Much Money Can I Get: $500
Whom Do I Contact: Scholarship Office, University of Texas, Box 19199, Arlington, TX 76019, (817) 273-2197.

894

UNIVERSITY OF TEXAS AT AUSTIN

Accounting Scholarship
Who Can Apply: Minority students majoring in Accounting.
How Much Money Can I Get: Varies
Whom Do I Contact: Office of Admissions, University of Texas at Austin, Austin, TX 78712, (512) 471-3434.

895

UNIVERSITY OF TEXAS AT AUSTIN

Minority Business Assistance
Who Can Apply: Students in the College of Business Administration.
How Much Money Can I Get: Varies
Whom Do I Contact: Office of Admissions, University of Texas at Austin, Austin, TX 78712, (512) 471-3434.

896

UNIVERSITY OF TEXAS AT AUSTIN

Texas Achievement Award
Who Can Apply: Minority freshmen who show academic potential.
How Much Money Can I Get: $1,000
Whom Do I Contact: Office of Admissions, University of Texas at Austin, Austin, TX 78712, (512) 471-3434.

897

UNIVERSITY OF TEXAS AT AUSTIN

Earl Campbell Endowed Presidential Scholarship
Who Can Apply: Deserving undergraduate minority students. Deadline February 15.
How Much Money Can I Get: $2,000
Whom Do I Contact: University of Texas at Austin, College of Communication, Austin, TX 78712, (512) 471-5775.

898

TEXAS SOUTHERN UNIVERSITY
The Julius A. Thomas Fellowship
Who Can Apply: Program was created to offer minority individuals an opportunity for master's-level education in a field to enable them to serve the career counseling and placement needs of minority and disadvantaged students. In addition, an allowance of up to $150 for approved books and materials is available. Persons interested should apply for the program at one of the six participating institutions and indicate an interest in the Thomas Fellowship Program. Contact the dean for instructional services at Texas Southern University for additional information. Deadline May 1.
How Much Money Can I Get: $3,000
Whom Do I Contact: Texas Southern University, 2300 Cleburne, Houston, TX 77004, (713) 527-7474.

899

UNIVERSITY OF TEXAS AT EL PASO
The Minority Engineering Award
Who Can Apply: Must show financial need and be majoring in one of the following engineering fields: civil, metallurgy, electrical, or mechanical.
How Much Money Can I Get: $250 to $1,000
Whom Do I Contact: University of Texas at El Paso, 500 W. University Avenue, El Paso, TX 79968, (915) 747-5204.

900

THURGOOD MARSHALL SCHOLARSHIP FUND
Who Can Apply: Available for students at historically black public colleges or universities with a 3.0 GPA and a 1000 SAT combined score (24 ACT). Deadline May 1.
How Much Money Can I Get: $16,000 over a four-year period
Whom Do I Contact: The Thurgood Marshall Scholarship Fund, 100 Park Avenue, 10th Floor, New York, NY 10017.

901

UNIVERSITY OF TOLEDO
Minority Scholarship
Who Can Apply: Applicants must be U.S. citizens, majoring in Engineering with a 3.0 GPA.
How Much Money Can I Get: $1,000
Whom Do I Contact: Office of Admissions, University of Toledo, 2801 W. Bancroft, Toledo, OH 43606, (419) 537-2696.

902

TOWSON UNIVERSITY

Minority Awards for Academic Excellence
Who Can Apply: Full-time freshman and transfer students. Academic achievement and leadership potential are criteria. Applicants must be Maryland residents with a 2.75+ GPA and a 1000 combined SAT score. Transfers must be Maryland residents with a 2.75 GPA and an associate's degree from a Maryland community college. Deadline January 1.
How Much Money Can I Get: $1,000 to full tuition and fees
Whom Do I Contact: Admissions Office, Towson University, Administration Building, Room 324, Towson, MD 21204-7097, (410) 830-2113.

903

TRINITY UNIVERSITY

Minority Scholarship
Who Can Apply: Students recognized through National Achievement or National Hispanic Scholarship programs.
How Much Money Can I Get: $1,000 to $4,000
Whom Do I Contact: Director, Trinity University, Minority Scholarships Financial Aid Office, 715 Stadium Drive, San Antonio, TX 78284, (512) 736-8315.

904

TUCSON DAILY STAR

Concerned Media Professional Scholarship
Who Can Apply: Minority students majoring in Journalism. Deadline in April.
How Much Money Can I Get: $500 to $1,000
Whom Do I Contact: *Tucson Daily Star*, P.O. Box 26887, Tucson, AZ 85726, (602) 573-4511

905

TUFTS UNIVERSITY

Summer Multicultural Teaching Fellowship Program
Who Can Apply: Underrepresented graduate students who are either entering or have completed the final year of their terminal degree program. Students must teach one course during a five- to six-week term. Candidates must be a U.S. citizen. Deadline November 7.
How Much Money Can I Get: $3,500
Whom Do I Contact: Summer Multicultural Teaching Fellowship Program, Office of Equal Opportunity, Tufts University, Medford, MA 02155, (617) 627-3298, (800) 611-5060.

906

TUSKEGEE UNIVERSITY

Who Can Apply: The United Negro College Fund is awarded to a black entering freshman. Must have a strong academic background. Apply early.
How Much Money Can I Get: $1,000 to $2,000
Whom Do I Contact: Office of Financial Aid, Tuskegee University, Tuskegee, AL 36088, (212) 867-1100.

907

UNION COLLEGE

The Chester Arthur Undergraduate Support of Excellence Awards (CAUSE)
Who Can Apply: Students engaging in public service-oriented activities.
How Much Money Can I Get: Varies
Whom Do I Contact: Admissions Office, Becker Hall, Union College, Schenectady, NY 12308, (518) 370-6131.

908

UNION COLLEGE

IBM Scholarship Fund
Who Can Apply: Women and minority engineering students. Financial need required.
How Much Money Can I Get: Varies
Whom Do I Contact: Union College, Stanley R. Becker Hall, Schenectady, NY 12308.

909

UNITED CHURCH OF CHRIST COMMISSION FOR RACIAL JUSTICE

Special Higher Education Program
Who Can Apply: Students demonstrating financial need. Awards are given each semester.
How Much Money Can I Get: Varies
Whom Do I Contact: United Church of Christ Commission for Racial Justice Special Higher Education Program, 475 Riverside Drive, Tenth Floor, New York, NY 10115-0122, (212) 870-2893.

910

UNITED CHURCH OF CHRIST, SOUTHERN CALIFORNIA

Seaman Scholarship
Who Can Apply: Open to female students. Deadline May 6.
How Much Money Can I Get: Varies

Whom Do I Contact: United Church of Christ, Southern California Conference, c/o Women in Mission Commission, Attn.: Josephine Seaman Scholarship Committee, 466 E. Walnut Street, Pasadena, CA 91101-1690, (818) 449-6026.

911

UNITED METHODIST CHURCH
Crusade Scholarship Program
Who Can Apply: Must show promise of providing leadership for the church and society. Deadline February 1.
How Much Money Can I Get: Varies
Whom Do I Contact: Mission Personnel Resources Program Department, General Board of Global Ministers, Suite 1470, 475 Riverside Drive, New York, NY 10115.

912

UNITED METHODIST CHURCH
Ethnic Minority Scholarship
Who Can Apply: Minority students who are active in the United Methodist Church, recommended by their pastor, enrolled in an accredited college, and in financial need.
How Much Money Can I Get: $100 to $1,000
Whom Do I Contact: United Methodist Church Board of Higher Education and Ministry, P.O. Box 871, Nashville, TN 37202, (615) 327-2700.

913

UNITED METHODIST CHURCH
HANA Scholars Program
Who Can Apply: Minority United Methodist Church members with financial need for undergraduate studies.
How Much Money Can I Get: Up to $1,000
Whom Do I Contact: United Methodist Church, Board of Higher Education and Ministry, P.O. Box 871, Nashville, TN 37202, (615) 327-2700.

914

UNITED METHODIST COMMUNICATION
Leonard M. Perryman Communication Scholarship
Who Can Apply: Minority students pursuing a career in religious communications. Deadline February 1.
How Much Money Can I Get: $2,500
Whom Do I Contact: Nelson Price, United Methodist Communication, Suite 1901, 475 Riverside Drive, New York, NY 10115.

915

UNITED METHODIST PUBLISHING HOUSE
MERIT SCHOLARSHIP PROGRAM

Who Can Apply: For those interested in employment with United Methodist Church or United Methodist Publishing House. Deadline March 15.
How Much Money Can I Get: Varies
Whom Do I Contact: Office of Loans & Scholarships, The United Methodist Church Merit Scholarship Program, P.O. Box 871, Nashville, TN 37202-0871, (615) 327-2700.

916

UNITED NEGRO COLLEGE FUND

Who Can Apply: Qualified applicants are considered without regard to race, creed, color, or national origin. Individual member colleges where students have applied for admission select scholarship recipients. Applications and selection of recipients are not administered by the United Negro College Fund. Students must take the SAT test (December exam). The United Negro College Fund administers full support MBA fellowships. Applicants must have a 3.0 GPA, majoring in engineering, and have financial need. Write for details.
How Much Money Can I Get: $1,000 to $2,000
Whom Do I Contact: UNCF, 8260 Willow Oaks Corporate Drive, Fairfax, VA 22031-4511, (703) 205-3400.

917

UNITED NEGRO COLLEGE FUND
General Motors Engineering Scholarship
Who Can Apply: Students must be enrolled in a UNCF college or university, demonstrate need, and have a 2.5 GPA. Inquiries must be made to the financial aid office at each school.
How Much Money Can I Get: Varies
Whom Do I Contact: UNCF, 8260 Willow Oaks Corporate Drive, Fairfax, VA 22031-4511, (703) 205-3400.

918

UNITED NEGRO COLLEGE FUND
Janet Jackson Rhythm Nation Scholarship for Performing Arts
Who Can Apply: Students must be enrolled in a UNCF college or university, demonstrate need, and have a 2.5 GPA. Inquiries must be made to the financial aid office at each school.
How Much Money Can I Get: Varies
Whom Do I Contact: UNCF, 8260 Willow Oaks Corporate Drive, Fairfax, VA 22031-4511, (703) 205-3400.

919

THE UNITED NEGRO SCHOLARSHIP FUND

Michael Jackson Scholarship for Performing Arts

Who Can Apply: Students must be enrolled in a UNCF college or university, demonstrate need, and have a 2.5 GPA. Inquiries must be made to the financial aid office at each school.

How Much Money Can I Get: Varies

Whom Do I Contact: UNCF, 8260 Willow Oaks Corporate Drive, Fairfax, VA 22031-4511, (703) 205-3400.

920

UNITED NEGRO COLLEGE FUND

Johnson & Johnson Awards Program

Who Can Apply: This program is available to minority men and women holding an undergraduate degree in any discipline for graduate study toward an MBA degree at one of seven selected institutions. Selection is based upon exceptional leadership ability and a strong interest in corporate management. Deadline January 31.

How Much Money Can I Get: $30,000

Whom Do I Contact: Johnson & Johnson Awards, United Negro College Fund, 500 E. 62nd Street, New York, NY 10021, (212) 326-1239.

921

UNITED NEGRO COLLEGE FUND

Stan Scott Endowed Scholarship for Journalism

Who Can Apply: Students must be enrolled in a UNCF college or university, demonstrate need, and have a 2.5 GPA. Inquiries must be made to the financial aid office at each school.

How Much Money Can I Get: Varies

Whom Do I Contact: UNCF, 8260 Willow Oaks Corporate Drive, Fairfax, VA 22031-4511, (703) 205-3400.

922

THE UNITED PRESBYTERIAN CHURCH IN THE U.S.A.

National Presbyterian College Scholarship

Who Can Apply: Awarded to superior young people preparing to enter as freshmen at one of the participating colleges related to the United Presbyterian Church in the U.S.A. Students must be a communicant member of the United Presbyterian Church and must demonstrate financial need. Deadline December 1.

How Much Money Can I Get: $100 to $1,400

Whom Do I Contact: The United Presbyterian Church in the U.S.A., 475 Riverside Drive, Room 430, New York, NY 10027, (212) 870-2618.

923
THE UNITED PRESBYTERIAN CHURCH IN THE U.S.A.

Student Opportunity Scholarship
Who Can Apply: For young persons of limited opportunities who are of ethnic minority groups and are related to the United Presbyterian Church in the U.S.A. Students must be a U.S. citizen, be entering as a freshman, be a full-time student, and apply to the college for financial aid.
How Much Money Can I Get: $100 to $1,400
Whom Do I Contact: The United Presbyterian Church in the U.S.A., 475 Riverside Drive, Room 430, New York, NY 10027, (212) 870-2618.

924
UTAH STATE UNIVERSITY

Minority Engineering Scholarship
Who Can Apply: For those majoring in one of the following engineering areas: civil, metallurgy, electrical, mechanical, or agriculture. Financial need required. Deadline September 1.
How Much Money Can I Get: $250 to $2,500
Whom Do I Contact: Utah State University, Logan, UT 84322-7700, (801) 797-1000.

925
UNIVERSITY OF UTAH

Who Can Apply: Achievement Award for Culturally Diverse Students, Meritorious Award for Culturally Diverse Students, John A. Moran Scholarship, Ken Winsness Scholarship, and Margaret E. Oser Foundation Scholarship available to matriculated freshman or transfer students, who on account of their geographic, ethnic, or cultural background will contribute to an educationally diverse environment. Deadline February 1.
How Much Money Can I Get: Varies
Whom Do I Contact: University of Utah, Office of Financial Aid and Scholarships, 201 South 1460, East Room 105, Salt Lake City UT 84112-9055, (801) 581-6211, (800) 868-5618, TTY: (801) 585-3665, fax: (801) 585-6350.

926
VALENCIA COMMUNITY COLLEGE

The African American Heritage Scholarship
Who Can Apply: Students of African American heritage with financial need and who graduated in the top 25 percent of their high school class.

How Much Money Can I Get: Tuition, renewable
Whom Do I Contact: Financial Aid Office, Valencia Community College, P.O. Box 3028, Orlando, FL 32802-3028 (407) 317-7950, E-mail Valencia3@aol.com.

927

VALPARAISO UNIVERSITY
The Henry L. Prahl Scholarship Fund
Who Can Apply: Minority student majoring in Education.
How Much Money Can I Get: Varies
Whom Do I Contact: Financial Aid Director, Valparaiso University, Valparaiso, IN 46383, (219) 464-5000.

928

VILLANOVA UNIVERSITY
Who Can Apply: Scholarships for black Americans are for students who wish to attend Villanova University as commuters. Applicants must be a U.S. citizen and in the upper fifth of their class.
How Much Money Can I Get: Tuition
Whom Do I Contact: Villanova University, Minority Recruiter, Villanova, PA 19085-1672, (215) 645-4004.

929

VIRGINIA COMMONWEALTH UNIVERSITY
The Black Freshman Scholarship Program
Who Can Apply: Entering freshmen with a 3.0 GPA. Applicants must be U.S. citizens and in the upper fifth of their class. Deadline March 1.
How Much Money Can I Get: $1,000 to $1,200
Whom Do I Contact: UES/Admissions, Virginia Commonwealth University, 821 W. Franklin Street, Box 2526, Richmond, VA 23284, (804) 367-1222.

930

VIRGINIA COMMONWEALTH UNIVERSITY
The Coca-Cola Scholarship
Who Can Apply: Entering black students who are U.S. citizens. Applicants must have a 3.5 GPA, be in the upper fifth of their class, and major in Accounting, Art, Marketing, or Business Administration/Management, and a 1000 SAT (23 ACT). Deadline March 1.
How Much Money Can I Get: $2,415
Whom Do I Contact: UES/Office of Admissions, Virginia Commonwealth University, 821 W. Franklin Street, Box 2526, Richmond, VA 23284, (804) 367-1222.

931

VIRGINIA POLYTECHNIC INSTITUTE & STATE UNIVERSITY

Minority Fellowship
Who Can Apply: Undergraduate and graduate students of urban and regional planning, urban affairs, and urban design. Students must have a minimum 3.0 GPA during the last two years of study. Deadline July 15.
How Much Money Can I Get: $2,100 for nine months
Whom Do I Contact: Virginia Polytechnic Institute & State University, Division of Environment & Urban Systems, College of Architecture & Urban Studies, Blacksburg, VA 24061, (703) 951-5582.

932

VIRGINIA UNION UNIVERSITY

John Gyles Education Award
Who Can Apply: High school seniors with a minimum 2.7 GPA.
How Much Money Can I Get: Up to 3,000 in yearly scholarship.
Whom Do I Contact: Virginia Union University, 1500 N. Lombardy Street, Richmond, VA 23220, (804) 257-5881 or (800) 368-3227.

933

VIRGINIA UNION UNIVERSITY

Health and Medical Scholars Program – Ronald McDonald House Charities and UNCF/The College Fund
Who Can Apply: Students must be studying at a HBCU that is a member of the UNCF.
Deadline April 1.
How Much Money Can I Get: $1,000 to full tuition
Whom Do I Contact: Virginia Union University, 1500 N. Lombardy Street, Richmond, VA 23220, (804) 257-5881 or (800) 368-3227.

934

VIRGINIA UNION UNIVERSITY

United Negro College Fund
Who Can Apply: Black freshmen. Must have a strong academic background. Apply early.
How Much Money Can I Get: $100 to $2,000
Whom Do I Contact: Virginia Union University, 1500 N. Lombardy Street, Richmond, VA 23220, (804) 257-5881 or (800) 368-3227.

935

VIRGINIA UNION UNIVERSITY
Scott L. Henderson Award
Who Can Apply: Needy black students majoring in journalism, English, or taking courses leading to a degree in journalism
How Much Money Can I Get: Varies
Whom Do I Contact: Virginia Union University, 1500 N. Lombardy Street, Richmond, VA 23220, (804) 257-5881 or (800) 368-3227.

936

VIRGINIA UNION UNIVERSITY
The J. Raymond Henderson Award
Who Can Apply: Students interested in the Christian ministry.
How Much Money Can I Get: Varies
Whom Do I Contact: Virginia Union University, 1500 N. Lombardy Street, Richmond, VA 23220, (804) 257-5881 or (800) 368-3227.

937

VIRGINIA UNION UNIVERSITY
The Benjamin F. Bunn Award
Who Can Apply: students enrolled in the School of Theology.
How Much Money Can I Get: Varies
Whom Do I Contact: Virginia Union University, 1500 N. Lombardy Street, Richmond, VA 23220, (804) 257-5881 or (800) 368-3227.

938

VIRGINIA UNION UNIVERSITY
The Lucille Murray Brown Award
Who Can Apply: Sophomore students majoring in teacher education who graduated from the Richmond Public School system.
How Much Money Can I Get: Varies
Whom Do I Contact: Virginia Union University, 1500 N. Lombardy Street, Richmond, VA 23220, (804) 257-5881 or (800) 368-3227.

939

VIRGINIA UNION UNIVERSITY
The Academic Excellence Endowed Scholarship
Who Can Apply: Worthy and deserving students enrolled in English, foreign languages of business courses in accordance with the wishes of Mr. Arthur Ashe, Jr.
How Much Money Can I Get: Varies
Whom Do I Contact: Virginia Union University, 1500 N. Lombardy Street, Richmond, VA 23220, (804) 257-5881 or (800) 368-3227.

940

VIRGINIA UNION UNIVERSITY
The John A. Inez C. Bacoats Award
Who Can Apply: Deserving students who are preparing for a career in the Christian Ministry of who are majoring in Church Music.
How Much Money Can I Get: Varies
Whom Do I Contact: Virginia Union University, 1500 N. Lombardy Street, Richmond, VA 23220, (804) 257-5881 or (800) 368-3227.

941

VIRGINIA UNION UNIVERSITY
The Michael A. Bradford Award
Who Can Apply: Needy and deserving children students dedicated to Christian Service
How Much Money Can I Get: Varies
Whom Do I Contact: Virginia Union University, 1500 N. Lombardy Street, Richmond, VA 23220, (804) 257-5881 or (800) 368-3227.

942

VIRGINIA UNION UNIVERSITY
The Dr. and Mrs. Lyman Beecher Brooks Award
Who Can Apply: Students majoring in mathematics.
How Much Money Can I Get: Varies
Whom Do I Contact: Virginia Union University, 1500 N. Lombardy Street, Richmond, VA 23220, (804) 257-5881 or (800) 368-3227.

943

VIRGINIA UNION UNIVERSITY
The Dorothy N. Cowling Award
Who Can Apply: Worthy and deserving seniors majoring in Education and Psychology.
How Much Money Can I Get: Varies
Whom Do I Contact: Virginia Union University, 1500 N. Lombardy Street, Richmond, VA 23220, (804) 257-5881 or (800) 368-3227.

944

VIRGINIA UNION UNIVERSITY
The Jerry C. Crews Award
Who Can Apply: Preference given to a Junior male student living in Richmond, VA.
How Much Money Can I Get: Varies
Whom Do I Contact: Virginia Union University, 1500 N. Lombardy Street, Richmond, VA 23220, (804) 257-5881 or (800) 368-3227.

945

VIRGINIA UNION UNIVERSITY
The Endowed Teacher Education Scholarship
Who Can Apply: Industrious and deserving sophomores and juniors majoring in the field of teacher education.
How Much Money Can I Get: Varies
Whom Do I Contact: Virginia Union University, 1500 N. Lombardy Street, Richmond, VA 23220, (804) 257-5881 or (800) 368-3227.

946

VIRGINIA UNION UNIVERSITY
The Ada Virginia Foster Fisher Award
Who Can Apply: The graduating valedictorian and the graduating senior majoring in French with the Highest GPA.
How Much Money Can I Get: Varies
Whom Do I Contact: Virginia Union University, 1500 N. Lombardy Street, Richmond, VA 23220, (804) 257-5881 or (800) 368-3227.

947

VIRGINIA UNION UNIVERSITY
The Dr. and Mrs. M. Gordon Award
Who Can Apply: senior students enrolled in the Sydney Lewis School of Business Administration.
How Much Money Can I Get: Varies
Whom Do I Contact: Virginia Union University, 1500 N. Lombardy Street, Richmond, VA 23220, (804) 257-5881 or (800) 368-3227.

948

VIRGINIA UNION UNIVERSITY
The Zenobia Gilpin Henderson Award
Who Can Apply: Students evidencing a potential for careers in public service.
How Much Money Can I Get: Varies
Whom Do I Contact: Virginia Union University, 1500 N. Lombardy Street, Richmond, VA 23220, (804) 257-5881 or (800) 368-3227.

949

UNIVERSITY OF VIRGINIA
J. H. Holland Scholarship
Who Can Apply: Black students who are U.S. citizens. Applicants must reside outside Virginia. Deadline January 15.
How Much Money Can I Get: $5,000

Whom Do I Contact: Director of Financial Aid, University of Virginia, P.O. Box 9021, Miller Hall, Charlottesville, VA 22906, (804) 924-3725.

950

UNIVERSITY OF VIRGINIA

The University Achievement Award
Who Can Apply: Exceptional black students in Virginia. Award is renewable with satisfactory academic progress.
How Much Money Can I Get: Tuition
Whom Do I Contact: University of Virginia—Charlottesville, Office of Financial Aid, P.O. Box 9021, Miller Hall, Charlottesville, VA 22906, (804) 924-3725.

951

UNIVERSITY OF VIRGINIA

Who Can Apply: Financial need required. Must be majoring in one of the following engineering areas: aerospace, civil, mechanical, chemical, or electrical.
How Much Money Can I Get: $250 to $2,500
Whom Do I Contact: Financial Aid Director, University of Virginia, P.O. Box 9021, Miller Hall, Charlottesville, VA 22906, (804) 924-3725.

952

VOORHEES COLLEGE

The United Negro College Fund
Who Can Apply: Entering freshmen. Must have a strong academic background. Apply early.
How Much Money Can I Get: $100 to $2,000
Whom Do I Contact: Voorhees College, Voorhees Road, Denmark, SC 29042.

953

W. W. SMITH FOUNDATION

Who Can Apply: Awards for students attending Cheyney University.
How Much Money Can I Get: $2,000 renewable
Whom Do I Contact: James Brown, Cheyney University of Pennsylvania, Cheyney, PA 19319, (215) 399-2302.

954

WARREN WILSON COLLEGE

Who Can Apply: Students must rank in the top 20 percent of their class and must submit an essay and letters of recommendation.
How Much Money Can I Get: $1,500

Whom Do I Contact: Warren Wilson College, Admissions Office, 701 Warren Wilson College Road, Swannanoa, NC 28778, (704) 298-3325.

955

WASHINGTON STATE NEED GRANT

Who Can Apply: Student must be needy or disadvantaged, a Washington resident, and enrolled or accepted as a full-time undergraduate student.
How Much Money Can I Get: $300 to $570
Whom Do I Contact: Washington Council for Postsecondary Education, 908 E. Fifth Street, Olympia, WA 98504, (206) 753-3571.

956

WASHINGTON STATE UNIVERSITY

Multicultural Scholars Program
Who Can Apply: Entering freshmen and community college students who are African American, Asian Pacific American, Latino, Native American Indian, or Alaskan native with at least a 3.0 cumulative GPA. Students must be U.S. citizens or permanent residents of the United States. Selection is based on GPA, standardized test scores, and other indicators of potential achievement. Selection Committee may also consider leadership or service activities.
How Much Money Can I Get: $1,500 to $3,000 annually, renewable
Whom Do I Contact: Office of Multicultural Student Recruitment and Community Relations, Washington State University, Pullman, WA 99164-2329, (509)-335-8678.

957

WASHINGTON UNIVERSITY

John B. Ervin Scholarship Competition for Black Americans
Who Can Apply: High school seniors who apply and are admitted as freshmen to Washington University. Deadline January 15.
How Much Money Can I Get: Tuition plus stipend
Whom Do I Contact: John B. Ervin Scholarship Competition, Washington University, Campus Box 1089, One Brookings Drive, St. Louis, MO 63130, (800) 638-0700.

958

WASHINGTON URBAN LEAGUE GRANDMET/ NATIONAL URBAN LEAGUE, ESSAY CONTEST

Who Can Apply: Participants must be entering college freshmen or undergraduate college students who will be attending an accredited institution of higher learning. Awards will be made payable to the institution. Essays must be between 500 and 1,000 words and be typewritten and double-spaced or legibly handwritten and must include participant's full name and permanent address. Entries will be judged for content, originality, organization, style, grammar, spelling, punctuation, and neatness. Contact your high school guidance counselor or college counselor for additional information and this year's topic and deadline.

How Much Money Can I Get: $1,000

Whom Do I Contact: Deputy Director, Northern Virginia Branch, Washington Urban League, Inc., 901 N. Washington Street, #202, Alexandria, VA 22314, (703) 836-2858.

959

WEST CHESTER UNIVERSITY

Minority Academically Talented Award

Who Can Apply: Evaluation includes successful completion of an academic high school program, successful high school class rank, satisfactory SAT or ACT scores, an essay discussing contribution to the school/community, and three letters of recommendation. Deadline March 1.

How Much Money Can I Get: Varies

Whom Do I Contact: Director of Admissions, West Chester University Office of Admissions, 110 Rosedale Avenue, West Chester, PA 19383, (610) 436-2627.

960

UNIVERSITY OF WEST FLORIDA

Equal Education Opportunity Grant

Who Can Apply: Renewable with a 2.3 GPA for undergraduates and 3.2 for graduate students.

How Much Money Can I Get: $500

Whom Do I Contact: Financial Aid Director, The University of West Florida, 11000 University Parkway, Pensacola, FL 32514, (904) 474-2400.

961

WEST GEORGIA COLLEGE

Who Can Apply: These minority scholarships are awarded to black students who have demonstrated outstanding academic achievement. Entering freshman will receive a total of $3,000 over four years. Deadline March 1.

How Much Money Can I Get: $750 per year

Whom Do I Contact: Director of Admissions, West Georgia College, Carrollton, GA 30118, (404) 836-6416.

962

WEST VIRGINIA STATE COLLEGE
Marguerite Thornton Scholarship
Who Can Apply: Full-time black students with a 2.0 GPA. Applicant must be a resident of Pennsylvania and show financial need. Three letters of recommendation required. Deadline April 22.
How Much Money Can I Get: Varies
Whom Do I Contact: Marguerite Brower Thornton Family, Attn.: Marguerite Thornton Scholarship, 1517 W. Pike Street, Philadelphia, PA 19140, (215) 225-4462.

963

WESTERN MICHIGAN UNIVERSITY
Who Can Apply: Approximately 55 predoctoral fellowships and 20 dissertation fellowships for designated minorities to be awarded in a nationwide competition sponsored by the Ford Foundation and administered by the National Research Council. Each predoctoral award includes an annual stipend of $11,000 to the fellow. Each predoctoral award provides up to a maximum of three years of support. Each dissertation award consists of an annual stipend of $18,000 to the fellow. Dissertation awards are not renewable. There will be no dependency or travel allowances for predoctoral and dissertation fellows. Must be a U.S. citizen and majoring in social science, engineering, science, humanities, or mathematics.
How Much Money Can I Get: $10,350 to $18,000
Whom Do I Contact: Western Michigan University, Office of Financial Aid, Kalamazoo, MI 49008-3899, (616) 383-1806.

964

WESTERN MICHIGAN UNIVERSITY
The Alfred Griffin Scholarship Fund
Who Can Apply: Seniors in early elementary education. Black or Native American Indian preferred. Must have a 2.5 GPA.
How Much Money Can I Get: Half tuition
Whom Do I Contact: Western Michigan University, College of Education, 2306 Sangren Hall, Kalamazoo, MI 49008-3899, (616) 387-3465.

965

WESTERN MICHIGAN UNIVERSITY
The Ann C. Mountjoy Memorial Scholarship
Who Can Apply: Outstanding minority, undergraduate Psychology major.
Whom Do I Contact: Department Chairman, Western Michigan University, Department of Psychology, Kalamazoo, MI 49008-3899, (616) 387-4498.

966

WESTERN MICHIGAN UNIVERSITY
Higher Education Incentive Scholarship
Who Can Apply:. This renewable award is based on academic excellence and a competition. Extracurricular activities are considered. A 3.5 GPA computed by Western Michigan is a requirement.
How Much Money Can I Get: $3,000
Whom Do I Contact: Incentive Scholarship Officer, Western Michigan University, WMU Minority Student Services, Kalamazoo, MI 49008, (616) 383-1806.

967

WESTERN MICHIGAN UNIVERSITY
Martin L. King, Jr.—Cesar Chavez—Rosa Parks Scholarship
Who Can Apply: For minority undergraduates declaring education as their area of study.
How Much Money Can I Get: $1,500
Whom Do I Contact: Education Dean's Office, Western Michigan University, College of Education, 2306 Sangren Hall, Kalamazoo, MI 49008-3899, (616) 387-3465.

968

WESTERN MICHIGAN UNIVERSITY
The Thurgood Marshall Assistantship
Who Can Apply: Students from minority groups admitted to degree program with demonstrated scholarship and financial need and who participate in the professional activities of the department are eligible.
How Much Money Can I Get: $6,900/three semesters
Whom Do I Contact: Marshall Assistantships Administration, Western Michigan University, The Graduate College, Kalamazoo, MI 49008, (616) 383-1806.

969

WESTERN MICHIGAN UNIVERSITY
Whitney Young Scholar's Program
Who Can Apply: Applicants must be either seniors or first-year graduate students and must have demonstrated excellence in scholarship and community service. Applicants are recommended by university personnel and must major in social work.
How Much Money Can I Get: Varies
Whom Do I Contact: Western Michigan University, School of Social Work, College of Health & Human Services, Kalamazoo, MI 49008-3899, (616) 387-3180.

970

WESTERN WASHINGTON UNIVERSITY
Ford Foundation Postdoctoral Fellowships for Minorities
Who Can Apply:. In this national competition sponsored by the Ford Foundation, citizens of the U.S. who are members of one of the designated minority groups, who are preparing for or already engaged in college or university teaching, and who have held the Ph.D. or Sc.D. degree for less than seven years, may apply for a fellowship award of one year's duration. Must be majoring on one of the following: science, humanities, physical science, engineering, social science, or mathematics. Deadline January 12.
How Much Money Can I Get: $25,000
Whom Do I Contact: Multi-Cultural Center, 516 High Street, Western Washington University, Bellingham, WA 98225, (206) 676-3843.

971

WESTERN WASHINGTON UNIVERSITY
The Martin Luther King, Jr., Scholarship
Who Can Apply: Black American attending Western. Selection is based on leadership ability, academic achievement, community activities, and club participation. Applicant must be in the upper fifth of the class. Deadline April 15.
How Much Money Can I Get: Varies
Whom Do I Contact: Multi-Cultural Center, 516 High Street, Western Washington University, Bellingham, WA 98225, (206) 676-3843.

972

WESTERN WASHINGTON UNIVERSITY
Minority Achievement Program Scholarships
Who Can Apply: Applicants may be freshman or transfer students with strong academic promise. A faculty mentor program matches students with faculty of the student's academic interest. Deadline April 15.
How Much Money Can I Get: $1,000
Whom Do I Contact: Multi-Cultural Center, 516 High Street, Western Washington University, Bellingham, WA 98225, (206) 676-3843.

973

WICHITA STATE UNIVERSITY
The Minority Engineering Scholarship
Who Can Apply: Minority students majoring in one of the following engineering fields: electrical, mechanical, aerospace, or geological. Deadline September 1.
How Much Money Can I Get: Varies

Whom Do I Contact: Wichita State University, Campus Box 24, 1845 N. Fairmount, Wichita, KS 67208-1595, (316) 689-3430.

974
WILBERFORCE UNIVERSITY
The United Negro College Fund
Who Can Apply: Black Wilberforce students. Must have a strong academic background. Apply early.
How Much Money Can I Get: $100 to $2,000
Whom Do I Contact: Wilberforce University, Wilberforce, OH 45384, (513) 376-2911.

975
WILLIAMS COLLEGE
Gaius Charles Bolin Fellowships for Minority Graduate Students
Who Can Apply: Candidates interested in pursuing careers in college teaching. The fellowship gives a minority graduate student time to complete dissertation work while working toward the Ph.D. in the humanities or in the natural, social, or behavioral sciences. Additionally, fellows teach a one-semester course and are assigned a faculty adviser during the year of residence.
Whom Do I Contact: John Reichert, Dean of the Faculty, Hopkins Hall, Williams College, Williamstown, MA 01267, (413) 597-4351.

976
WILMINGTON COLLEGE
Minority Leader Scholarship
Who Can Apply: Candidates must be involved in a leadership capacity in an extracurricular activity and rank in the upper three-fifths of the class. Must have a 2.5 GPA. Deadline November 15 and January 15.
How Much Money Can I Get: $3,000
Whom Do I Contact: Office of Admissions, Wilmington College, Pyle Center, Box 1325, Wilmington, OH 45177, (513) 382-1661.

977
WISCONSIN MINORITY STUDENT GRANT PROGRAM
Who Can Apply: Black students enrolled in a private, nonprofit institutions of higher education in Wisconsin may apply.
How Much Money Can I Get: Varies
Whom Do I Contact: Higher Education Aids Board, P.O. Box 7885, Madison, WI 53707-7885, (608) 267-2206.

978

UNIVERSITY OF WISCONSIN AT MADISON
The Grant Foundation Scholarship
Who Can Apply: Minority students studying journalism.
How Much Money Can I Get: $800
Whom Do I Contact: Office of Admissions, University of Wisconsin at Madison, 500 Lincoln Drive, Madison, WI 53706, (608) 262-1234.

979

UNIVERSITY OF WISCONSIN AT MILWAUKEE
Advanced Opportunity Program Fellowship
Who Can Apply: Minority or disadvantaged graduate students in full-time degree programs. Preference is given to Wisconsin residents. Deadline early February.
How Much Money Can I Get: $12,816 academic year, $3,000 summer;75 awards, renewable
Whom Do I Contact: Karen Levy, Graduate Fellowship Coordinator, Mitchell 261, University of Wisconsin-Milwaukee, Milwaukee, WI 53201.

980

UNIVERSITY OF WISCONSIN AT MILWAUKEE
Findorff Construction Company Minority Scholarship
Who Can Apply: Level 1 students with academic merit and demonstrated financial need. Deadline March 1.
How Much Money Can I Get: $1,000
Whom Do I Contact: School of Architecture and Urban Planning, AUP 225, University of Wisconsin at Milwaukee, P.O. Box 469, Milwaukee, Wisconsin 53201, (414) 229-4541, E-mail: finaid@des.uwm.edu.

981

UNIVERSITY OF WISCONSIN AT MILWAUKEE
Firstar Milwaukee Foundation Scholarship
Who Can Apply: BBA students nominated by school. No deadline.
How Much Money Can I Get: $5,000
Whom Do I Contact: Robert Ellis, BUS N25, University of Wisconsin-Milwaukee, Milwaukee, WI 53201

982

UNIVERSITY OF WISCONSIN AT MILWAUKEE
Mayor's Scholarship for Excellence
Who Can Apply: Minority students with junior or senior status, Milwaukee residency, and a minimum 2.75 GPA, nominated by school. No deadline.

How Much Money Can I Get: $2,000
Whom Do I Contact: Robert Ellis, BUS N251, University of Wisconsin-Milwaukee, Milwaukee, WI 53201.

983

UNIVERSITY OF WISCONSIN AT MILWAUKEE
Milwaukee Police Athletic League Criminal Justice Scholarship
Who Can Apply: High school senior or enrolled undergraduate student. Must be a participant in PAL and planning to major in criminal justice. Preference is given to minority students. Deadline varies.
How Much Money Can I Get: Full tuition, renewable
Whom Do I Contact: Ellen Lafouge, Enderis Hall 1123, University of Wisconsin at Milwaukee, Milwaukee, WI 53201.

984

UNIVERSITY OF WISCONSIN AT MILWAUKEE
Minority Academic Achievement Scholarship
Who Can Apply: African American, Hispanic, Southeast Asian, Native American Indian, or Alaskan Native high school seniors with academic excellence extracurricular activities. Deadline rolling.
How Much Money Can I Get: Up to full tuition
Whom Do I Contact: Leonard C. White, Jr., Department of Enrollment Services, Mitchell Hall 161, or Scholarship Coordinator, Financial Aid Office, Mellencamp Hall 162, University of Wisconsin at Milwaukee, Milwaukee, WI 53201.

985

UNIVERSITY OF WISCONSIN AT OSHKOSH
Minority Honor Scholarship
Who Can Apply: Minority students in the top 25 percent of high school class. Must be a U.S. citizen or have permanent residency. Deadline February 15.
How Much Money Can I Get: $500 to $2,000
Whom Do I Contact: University of Wisconsin, Attn.: Director of Admissions, 800 Algoma Boulevard, Oshkosh, WI 54901, (414) 424-0202.

986

UNIVERSITY OF WISCONSIN AT PLATTEVILLE
The Engineering Development Scholarship
Who Can Apply: Entering minority women majoring in one of the following engineering fields: civil, industrial, electrical, or mechanical.
How Much Money Can I Get: $200

Whom Do I Contact: University of Wisconsin, Platteville Campus, 1 University Plaza, Platteville, WI 53818, (608) 342-1125.

987

THE WOODROW WILSON
NATIONAL FELLOWSHIP FOUNDATION

Who Can Apply: Awards for minority students who have completed their junior year in college and are interested in government careers. Students must attend an accredited summer institute.

How Much Money Can I Get: $6,000

Whom Do I Contact: Judith Pinch, Vice President, The Woodrow Wilson National Fellowship Foundation, 330 Alexander Street, Box 642, Princeton, NJ 08542, (609) 924-4666.

988

WORLD INSTITUTE OF
BLACK COMMUNICATIONS, INC.

A's African American Student Scholarship

Who Can Apply: Black American men and women interested in advertising. Students must have been participants in the American Association of Advertising Agencies' Minority Advertising Intern Program.

How Much Money Can I Get: $1,000 to $2,000

Whom Do I Contact: World Institute of Black Communications, Inc., 10 Columbus Circle, New York, NY 10019, (212) 586-1771.

989

WRIGHT STATE UNIVERSITY

Paul Laurence Dunbar Scholarship

Who Can Apply: African-American students who score an 870 SAT (20 ACT), or complete a college prep curriculum and rank in top 20 percent at the end of their seventh semester or have a 3.0 GPA. Deadline March 31 for application and Financial Aid Form.

How Much Money Can I Get: $2,000

Whom Do I Contact: Coordinator of Scholarships, Office of Financial Aid, Wright State University, Dayton, OH 45401, (513) 873-2321.

990

XAVIER UNIVERSITY

Fr. Pedro Arrupe, S. J. Scholarship

Who Can Apply: African-American students. Scholarships are awarded every four years.

How Much Money Can I Get: Tuition

Whom Do I Contact: Xavier University, Attn.: Director of Admissions, 3800 Victory Parkway, Cincinnati, OH 45207-5311, (513) 745-3301.

991
XAVIER UNIVERSITY

United Negro College Fund
Who Can Apply: Black college freshmen. Must have a strong academic background. Apply early.
How Much Money Can I Get: $100 to $2,000
Whom Do I Contact: Xavier University, 7325 Palmetto Street, New Orleans, LA 70125, (504) 486-7411.

992
XAVIER UNIVERSITY

Xavier Academic Award
Who Can Apply: The award is given to a student with a math SAT score of at least 400, a verbal SAT score of at least 400, and an ACT score of at least 20. Student must be ranked in the top 20 percent of his or her class. Deadline April 15.
How Much Money Can I Get: $2,500
Whom Do I Contact: Xavier University, Attn.: Director of Admissions, 3800 Victory Parkway, Cincinnati, OH 45207-5311, (513) 745-3301.

993
XEROX CORPORATION

Who Can Apply: Scholarships to minority students studying engineering or science.
How Much Money Can I Get: Up to $4,000 a year
Whom Do I Contact: Xerox Corporation, P.O. Box 1600, Stamford, CT 06904.

994
XEROX TECHNICAL SCHOLARSHIPS

Who Can Apply: Awards to minority students enrolled full-time in science or engineering college programs. Deadline August 1.
How Much Money Can I Get: Varies
Whom Do I Contact: Xerox Technical Scholarships, College Relations, Xerox Corporation, Building 205LL, 800 Phillips Road, Webster, NY 14580.

995

YMCA KATE H. ATHERTON SCHOLARSHIP

Who Can Apply: Grants are available only to female residents of Hawaii (preferably minorities), who are pursuing a college education in Hawaii or in the continental United States.
How Much Money Can I Get: Up to $1,500
Whom Do I Contact: Hawaiian Trust Company, Ltd., P.O. Box 3170, Honolulu, HI 96802, (808) 525-8511.

996

ZETA DELTA PHI SORORITY

Who Can Apply: This sorority promotes academic excellence and offers scholarships to qualified black high school students.
How Much Money Can I Get: Varies
Whom Do I Contact: Zeta Delta Phi Sorority, Inc., P.O. Box 157, Bronx, NY 10469, (212) 407-8288.

997

ZETA PHI BETA SORORITY
African Fellowship
Who Can Apply: Active black members of Zeta Phi Beta Sorority. Official application form should be secured from national headquarters of Zeta Phi Beta Sorority or directly from the chairperson of the scholarship committee. Applicant must supply proof of matriculation. Deadline February 1.
How Much Money Can I Get: Not to exceed $1,000
Whom Do I Contact: Zeta Phi Beta Sorority, c/o Brenda K. Green, 1514 N. 25th Street, Baton Rouge, LA 70802.

998

ZETA PHI BETA SORORITY
The Deborah P. Wolfe International Fellowship
Who Can Apply: Black women for a full academic year for full-time study in the U.S. for a foreign student. Deadline February 1.
How Much Money Can I Get: Varies
Whom Do I Contact: Zeta Phi Beta Sorority, 1201 Boynton Avenue, Westfield, NJ 07090.

999

ZETA PHI BETA SORORITY
The Mildred C. Bradham Social Work Fellowship
Who Can Apply: Applicants must be of good character, have an outstanding academic record, demonstrate leadership ability, and be recommended by a

graduate chapter of Zeta Phi Beta Sorority. Applicants must write a 10-page essay on why the scholarship request is being made. Award is renewable. Write for details. Deadline March 1.
How Much Money Can I Get: Varies
Whom Do I Contact: Zeta Phi Beta Sorority, 1734 New Hampshire Avenue, NW, Washington, DC 20009, (202) 387-3103.

1000
ZETA PHI BETA SORORITY
The Nancy B. Woolridge Graduate Fellowship
Who Can Apply: Zeta Phi Beta members in good standing. Must show good character, exemplify high ideals, and be active in the sorority. Applicants must write a 10-page essay on why the scholarship request is being made. Applicants must have a minimum 2.0 GPA. Write for details.
How Much Money Can I Get: Varies
Whom Do I Contact: Zeta Phi Beta Sorority, Inc., 1734 New Hampshire Avenue, NW, Washington, DC 20009, (202) 387-3103.

1001
ZETA PHI BETA SORORITY
The National Education Foundation
Who Can Apply: Applicants may or may not be members of Zeta Phi Beta. This is for graduate women who are working on a professional degree, master's, doctorate, or postdoctoral study.
How Much Money Can I Get: Up to $2,500
Whom Do I Contact: Zeta Phi Beta Sorority, 1827 79th Avenue, Baton Rouge, LA 70807.

INDEX BY DISCIPLINE

Dental Health/Oral Health: 001, 069, 072, 073, 418, 531, 641, 654

Economics: 070, 269, 350, 446, 513

Education/Teaching: 032, 036, 042, 053, 163, 164, 166, 180, 193, 256, 198, 219, 220, 222, 320, 321, 322, 408, 493, 502, 562, 640, 646, 690, 704, 754, 766, 783, 848, 857, 876, 878, 927, 967 , 964

Engineering: 028, 062, 115, 117, 120, 121, 138, 149, 214, 227, 228, 231, 268, 288, 290, 297, 300, 303, 306, 307, 323, 340, 341, 348, 350, 364, 365, 386, 394, 401, 403, 416, 418, 421, 454, 456, 464, 478, 479, 483, 499, 510, 516, 518, 511, 535, 543, 551, 552, 558, 559, 563, 564, 566, 579, 581, 583, 600, 601, 614, 615, 616, 617, 620, 623, 635, 636, 637, 660, 674, 676, 686, 683, 684, 690, 706, 711, 823, 829, 834, 838, 839, 842, 861, 879, 883, 885, 888, 890, 899, 901, 908, 916, 917, 924, 951, 963, 970, 973, 960, 986, 993, 994

English: 032, 169, 388, 800, 872

Environment: 107, 371, 579, 632

Forestry: 554

Genealogy: 327

General: 002, 003, 004, 006, 007, 008, 019, 020, 021, 022, 023, 024, 025, 026, 027, 035, 037, 038, 039, 040, 042, 043, 044, 046, 047, 048 049, 051, 052, 055, 058, 059, 060, 061, 063, 064, 088, 092, 101, 103, 104, 106, 108, 109, 110, 113, 114, 118, 122, 123, 128, 129, 130, 132, 133, 134, 135, 137, 139, 141, 142, 143, 144, 145, 146, 147, 148, 151, 152, 153, 160, 165, 167, 168, 170, 171, 172, 173, 174, 175, 176, 177, 178, 179, 181, 182, 183, 184, 185, 186, 187, 188, 189, 190, 191, 192, 194, 196, 197, 200, 201, 202, 203, 204, 205, 206, 218, 223, 224, 227, 229, 232, 233, 234, 235, 236, 237, 239, 240, 249, 250, 251, 252, 253, 254, 257, 258, 259, 262, 263, 264, 270, 271, 280, 284, 287, 289, 292, 294, 295, 296, 298, 301, 304, 308, 309, 319, 325, 330, 331, 333, 335, 336, 337, 338, 343, 344, 347, 349, 351, 353, 355, 356, 358, 359, 363, 367, 368, 370, 372, 374, 375, 376, 378, 379, 380, 381, 383, 384, 387, 391, 393, 397, 398, 400, 409, 410, 411, 413, 415, 417, 419, 423, 424, 425, 428, 429, 430, 432, 434, 435, 438, 440, 441, 442, 455, 457, 458, 459, 462, 463, 469, 472, 474, 475, 480, 481, 482, 484, 485, 487, 488, 489, 491, 492, 494, 495, 496, 498, 500, 501, 503, 504, 505, 506, 507, 508, 509, 512, 514, 515, 519, 521. 522, 523, 524, 525, 526, 533, 534, 536, 537, 538, 539, 540, 541, 542, 544, 548, 549, 555, 556, 557, 559, 560, 565, 568, 569, 570, 571, 571, 577, 578, 582, 589, 613, 622, 624, 626, 627, 628, 629, 630, 631, 633, 638,

644, 647, 648, 649, 651, 652, 653, 657, 658, 659, 661, 663, 664, 665, 666, 667, 669, 670, 673, 675, 677, 679, 691, 685, 687, 682, 689, 691, 692, 693, 694, 695, 697, 699, 705, 707, 708, 709, 710, 713, 714, 715, 716, 719, 720, 721, 723, 724, 725, 726, 727, 728, 729, 730, 732, 733, 734, 759, 760, 761, 762, 763, 767, 768, 769, 771, 772, 773, 776, 777, 778, 779, 780, 781, 786, 787, 788, 789, 790, 791, 792, 793, 794, 796, 797, 798, 799, 801, 802, 803, 806, 807, 815, 816, 817, 820, 821, 822, 824, 826, 827, 833, 835, 836, 837, 840, 844, 845, 847, 851, 852, 853, 858, 859, 862, 863, 864, 865, 866, 867, 868, 869, 870, 871, 873, 874, 877, 882, 884, 887, 889, 891, 892, 893, 896, 897, 900, 902, 903, 905, 906, 907, 909, 910, 911, 912, 913, 920, 922, 923, 925, 926, 928, 929, 932, 963, 950, 952, 953, 968, 970, 957, 958, 959, 960, 961, 962, 964, 966, 971, 972, 974, 976, 977, 979, 980, 981, 982, 984, 985, 989, 990, 991, 992, 995, 996, 997, 998, 999, 1000, 1001

Geography: 269

Geology: 074, 075, 268, 437

Government: 032, 054, 140, 315, 688, 987

Health Care: 382, 407, 433, 545, 547, 604, 605, 606

History: 032, 267, 269, 875

Home Economics: 076, 077, 156, 158, 159, 162

Hotel and Restaurant Management: 018, 554

Humanities: 107, 239, 240, 267, 304, 332, 576, 643, 680, 755, 909, 925, 963, 970, 975

Information Systems: 062, 117, 195, 290

Insurance: 230

Journalism: 031, 057, 112, 124, 126, 215, 216, 217, 265, 282, 291, 312, 313, 314, 323, 324, 328, 329, 342, 345, 349, 360, 361, 362, 377, 389, 390, 392, 395, 396, 399, 402, 404, 412, 466, 476, 477, 497, 513, 528, 529, 530, 532, 553, 585, 609, 612, 639, 642, 655, 662, 678, 756, 831, 832, 860, 861, 881, 886, 904, 921, 978

Languages: 267, 310, 327

Law Enforcement: 326, 339, 346, 352, 406, 418, 420, 587, 598,

Library Science: 086, 085, 125, 209, 211, 212, 281, 427, 593, 680, 810, 841, 849

Maritime Studies: 572

Mathematics: 013, 032, 268, 385, 486, 563, 566, 569, 581, 614, 680, 722, 764, 800, 842, 963, 970

Medical: 071, 096, 241, 242, 243, 244, 245, 246, 247, 248, 316, 527, 545, 546, 599, 600, 602, 604, 605, 606, 607, 608, 650, 654, 656, 738, 744, 758, 770, 800

Meteorology: 075, 600, 615

Microbiology: 097, 554, 602, 603

Ministry/Seminary/Theology: 002, 003, 127, 182, 225, 226, 266, 267, 293, 414, 426, 914, 915

Music: 016, 032, 154, 193, 267, 573, 574, 575, 592, 846, 862

Nursing: 087, 089, 465, 595, 596, 597, 618, 619, 672, 775, 784, 793

Performing Arts: 161, 193, 334, 373, 576, 782, 828 918, 919

Pharmacy: 467, 610

Philanthropy: 445

Physical Therapy: 718

Physics: 090, 091, 120, 268, 418, 563, 566, 581, 600, 839

Planning: 012, 017, 136, 774, 931

Political Science: 032, 093, 238, 269, 365, 754

Public Relations: 405, 752

Psychology: 032, 094, 095, 210, 269, 671, 731, 800, 965, 975

Real Estate: 083, 448

INDEX BY STATE

Florida: 172, 173, 174, 175, 176, 177, 178, 179, 180, 181, 182, 183, 184, 185, 238, 241, 242, 243, 244, 245, 246, 248, 310, 311, 320, 376, 377, 378, 379, 380, 381, 382, 383, 384, 386, 387, 388, 389, 391, 392, 393, 394, 395, 396, 397, 398, 399, 400, 401, 402, 403, 404, 405, 406, 506, 385, 622, 658, 659, 670, 671, 693, 741, 742, 800, 926, 960

Georgia: 033, 034, 035, 036, 037, 038, 039, 040, 041, 042, 043, 044, 045, 046, 047, 048, 049, 050, 051, 052, 053, 281, 282, 324, 370, 402, 568, 590, 591, 811, 812, 813, 814, 961

Hawaii: 995

Idaho: 442

Illinois: 001, 055, 056, 069, 072, 073, 083, 085, 086, 122, 265, 360, 361, 362, 407, 418, 446, 448, 524,

525, 526, 527, 582, 592, 593, 594, 752, 753, 754, 801, 802

Indiana: 123, 124, 125, 266, 267, 268, 269, 323, 338, 353, 354, 372, 425, 426, 443, 444, 445, 461, 486, 601, 669, 706, 722, 763, 764, 857, 927

Iowa: 204, 235, 237, 295, 344, 345, 346, 446, 452, 453, 454, 455, 456, 496, 508, 698, 762, 843, 848

Kansas: 413, 415, 462, 463, 464, 465, 466, 467, 468, 973

Kentucky: 323, 476, 609

Louisiana: 074, 497, 500, 644, 991

Maine: 201, 296, 803

Maryland: 068, 090, 091, 099, 100, 126, 227, 335, 433, 498, 509, 510, 511, 512, 513, 514, 516, 517, 518, 519, 520, 521, 514, 547, 566, 570, 576, 577, 578, 579, 580, 581, 599, 602, 603, 604, 605, 606, 607, 616, 716, 844, 902

Massachusetts: 110, 170, 171, 197, 198, 199, 200, 234, 369, 375, 424, 427, 428, 435, 446, 535, 595, 596, 597, 628, 629, 631, 660, 661, 711, 761, 905, 975

Michigan: 225, 226, 239, 240, 421, 446, 470, 471, 483, 524, 541, 542, 543, 544, 545, 664, 668, 747, 963, 964, 965, 966, 967, 968, 969

Minnesota: 229, 293, 446, 567

Mississippi: 450, 460, 551, 552

Missouri: 0087, 317, 490, 524, 553, 554, 555, 556, 557, 558, 559, 560, 561, 563, 562, 586, 665, 666, 667, 740, 842, 957

Nebraska: 325, 326, 624, 625, 626

New Jersey: 119, 120, 121, 332, 366, 367, 414, 532, 531, 564, 639, 735, 736, 738, 745, 846, 987

New Mexico: 320, 611, 632, 633, 634, 635, 636, 637

New York: 054, 080, 081, 082, 297, 319, 321, 322, 352, 364, 365, 366, 416, 424, 433, 458, 459, 484, 494, 524, 548, 573, 574, 583, 608, 613, 619, 621, 638, 640, 641, 642, 643, 718, 730, 732, 739, 744, 755, 849, 850, 851, 852, 840, 841, 856, 860, 861, 900, 907, 908, 909, 911, 914, 920, 922, 923, 988

North Carolina: 109, 128, 153, 154, 155, 156, 157, 158, 159, 160, 161, 162, 163, 164, 165, 166, 167, 168, 169, 320, 348, 349, 351, 368, 373, 493, 550, 588, 612, 651, 652, 653, 654, 655, 656, 657, 672, 673, 723, 737, 816, 817, 818, 819, 820, 821, 822, 823, 824, 825, 826, 827, 828, 829, 830, 831, 832, 833, 834, 835, 836, 837, 838, 839, 954

Ohio: 004, 104, 105, 106, 107, 108, 115, 116, 118, 202, 203, 231, 232, 270, 271, 290, 291, 331, 336, 337, 446, 473, 474, 475, 482, 537, 538, 539, 540, 571, 623, 670, 677, 678, 695, 756, 901, 974, 976, 989, 990, 992

Oklahoma: 662, 679, 680, 681

Oregon: 417, 446, 715

Pennsylvania: 003, 071, 117, 129, 205, 206, 230, 249, 250, 251, 252, 253, 254, 255, 256, 257, 258, 259, 260, 261, 262, 263, 264, 280, 339, 347, 359, 411, 424, 430, 431, 432, 469, 478, 480, 481, 487, 488, 489, 490, 491, 492, 502, 504, 505, 524, 533, 534, 536, 565, 627, 694, 699, 700, 701, 702, 712, 713, 714, 743, 815, 858, 859, 928, 953, 959, 962

Rhode Island: 719, 720, 721,

South Carolina: 129, 130, 131, 132, 133, 134, 135, 136, 137, 138, 139, 140, 141, 142, 143, 144, 415, 146, 147, 148, 149, 150, 151, 152, 272, 273, 274, 275, 276, 277, 278, 279, 283, 284, 285, 286, 287, 288, 289, 290, 309, 446, 758, 766, 767, 768, 769, 770, 771, 772, 773, 774, 775, 776, 777, 778, 779, 780, 781, 782, 783, 784, 785, 786, 787, 788, 789, 790, 791, 792, 793, 794, 795, 796, 797, 798, 952

South Dakota: 799

Tennessee: 355, 374, 447, 523, 528, 529, 530, 674, 733, 861, 880, 881, 877, 878, 879, 913, 912, 915

Texas: 032, 096, 127, 318, 320, 330, 356, 357, 358, 429, 436, 437, 438, 439, 440, 441, 442, 734, 804, 805, 806, 807, 847, 882, 883, 884, 885, 886, 887, 888, 889, 890, 891, 892, 893, 894, 895, 896, 897, 898, 899, 903

Utah: 924, 925

Vermont: 233, 424

Virginia: 075, 292, 320, 328, 363, 409, 410, 412, 451, 479, 504, 507, 522, 585, 646, 647, 648, 649, 650, 663, 682, 684, 685, 686, 687, 688, 727, 728, 729, 845, 916, 917, 918, 919, 921, 929, 930, 931, 932, 949, 950, 951, 958

Washington: 955, 956, 970, 971, 972

Wisconsin: 058, 059, 060, 061, 062, 063, 064, 065, 546, 569, 725, 726, 977, 978, 979, 980, 981, 982, 983, 984, 985, 986

NOTES